In the 1950s, Brazil prohibited car imports and forced trans-national auto companies either to abandon the market or to manufacture vehicles within the country. Although currently contending approaches to economic development would suggest that this type of industrialization policy would fail in the political-economic context of postwar Brazil, the plan was successful according to a variety of criteria. The Brazilian auto industry would become the largest in the periphery.

The book explains the economic and political motivations behind the plan, and why Brazil relied on foreign firms to do the job. It documents the bargaining process between the Brazilian government and transnational firms, estimates the cost incurred by the government as a result of the plan, and provides new archival evidence that shows that firms would not have invested without government pressure. It argues that the current, polarized debate on the role of the state in economic development must become more nuanced, as the Brazilian auto case suggests that the effectiveness of state policy can vary greatly across sectors and over time.

Engines of Growth

ENGINES OF GROWTH

THE STATE AND TRANSNATIONAL AUTO COMPANIES IN BRAZIL

Helen Shapiro

Harvard Business School

CAMBRIDGE
UNIVERSITY PRESS

Published by the Press Syndicate of the University of Cambridge
The Pitt Building, Trumpington Street, Cambridge CB2 1RP
40 West 20th Street, New York, NY 10011-4211, USA
10 Stamford Road, Oakleigh, Melbourne 3166, Australia

First published 1994

Printed in the United States of America

Library of Congress Cataloging-in-Publication Data
Shapiro, Helen.
Engines of growth : the state and transnational auto companies in Brazil /
Helen Shapiro.
p. cm.
Revision of the author's thesis (doctoral) – Yale University.
Includes index.
ISBN 0-521-41640-x (hc)
1. Automobile industry and trade – Government policy – Brazil.
2. International business enterprises – Brazil. I. Title.
HD9710.B82S48   1993
338.8'87292'0981 – dc20   92-39226
                                                                CIP

A catalog record for this book is available from the British Library.

ISBN 0-521-41640-x hardback

CONTENTS

v

TABLES AND FIGURES

Tables

vi

Figure

ACKNOWLEDGMENTS

This book originated as a doctoral dissertation at Yale University. During those years, I had the honor of working closely with two unique scholars, William Parker and Albert Fishlow, and would like to thank them both for their support and friendship. They supported my choice of a time-consuming and risky thesis topic and constantly challenged my abilities and assumptions. Albert Fishlow was largely responsible for pushing me in the direction of Brazil, for which I shall always be grateful.

I gratefully acknowledge the institutional support provided by the Instituto de Planejamento Econômico e Social (IPEA) during my first extended stay in Brazil. Special thanks are due to Marcelo Lara Resende for facilitating my entry into the Brazilian research community. My research on the auto industry would not have been possible without the help of those who participated in its early formation. I extend special thanks to Sydney Latini, who guided me through the labyrinth of Brazilian data collection, and Admiral Lúcio Meira, who graciously provided me with an oral history of the industry. Their ongoing enthusiasm for the industry and its history is remarkable. I am also indebted to José Almeida, who shared with me the original, unpublished study on which his subsequent book was based, and to Eduardo Augusto de Almeida Guimarães for his advice. I also thank José Mindlin, Jacy de Souza Mendonça, Jacques Nasser, Ricardo Strunz, and all of the other representatives of the industry – past and present – who shared their thoughts and experiences with me.

I would also like to pay special tribute to the many librarians and archivists, the unsung heroes of historical research, who assisted me. I especially thank Mariangela Besse Antunes, the librarian at the National Association of Motor Vehicle Manufacturers (ANFAVEA) at the time of my field work, and Maria Angélica Brandão Varela, the director of the Executive Group for the Automotive Industry (GEIA) archives at the Rio branch of the Industrial Development Council (CDI), who was particularly helpful and who demonstrated a commitment to preserving and organizing the historical record against great odds. I also thank the archivists at Volkswagen for providing me access to the company's materials, and Darleen Flaherty of the Ford Industrial Archives. I am grateful to Mira Wilkins for giving me free access to her personal files on Ford. I would also like to acknowledge the New York Public Library, a wondrous institution, which, to my astonishment, has one of the best and most accessible collections of Brazilian government records for this period, anywhere.

Over the years and the miles, many people have been pulled into the book-writing process, both in the United States and Brazil. Special thanks are due to Ben Schneider, who accompanied this project at every stage of its long life and who provided commentary on various drafts. I would also like to thank Lance Taylor, who was especially helpful with the theoretical framework. Jonathan Fox provided critical feedback and support in the final revisions of the manuscript.

There are many people who have made my visits to Brazil happy and productive. I would like to thank Luiz Carlos Bresser Pereira, Armando Castellar, M. Teresa Citeli, Sergio Crivorot, Philippe Faucher, Claudia Garcia, Antônio Kandir, and Wilson Suzigan. The following friends and colleagues provided support and critical feedback here in the United States: Paula Berg, John Evansohn, Daniel Gleizer, Marg Hainer, Connie Helfat, Richard Kohl, Gesner Oliveira, and Paula Weinbaum.

For their comments on earlier drafts, I would like to thank George Lodge, Elizabeth Silva, Steve Tolliday, Lou Wells, and especially Tom McCraw. I would also like to thank David Yoffie and the World Trade and Global Competition Project at the Harvard Business School for giving me the opportunity to look at recent developments in the Brazilian auto industry and to clarify further my understanding of firm strategy.

Field research was originally funded by the Yale Center for International and Area Studies and subsequently by the Division of Research of the Harvard Business School. Miguel Lengyel, Laura Hastings, Antônio Botelho, and Clemencia Torres provided excellent research assistance. Ricardo Dominguez and Lisa Wells helped with the tables, and Pat Denault assisted with the copy-editing and proofreading. Mary Alice Wood provided unwavering secretarial support.

Finally I would like to thank the members of my extended family, too numerous to name here, whose encouragement and patience were crucial to this book's completion. This book is dedicated to my parents,

Sol and Lena Shapiro, who valued education for their daughters as well as their son. The book is in memory of my uncle, Jack Shapiro, who, despite our disagreements about almost everything, would have been very proud.

1
APPROACHES TO STATE INTERVENTION

In 1956, the Brazilian government banned all car imports. Foreign automobile companies faced an official ultimatum: Either they abandon the lucrative Brazilian market or they invest to manufacture vehicles with 90–95 percent Brazilian-made content within five years. The timing for such an initiative did not appear propitious. Brazil had only the beginnings of an industrial base, and until that point, virtually all vehicles had been imported as knocked-down kits and assembled locally. Steel production had begun only nine years earlier, and coffee still accounted for more than 50 percent of the country's exports. Indeed, the auto plan was part of a general import-substituting development strategy to shift the economy's focus from raw material exports to domestic industrialization. Moreover, as the first country in Latin America to insist upon domestic auto production, Brazil was entering uncharted territory. There was little precedent in Brazil or in the region for negotiating with transnational firms in any manufacturing activity. Foreign investment had been largely restricted to public utilities, railroads, and raw materials. Despite the intensification of international competition among the large auto manufacturers, cross-national investment in production facilities was occurring primarily within Europe. In the 1950s, firms competed for peripheral markets such as Brazil through exports.

In addition to these challenges, the Brazilian state's industrialization effort was constrained by chronic balance-of-payments difficulties, limited fiscal capacity, and internal divisions. The executive branch, the agent of the industrialization drive, was not hegemonic within the government apparatus and lacked full autonomy over existing resources. Congress had budgetary control, and much of the executive's revenues came in the form of "earmarked funds," the allocation of which was predetermined. As president, Juscelino Kubitschek (1956–61) was able to unite different sectors and classes around an ideology of "national developmentalism," but the industrial elite was by no means in firm control. Both corporatist and clientelistic tactics were

1

used to consolidate political support and to mute opposition. The broad political coalition that supported Kubitschek precluded a direct squeeze on consumption to finance industrial investment.

These attributes of the Brazilian state molded its intervention. In general, the lack of direct access to resources caused the state to resort to indirect financing methods. Because of the executive branch's control over access to scarce foreign exchange, trade policy played a developmental role in Brazil. Moreover, the economic and political power of the agro-export sector precluded the use of direct export taxes. As a result, the state relied on the "second-best" alternative to transfer resources from agriculture to industry, that is, differential exchange rates on imports and exports. In addition to protection from imports, therefore, the government offered the auto companies incentives and subsidies, largely in the form of beneficial exchange rates on investment and foreign financing, as well as exemptions from various duties and taxes.

Neither of the currently contending approaches to economic development would suggest that this type of import-substitution program would succeed in the context of Brazil's political economy. On the one hand, neoclassical, market-oriented explanations of economic development challenge both the necessity and the efficacy of state intervention. Traditional orthodox trade theory predicts that such deviation from free-trade policies is likely to lead to suboptimal results; reliance on "second-best" trade policies as indirect instruments of industrial policy is especially suspect. According to a more recent neoclassical political economy literature that focuses on the dynamics of state intervention, import-substitution policies of protective tariffs and subsidies are more likely than externally oriented strategies to induce nonproductive, rent-seeking activity by private actors. On the other hand, state-centered approaches that emphasize the importance of institution building over market forces typically assume that effective state policy requires a highly autonomous state to insulate economic decision making and implementation from clientelistic politics. However, the Brazilian state had neither the fiscal authority nor the disciplinary power over the private sector associated with late developers such as Japan, South Korea, and other East Asian newly industrializing countries (NICs), which are often the models for this type of approach.

This book will show that, despite these constraints, the Brazilian strategy to install a domestic automotive industry successfully forced transnational firms to invest rapidly and allowed the country to capture the economic rents and positive externalities associated with the industry. Most production targets were achieved. By 1961, only six years after the plan's initiation, eleven firms were producing over 145,000 vehicles with an average domestic-content share of 93 percent by weight and 87 percent by value. Most of the major players in the international auto industry, including Ford, General Motors, Volkswagen, and Mercedes-Benz, participated. Production reached 280,000 by 1968, and eight firms, all foreign controlled, remained, although only three were responsible for 89 percent of all vehicles produced. This consolidation allowed some firms to attain economies of scale, and production costs declined. Subsequently, the industry entered a second phase of growth, leading the Brazilian economic "miracle" of 1968–73 with annual growth rates topping 20 percent. By 1975, annual production approached one million vehicles, making Brazil's industry the largest in the periphery and the ninth largest in the world.

More surprising are the results with respect to state financing of the auto plan. The state's subsidies, though substantial, were smaller than other analysts have previously assumed. Moreover, in contrast to many contemporary Latin American experiences that better fit the rent-seeking paradigm, the initial subsidies did not lead to ongoing resource transfers to the sector. The taxes paid by the vehicle assemblers more than compensated for the indirect subsidies they received, even within the industry's first five years. A circular self-financing program can be observed from the data: Firms were given indirect subsidies, and consumers reimbursed the government through production and sales taxes. The share of oligopolistic rents accruing to the firms decreased over time, as companies were forced to lower prices and as an increasing tax bite was taken by the state. The sector thus became a significant source of revenue for a state with limited sources of fiscal income. The data reveal a form of rent redistribution usually found between peripheral states and transnational firms exporting raw materials. The evidence also shows that the automotive industry had relatively high linkage effects. It generated the development of new sectors to produce parts and intermediate inputs. Brazil's policy was successful in generating the production externalities of the industry and in increasing the capacity of the state to capture rents accruing to the firms, benefits it would have sacrificed had it continued to import from the oligopolized firms.

Historical evidence also shows that transnational automotive firms would not have invested in manufacturing capacity or complied with domestic-content requirements in the absence of government policies. Even if the auto program may have "anticipated an existing trend" in foreign direct investment, as some claim, firms were compelled to invest according to a Brazilian-imposed schedule, which greatly accelerated the speed and diffusion of industrialization more generally.

Brazil's success in establishing an automotive industry was determined by a favorable combination of market and institutional variables. It was dependent on the capacity of a segment of the state apparatus to formulate and implement a sectoral policy consistent with the country's underlying economic structure and to bargain effectively with transnational firms. The Brazilian case demonstrates that, while the institutional actors and the environment are critical to success, strongly compatible underlying economic conditions provide crucial leeway for policy manipulation. It also suggests that the effectiveness of state policy can vary greatly across sectors and over time depending on demand conditions, the nature of technological change, transnational firm strategy, and the domestic and international macroeconomic environment.

Contending Paradigms

The fact that Brazil's successful experience with automobiles cannot be fully accounted for by either of the dominant contending paradigms of economic development reflects their failure to articulate fully the interaction between the economic and political spheres. Although the terms of the debate on economic development have shifted over the years from the capacity of markets to the capacity of states, the essence of the controversy still centers on the relative importance of market versus institutional factors in determining economic performance. Currently, two contending paradigms dominate social science, one that ultimately argues for removing the state from the development process, and another that argues for putting it "back in."[1] Although each offers important insights, the debate over state intervention and industrial policy remains polarized between "all or nothing" theories and caricatured portrayals of both states and markets. As a result, neither paradigm alone can account for Brazil's experience with automobiles or, more generally, why some cases of intervention by particular states succeed while others fail.

The Neoclassical, Market-Oriented Approach

In the 1960s, development economists highlighted the greater scope of market failure in less-developed as compared with developed econ-

---

[1] The term is borrowed from Peter Evans, Dietrich Rueschemeyer, and Theda Skocpol, eds., *Bringing the State Back In* (Cambridge: Cambridge University Press, 1985).

omies, thereby providing a rationale for enlarging the scope of state intervention. Although distinct viewpoints were evident in the literature, these theorists all saw development as a process of dynamic, nonmarginal change.[2] The price mechanism alone was deemed insufficient to induce the resource transfer necessary for industrialization to occur.

This paradigm of economic development provoked two waves of neoclassical dissent. The thrust of the first wave was aimed at the state's capacity to guide structural change. Using new analytical tools from trade theory such as effective rates of protection and domestic resource costs, Ian M. D. Little, Tibor Scitovsky, and Maurice Scott showed that national industrial strategies were inefficient – the incentives they created were highly unequal for different economic actors.[3] Based on the neoclassical assumption that allocational inefficiencies always lead to production inefficiencies, this approach sought to correlate "distorted" policy regimes with poor economic performance, advocating domestic laissez-faire and free trade as the only viable alternatives.

This neoclassical critique was bolstered by the success of export-oriented countries such as South Korea and Taiwan. Their rapid growth in comparison to economies that followed import-substitution strategies seemed to provide empirical validation for Harry Johnson's earlier claims, which many development economists had denied, that dynamic gains could be had from free trade.[4] An avid supporter,

---

[2] Tibor Scitovsky, "Two Concepts of External Economies," *Journal of Political Economy* 62 (1954):143–51, explained the conditions required for the price mechanism to achieve dynamic allocation, such as complete and functioning markets, an absence of increasing returns, and complete tradability; empirical study showed that these conditions did not obtain in less-developed countries (LDCs). Albert O. Hirschman, *The Strategy of Economic Development* (New York: W. W. Norton, 1978), and others saw development as a sequence of punctuated disequilibria. For more on the early development theorists and the subsequent debates, see Helen Shapiro and Lance Taylor, "The State and Industrial Strategy," *World Development* 18, no. 6 (1990):861–78; John Toye, *Dilemmas of Development* (Oxford: Basil Blackwell, 1987); and Wing Thye Woo, "The Art of Economic Development: Markets, Politics, and Externalities," *International Organization* 44, no. 3 (1990):403–29.

[3] Ian M. D. Little, Tibor Scitovsky, and Maurice Scott, *Industry and Trade in Some Developing Countries: A Comparative Study* (London: Oxford University Press, 1970).

[4] Harry G. Johnson, *Economic Policies toward Less Developed Countries* (Washington, D.C.: Brookings Institution, 1967). From a planning perspective, Hollis Chenery, in "Comparative Advantage and Development Policy," *American Economic Review* 51 (1961):18–51, argued that the optimality of a free-trade regime was contingent on the absence of market imperfections. Hans Singer's "The Distribution of Gains between Investing and Borrowing Countries," *American Economic Review* 40 (1950):473–85; and Raul Prebisch's "Commercial Policy in the Underdeveloped Countries," *Amer-*

Anne Krueger, later explained that: "From a theory without any evidence in the early 1960s suggesting departures from free trade for dynamic reasons, the tables are turned: empirical evidence strongly suggests dynamic factors that may be associated with export-led growth."[5] Export expansion spurred by market liberalization became the industrialization strategy of choice.

Work in the 1970s by Krueger, Bela Balassa,[6] and others was not so much anti-interventionist as anti–import substitution. The debate between old-style development economists and more orthodox theorists still centered on market failure. It focused on whether to intervene and, with few exceptions,[7] the protagonists stopped well short of denying the state's institutional capacity to promote economic development. That more radical claim came with the second phase of neoclassical counterrevolution against heterodoxy.

The neoclassical political economy literature of the 1980s explicitly attacks the early development economists' implicit belief in the efficacy of government intervention. It argues that the existence of market failure is not sufficient to justify state intervention. Formal models of the interaction between state and economy have been devised to show theoretically and not just empirically how government intervention is likely to produce inefficiencies. State policy is endogenized to the general equilibrium system by depicting it as the outcome of individual optimizing behavior in the political realm. In contrast to traditional

---

ican Economic Review 49 (1959):257–69, embellished this work by arguing that static comparative advantage as revealed by current prices could not capture secular trends. These articles argued that raw material exports could not finance manufactured imports in the long term because of the differences in price and income elasticities for primary and manufactured goods. The inevitability of future foreign-exchange shortages thus provided a rationale for industrialization.

[5] Anne O. Krueger, "Comparative Advantage and Development Policy 20 Years Later," in Moshe Syrquin, Lance Taylor, and Larry Westphal, eds., *Economic Structure and Performance: Essays in Honor of Hollis B. Chenery* (New York: Academic Press, 1984), p. 139.

[6] Bela Balassa, "Trade Policies in Developing Countries," *American Economic Review* 61 (1971):178–87.

[7] These include P. T. Bauer, *Dissent on Development* (London: Weidenfeld and Nicolson, 1972); and *Reality and Rhetoric: Studies in the Economics of Development* (London: Weidenfeld and Nicolson, 1984). Bauer was one of the first to argue that government failure was worse than market failure, and that intervention caused and did not cure market imperfections. A few isolated voices from the other side of the spectrum include John Kenneth Galbraith, *Economic Development in Perspective* (Cambridge, Mass.: Harvard University Press, 1964); and Gunnar Myrdal, "The 'Soft State' in Underdeveloped Countries," in Paul Streeten, ed., *Unfashionable Economics: Essays in Honor of Lord Balogh* (London: Weidenfeld and Nicolson, 1970).

arguments of administrative incompetence and corruption, recent theorists argue that state policies such as subsidies and quotas distort incentives to the private sector and generate competition for the excess returns that accrue to the winners of government largesse. Because almost any state intervention opens space for a "rent,"[8] seeking government favors will divert resources away from productive market activity. Firms will engage instead in activities such as lobbying and bribery to garner and maintain these rents. The rational pursuit of these favors on an individual level produces a nonoptimal result for the economy as a whole.[9]

These arguments suggest that industrialization strategies oriented to the national market, which, by definition, rely upon market restrictions and government intervention, create a more conducive climate for rent-seeking activity than the more open, export-promoting strategies. This presents a different explanation for the relative success of export-promoting countries: The state is less involved, so the economy is less prone to rent-seeking activity. The pressures of international competition are supposed to mitigate the worst sort of rent seeking observed in countries practicing pure import-substituting industrialization. Free trade and factor mobility reduce rent seeking by restraining special interests and making cartels harder to maintain.

---

[8] In this context, a rent is earned on a given resource when its return is higher than its opportunity cost, that is, the return it would generate in an alternative activity.

[9] If one follows the categorization used by T. N. Srinivasan in "Neoclassical Political Economy: The State and Economic Development," Yale University, Economic Growth Center Paper no. 375 (New Haven, 1985), three different strands can be discerned in the neoclassical political economy literature: Mancur Olson's collective action framework, James Buchanan's public choice school, and Jagdish N. Bhagwati's and Anne O. Krueger's related work on trade and development. In *The Rise and Decline of Nations* (New Haven: Yale University Press, 1983), Olson argues that because of bargaining costs and the problem of free riders, individuals are unlikely to organize in their collective interest unless they are in small groups and/or can impose selective incentives on group members. Such coalitions of self-interested persons are likely to try to redistribute income toward themselves instead of working to raise efficiency and national income, the full benefits of which they would not receive. In "Rent Seeking and Profit Seeking," in J. M. Buchanan, R. D. Tollison, and G. Tullock, eds., *Toward a Theory of Rent-Seeking Society* (College Station: Texas A & M University Press, 1980), pp. 3–15, Buchanan argues that the emergence of monopoly and other distortions created by public policy does more than impose a deadweight loss on the economy, because it directs resources into what Bhagwati referred to as "directly unproductive profit-seeking activities" (in "Directly Unproductive Profit Seeking [DUP] Activities," *Journal of Political Economy* 90 [1982]:988–1002). In "The Political Economy of the Rent-Seeking Society," in *American Economic Review* 64 (1974):291–303, Krueger emphasized the consequences of quantitative import restrictions.

In development economics, therefore, the operating assumption of imperfect markets has been replaced by the presumed inevitability of imperfect states, lacking the wherewithal to counteract rent-seeking behavior. The neoclassical political economy literature has concluded that the former is the lesser of two evils. From this perspective, even if markets are imperfect, state intervention – due to its market-distorting, growth-inhibiting character – only makes things worse. As Deepak Lal contends, "bureaucratic failure" may be worse than "market failure."[10]

The State-Centric, Institutional Approach

Proponents of a statist approach to development are as impressed with East Asia's success as are market-oriented theorists, but they derive different conclusions from the experiences of these late industrializers. In the tradition of Alexander Gerschenkron, this eclectic group, drawn mostly from social science disciplines outside economics, sees effective institution building as the critical explanatory variable for relative growth rates among latecomers. According to its reading of history, what has distinguished countries such as Japan, South Korea, and even Taiwan from other twentieth-century industrializers has not been an unwillingness to subsidize and protect, but underlying productive structures and states with the fiscal and institutional capacity to discipline firms and to formulate coherent and strategic economic policy.[11]

A unifying theme among these theorists is that market forces alone will not lead to successful economic outcomes. There are differences among them, however, about the importance of using unfettered markets to set relative prices. Some argue that strong governments are required both to usurp the market's role in resource allocation

---

[10] Deepak Lal, *The Poverty of "Development Economics"* (Cambridge, Mass.: Harvard University Press, 1985), p. 14.

[11] See Gordon White and Robert Wade, eds., *Developmental States in East Asia* (Brighton: Institute of Development Studies, Research Report 16, 1985); Robert Wade, *Governing the Market: Economic Theory and the Role of Government in East Asian Industrialization* (Princeton: Princeton University Press, 1990); Gary Gereffi and Donald D. Wyman, eds., *Manufacturing Miracles: Paths of Industrialization in Latin America and East Asia* (Princeton: Princeton University Press, 1990); Leroy Jones and Il Sakong, *Government, Business, and Entrepreneurship in Economic Development: The Korean Case* (Cambridge, Mass.: Harvard University Press, 1980); and Peter Evans, "Predatory, Developmental and Other Apparatuses: A Comparative Political Economy Perspective on the Third World State," *Sociological Forum* 4, no. 4 (December 1989):561–87.

and to ignore standard indicators of static comparative advantage and nefficiency. Chalmers Johnson, for example, credits Japan's success to its "plan-rational" state, which took an active role in industrialization and was concerned with strategic outcomes, in contrast to a "market-rational" state's concern with rules of the game and traditional notions of efficient resource allocation.[12] Based on her study of South Korea, Alice Amsden even argues that late industrializers should get important prices "wrong" in order to direct resources into targeted activities that reflect a country's dynamic comparative advantage.[13] Others such as Stephan Haggard have supported the neoclassical contention that the success of East Asia's NICs resulted from economic liberalization and their quick adoption of export-oriented development strategies that were relatively less price-distorting than Latin American import-substitution schemes.[14]

Regardless of their attitude to market signals, these theorists are distinguished from their neoclassical adversaries by the contention that differences in state capacity largely explain variation in economic performance among latecomers. Although they acknowledge that "where there are rents, there are rent-seekers," their solution is not to remove the state but to build a competent bureaucracy to block rent-seeking behavior.[15] For those who defend price-distorting interventions, a state with enough countervailing power over the private sector is required to impose performance standards on firms receiving support.

Amsden, for example, argues that the source of South Korea's success, and what distinguishes it from other late-industrializing countries with similar strategies, is the state's power and willingness to discipline private firms. It rewarded firms with low-cost financing and access to foreign currency in exchange for increasingly stringent export requirements. It had a broad array of instruments at its disposal, including control of the banking system and prices, to curb monopoly power. It also had the fiscal authority to tax the middle class and the political leeway to keep social expenditures relatively low, which freed government funds for long-run investment. As a result, South Korea

---

[12] Chalmers Johnson, *MITI and the Japanese Miracle: The Growth of Industrial Policy, 1925–1975* (Stanford: Stanford University Press, 1982), pp. 19–20.
[13] Alice Amsden, *Asia's Next Giant: South Korea and Late Industrialization* (Oxford: Oxford University Press, 1989).
[14] Stephan Haggard, *Pathways from the Periphery: The Politics of Growth in the Newly Industrializing Countries* (Ithaca: Cornell University Press, 1990), p. 15.
[15] See Evans, "Predatory, Developmental and Other Apparatuses: A Comparative Political Economy Perspective on the Third World State."

did not degenerate into a pure rent-seeking society where the government distributed spoils only to politically favored groups. Despite a concentrated and protected industrial structure, government policies generated intense competition that forced firms to "learn" and become ever more productive.[16] Other countries have been less successful in creating this type of reciprocity between the state and private firms. Those who support the adoption of export-led industrial policies argue that this strategy, too, must be accompanied by economic and institutional reforms. Most less-developed country (LDC) states, for historical and political reasons, have not had the capacity with which to implement these reforms and to make hard policy choices.

Integrating Visions

The neoclassical political economy literature has correctly pinpointed the implicit assumption that the state has unlimited capacity to intervene effectively in the economic system as the major weakness of 1960s-era development economists. Those theorists had focused on whether to intervene, but they stopped short of explicitly considering the state's political and institutional capacity to meet its prescribed role. In so doing, much of development economics reproduced the neoclassical separation of the economic and political spheres, neglecting to incorporate a theory of the state. Traditional neoclassical theory at least assumed that markets function, presupposing a minimal role for the government. In contrast, the omission of the state as an explicit actor was a fundamental flaw in the development theorists' argument, because they relied on it as an agent of change and presumed that it had the requisite political autonomy and administrative tools to carry out the task. Because the academic debate concentrated only on the existence of market imperfections, the superior capacity of the state to allocate resources remained an article of faith.[17]

---

[16] Ha-Joon Chang makes the interesting argument that the dominance of large, industrial conglomerates, or *chaebols*, may have helped minimize the extent to which government subsidies turned into pure rents for the private sector. Given the *chaebols'* exclusive status, smaller players were unlikely to compete with them. Their involvement in multiple activities reduced the costs associated with start-up and with finding information about competitors. Furthermore, each *chaebol's* ability to move into almost any line of business generated competitive pressures to remain efficient. See Ha-Joon Chang, "Interpreting the Korean Experience – Heaven or Hell?" Faculty of Economics and Politics, University of Cambridge, Research Paper Series no. 42 (Cambridge, 1990).

[17] Implicit assumptions associated with early development frameworks increase the probability of efficient intervention. For a discussion of the political and technological

By challenging the underpinnings of this faith, the new literature has successfully shifted the terms of the debate from imperfect markets to imperfect states. It is no longer sufficient to justify state intervention by demonstrating market failure. Ironically, this shift comes at a time when the literature on potential market imperfections has become more extensive and theoretically sophisticated, as demonstrated by work on imperfect information and strategic trade. Exponents of strategic trade models have pointed out how economic rents need not be competed away in the presence of economies of scale, and intervention may be Pareto superior to laissez-faire. When international trade is driven by economies of scale rather than comparative advantage, and when international markets are dominated by oligopolistic firms earning excess returns, a "strategic trade policy" can shift the economic rents earned by foreign firms to domestically based firms. Commentators influenced by neoclassical political economy have been quick to point out the difficulties in devising policy prescriptions to overcome these market imperfections, thus relegating interventionist remedies to the realm of theory rather than of policy.[18]

assumptions of Alexander Gerschenkron, see Douglas C. Bennett and Kenneth E. Sharpe, "The State as Banker and as Entrepreneur: The Last Resort Character of the Mexican State's Economic Interventions, 1917–1976," *Comparative Politics* 12 (1980):165–89; Evans et al., *Bringing the State Back In;* and Helen Shapiro, "State Intervention and Industrialization: The Origins of the Brazilian Automobile Industry" (Ph.D. diss., Yale University, 1988). The Prebisch/Economic Commission on Latin America (ECLA) focus on the center–periphery dichotomy obfuscated internal, domestic contradictions of the type observed in Brazil, which affect the state's fiscal capacity. The lack of concern about relying on inflationary finance in the face of fiscal constraints reflected a generally shared view among Latin American structuralists of inflation as relatively benign or, at worst, a necessary evil. Dependency theorists were among the first to criticize ECLA and import-substitution strategies for ignoring the class nature of the peripheral state and for not fully analyzing the role of foreign capital. For a review, see Gabriel Palma, "Dependency: A Formal Theory of Underdevelopment or a Methodology for the Analysis of Concrete Situations of Underdevelopment," *World Development* 6, nos. 7–8 (1978):881–924.

[18] On the microeconomics of information, see Joseph E. Stiglitz, "The New Development Economics," *World Development* 14, no. 2 (1986):257–65; and "Economic Organization, Information and Development," in Hollis Chenery and T. N. Srinivasan, eds., *Handbook of Development Economics*, vol. 1 (Amsterdam: North-Holland, 1988), pp. 94–160. On strategic trade, see Paul R. Krugman, "Import Protection as Export Promotion," in H. Keirzkoski, ed., *Monopolistic Competition and International Trade* (Oxford: Oxford University Press, 1984), pp. 180–93; Paul R. Krugman, ed., *Strategic Trade Policy and the New International Economics* (Cambridge, Mass.: MIT Press, 1986); J. A. Brander and B. J. Spencer, "Export Subsidies and International Market Share Rivalry," *Journal of International Economics* 18 (1985):83–100; and Gerald K. Helleiner, ed., *Trade Policy Liberalization and Development: New Perspectives* (Oxford: Clar-

Despite these important contributions, however, many neoclassical theorists weaken their case by making ahistorical and universalistic claims, especially with respect to the international economy. Moreover, the approach generally has very limiting assumptions about the nature of the state. As a result, it virtually denies a priori the possibility of interventionist policies succeeding, and it cannot account for examples of success or failure. It therefore has only limited applicability to the Brazilian case.

The notion that eliminating distortions will enhance economic efficiency in Pareto's sense is a central tenet of the neoclassical perspective. However, a balanced judgment is that "getting the prices right" frequently may be a necessary condition for enhanced microeconomic supply performance but is seldom sufficient.[19] At issue is Alexander Gerschenkron's long-forgotten point about backwardness and inertia; more than a market signal is required to displace the previous "equilibrium" in order to make nontraditional export markets and industrial investment projects attractive. In many less-developed countries, the state has been the only entity with pockets deep enough to make beyond-market incentives sufficiently sweet.

More fundamentally, neoclassical political economy, despite the prominent contributions of economic historians and a concern with relative growth rates among countries, is strangely ahistorical and timeless. In fact, the recent neoclassical proponents tend to recast history to fit their assumptions. They attribute the high growth rates in East Asia and elsewhere to getting the prices "right." In so doing, they demonstrate asymmetric vision: if a country is growing rapidly, they see market forces at work; if it is not, they see bad public policy.

The question of whether enhanced microeconomic efficiency, if attained, significantly raises the growth rate is a methodologically thorny issue to address.[20] However, equating efficiency with growth fails to account for the experience of the advanced capitalist countries,

endon Press, 1992). For critiques of strategic trade, see Jagdish Bhagwati, *Protectionism* (Cambridge, Mass.: MIT Press, 1988); J. Eaton and G. M. Grossman, "Optimal Trade and Industrial Policy under Oligopoly," NBER Working Paper no. 1236 (Cambridge, Mass., 1983); and G. M. Grossman and J. D. Richardson, "Strategic Trade Policy: A Survey of Issues and Early Analysis," International Finance Section, Princeton University Special Paper 15 (Princeton, 1985).

[19] For example, such findings appear in eighteen country studies of stabilization and adjustment programs organized by the World Institute for Development Economics Research (WIDER) and reviewed by Lance Taylor, *Varieties of Stabilization Experience* (Oxford: Clarendon Press, 1988).

[20] For more on this point, see Shapiro and Taylor, "The State and Industrial Strategy."

as Joseph Schumpeter with his emphasis on entrepreneurs and innovations recognized long ago. Although failures abound, there are no "invisible hand" success stories. Virtually all cases of successful industrial development, including the United States, have involved state intervention.[21]

Moreover, the Latin American experiments with import-substitution policies have not been uniform failures. Performance has differed considerably across countries, and the abysmal record of the 1980s has obscured earlier successes. Brazilian and Mexican postwar growth rates, for example, rivaled those of the export-driven, high-growth economies of East Asia until 1980.[22] The world trend toward liberalization policies, as well as Brazil's current economic crisis, have obscured the fact that Brazil's interventionist policies and the intricate web of business–government interactions they spawned were once credited with bringing about the economic "miracle" of 1968–73 and sustaining high growth rates throughout the 1970s. Average annual growth rates averaged over 7 percent from 1940 to 1980, and real per capita income increased fivefold, from US$490 to US$2,450 in 1989 prices.[23] The country was included with the East Asian tigers among the NICs. Most accounts of Brazil's rapid growth gave primary credit to the state as a source of capital, as a bureaucratic administrator, and as a builder of effective alliances among state-owned enterprises, multinationals, and domestic firms.[24]

[21] M. Horowitz, *The Transformation of American Law* (Cambridge, Mass.: Harvard University Press, 1977), shows that U.S. courts restricted individuals' control over property; decisions came to favor community property over absolute domain. Although the court actions served the general welfare, they violated Buchanan's strict conditions for Pareto optimality. Oscar Handlin and Mary Flug Handlin, *Commonwealth: A Study of the Role of Government in the American Economy: Massachusetts 1774–1861* (Cambridge, Mass.: Belknap Press of Harvard University Press, 1969); and Louis Hartz, *Economic Policy and Democratic Thought: Pennsylvania 1776–1860* (Cambridge, Mass.: Harvard University Press, 1948), demonstrate that, although they were constrained by the Constitution in their choice of instruments, state legislatures controlled exports and granted monopoly power to public corporations.

[22] See Albert Fishlow, "Brief Comparative Reflections on Latin American Economic Performance and Policy," paper presented at the WIDER/UNU Conference, August 12–14, 1986, Helsinki.

[23] Dionisio D. Carneiro and Rogerio L. F. Werneck, "Brazil," in Lance Taylor, ed., *The Rocky Road to Reform: Adjustment, Income Distribution, and Growth in the Developing World* (Cambridge, Mass.: MIT Press, 1993), p. 415.

[24] See Werner Baer, Isaac Kerstenetsky, and Annibal V. Villela, "The Changing Role of the State in the Brazilian Economy," *World Development* 1, no. 11 (1973):23–4; Albert O. Hirschman, "The Political Economy of Import-Substituting Industrialization in Latin America," *Quarterly Journal of Economics* 82 (1968):1–32; Fernando Henrique

Although it is true that opportunities from international trade exist to a degree unforeseen by earlier theorists, gains from trade are not universally available to all countries at all times. In addition, the neoclassical focus on the advantages of economic openness often results in minimizing the extent to which the international arena presents constraints to less-developed countries as well. Dynamic gains from trade may not be available to, or the export-promotion strategy warranted for, every economy. Albert Fishlow and William Cline propose a series of counterarguments about the institutional requirements for export-led growth, the nature of the traditional export, and the potential fallacy of composition if all less-developed countries attempted trade expansion.[25] The international environment also complicates the task of neoclassical political theory. In particular, domestic rent-seeking activity is not the only distortion of free markets that occurs. The existence of strong oligopolies in certain world markets and of unequal access to technology contradicts the assumptions of free trade.

The basic problem is again one of counterfactuals: In attacking the government, neoclassical political economy posits an idealized market in its stead. But the market itself can generate its own rent-seeking entities and redistributions of income. There is a peculiar asymmetry in the neoclassical political economy models, whereby individuals coalesce to force a political redistribution but do not do the same in the marketplace. The political arena is depicted as one full of lobbyists and cartel builders, whereas the economy is presented as being more or less subject to competition.[26] Despite greater putative openness

Cardoso and Enzo Faletto, *Dependency and Development in Latin America* (Berkeley: University of California Press, 1979); and Peter Evans, *Dependent Development: The Alliance of Multinational, State, and Local Capital in Brazil* (Princeton: Princeton University Press, 1979). For an analysis of the more recent fiscal crisis of the Brazilian state, which takes many these political-economic issues into account, see Luiz Carlos Bresser Pereira, "Economic Reforms and Economic Growth: Efficiency and Politics in Latin America," in Luiz Carlos Bresser Pereira, José María Maravall, and Adam Przeworski, *Economic Reforms in New Democracies* (Cambridge: Cambridge University Press, 1993).

[25] Fishlow, "Brief Comparative Reflections"; and William Cline, "Can the East Asian Model of Development Be Generalized?" *World Development* 10 (1982):81–90.

[26] Olmstead's and Goldberg's comments with respect to this literature's stand on regulation are pertinent: "But this literature misses a crucial point, for it implicitly assumes that the alternative to regulation was either the world as it existed prior to regulation or a free market. However, in a dynamic world where groups can redirect their efforts to change the system there is no reason to expect that, having been frustrated in efforts to obtain regulation, they would not have invested resources to change some other aspect of the institutional structure. While the institutions of regulation can be manipulated in the producer's interest, so too can those of private contract. . . . This is not to say that regulation was the most desirable alternative in all cases. The point

under a liberal trade regime, there is no guarantee that an export-promotion strategy is any less subject to rent-seeking activity than import substitution.[27]

Generally, neoclassical political economy does not explicitly discuss the state itself, despite its claim to make public action an endogenous variable. Implicitly, however, it posits the state as a passive entity that is acted on by, and indeed becomes captive to, distributional coalitions.[28] As T. N. Srinivasan explains, instead of the benevolent and administratively competent state postulated in the development literature, "the state is seen to be pushed and pulled by lobbies and interest groups that are mostly interested in redistribution rather than growth and development."[29] Implicit in the approach is a peculiar counterfactual combining a nonpolitically organized society with the ideal liberal state, completely neutral with respect to distribution.[30]

State-centric theorists have made an enormous contribution to the

is simply that the current literature . . . makes a specious comparison between corrupt regulation and pristine private contract as if the latter were the feasible alternative to the former. The same forces that bend one also bend the other."Alan L. Olmstead and Victor P. Goldberg, "Institutional Change and American Economic Growth: A Critique of Davis and North," *Explorations in Economic History* 12 (1975):203–4.

[27] Boratav's study on Turkey illustrates that competition for rents can occur under an export-oriented strategy, and that the success of such a strategy is contingent on structural conditions that cannot be taken for granted. Turkey's export boom in the early 1980s rested upon a pre-existing industrial base created by import substitution, by policies leading to contraction of domestic demand for manufactures, by a general price reform, by subsidies of up to one-third of export sales, and by rapid growth in demand for Turkey's export products. See Korkut Boratav, "Turkey," Stabilization and Adjustment Policies and Programmes Country Study no. 5 (Helsinki: WIDER, 1988).

[28] Ake Blomqvist and Sharif Mohammad, "Controls, Corruption, and Competitive Rent-Seeking in LDCs," *Journal of Development Economics* 21 (1986):161–80, point out that the rent-seeking literature does not explicitly specify the type of directly unproductive profit seeking (DUP) activity involved, but usually assumes that rent-bearing assets are allocated to actors who withdraw factors from productive activity to seek rents. They show that the level of efficiency loss is affected by the type of productive activity in which the rent-receivers engage.

[29] Srinivasan, "Neoclassical Political Economy: The State and Economic Development," p. 45.

[30] Samuel Bowles and John Eatwell, "Between Two Worlds: Interest Groups, Class Structure, and Capitalist Growth," in Dennis C. Mueller, ed., *The Political Economy of Growth* (New Haven: Yale University Press, 1983), pp. 217–30; Brian Barry, "Some Questions about Explanation," *International Studies Quarterly* 27 (1983):17–27; and David Cameron, "Creating Theory in Comparative Political Economy: On Mancur Olson's Explanation of Growth", paper presented at the Annual Meeting of the American Political Science Association, Chicago, 1983, make this point with particular reference to Olson.

debate by reminding us of the multifaceted nature of economic development. They have corrected the historical record regarding the NICs by documenting the extent of state intervention in these countries and by demonstrating that their success was not simply the result of removing economic distortions or promoting exports. As a result of their efforts, the debate on East Asia has become less simplistic and has prompted some neoclassical-oriented economists to begin considering the institutional requirements of development more broadly.[31]

The state-centric literature has also countered the dependency theorists' presumption that the peripheral state is too weak vis-à-vis foreign capital to act as an independent agent in the development process. Early dependency theory had challenged the prevailing notion that foreign capital was inherently beneficial to less-developed countries and argued that economic and political dependency precluded the possibility of internally generated, sustainable development. Based on the experience of the East Asian NICs, statist theorists have illustrated that, under certain conditions, it is possible for governments in less-developed countries to shape the behavior of private firms in general and of foreign transnational firms in particular to fit into their own development strategies. As Barbara Stallings describes, "The state has been portrayed as capable of using foreign capital, rather than the other way around."[32]

The eclecticism within the statist approach leads to wide variation. In its extreme, however, the emphasis on the importance of institution building incorrectly reduces economic development to a domestic political problem. The implied solution for less-developed countries is a sufficiently autonomous state that is able to impose the necessary reforms and resource allocation. The "right" economic model is presumed as given, but the political variables necessary to implement it are not. The domestic and international economy may pose structural constraints, but in this framework, they are nonbinding; the problem is to derive the correct institutional mechanism to take advantage of the available economic opportunities. Chalmers Johnson's taxonomy of "plan-rational" versus "market-rational" states also poses a false dichotomy between rules and outcomes. For some economists, the market rules for allocating resources efficiently are also, theoretically,

[31] For example, see Pranab Bardhan, ed., "Symposium on the State and Economic Development," *Journal of Economic Perspectives* 4, no. 3 (1990):3–75.
[32] Barbara Stallings, "The Role of Foreign Capital in Economic Development," in Gereffi and Wyman, eds., *Manufacturing Miracles*, p. 58.

the best way to achieve goals, at least with respect to income max-
imization.

Those who have built on the work of Chalmers Johnson and others
by analyzing the historical and political conditions that provide particular states with particular capacities have shown that adopting the
"correct" economic policies or creating appropriate institutions is not
simply a question of political will.[33] However, their sample of successful cases is largely restricted to East Asian, export-oriented NICs,
with states powerful enough to discipline foreign and domestic capital.
Latin American states are generally characterized as being relatively
weak and their economies more structurally constrained, leaving less
room for policy manipulation.[34]

Brazilian Auto: A Case of Successful Intervention

Brazil's experience with the auto industry in the 1950s and 1960s does
not fit comfortably on either side of the dichotomous debate between
neoclassical political economy and state-centric approaches to economic development. It meets neither the economic nor the political
conditions for success postulated by either model.

This book is an attempt to bridge this conceptual gap. It starts from
the premise that in the 1950s, Brazil, like many less-developed countries, found itself in the world of second-best. Its domestic economy
was plagued with distortions and foreign-exchange constraints. On
the international front, it confronted an imperfectly competitive automotive industry, characterized by economies of scale and an oligopolized market structure. As exponents of strategic trade models
have pointed out, the installation of domestic productive capacity
would save Brazil the costs associated with imports. These costs included not only scarce foreign exchange but also the rents paid to
the importing firms, as well as the industry's production and technological externalities. These social benefits would not have been cap-
tured by individual investors; in the absence of intervention, there

[33] See Evans et al., *Bringing the State Back In;* Gereffi and Wyman, *Manufacturing Miracles;* and Haggard, *Pathways from the Periphery.*
[34] Latin American states have been depicted as being relatively weak with respect to
private domestic economic actors as well as to foreign firms, which have played a
more prominent role in Latin American development. For discussions of associated
dependent development models, see Cardoso and Faletto, *Dependency and Development
in Latin America;* Evans, *Dependent Development;* and Douglas C. Bennett and Kenneth
E. Sharpe, *Transnational Corporations versus the State: The Political Economy of the Mexican
Auto Industry* (Princeton: Princeton University Press, 1985).

would have been underinvestment in the sector. Therefore, according to both strategic trade arguments and traditional infant industry–externality arguments, protection and subsidization were warranted. For similar reasons, many countries in Europe, as well as Japan, protected their auto industries from U.S. exports in the 1920s and 1930s.

Brazil's political economy precluded the use of direct policy instruments to promote the industry; state intervention was not orchestrated by a planning agency with direct allocational control of economic resources analogous to Japan's Ministry of International Trade and Industry (MITI). The Kubitschek regime relied on indirect policy instruments such as exchange-rate manipulation to shift resources into the industrial sector. Brazil's domestic private sector was also relatively weak and its capital markets undeveloped.

As a result, and in contrast to countries such as Japan and South Korea, Brazil relied on foreign rather than domestic capital to build its domestic industry. This fact complicates the standard strategic trade model in two significant ways. First, these firms replicate oligopolistic behavior domestically. Therefore, the issue is not simply rent distribution between nations but the internal distribution among foreign firms, the state, and consumers. The notion of rent seeking must be expanded to the international arena by explicitly incorporating the behavioral characteristics of transnational firms, which are also powerful lobbyists for state privileges. Criteria for evaluating the success of Brazil's sectoral policies, therefore, must include the state's capacity to capture rents accruing to the firms, the possibility of which the neoclassical political economy model does not recognize.[35]

Second, because the industry was to be built by foreign capital, its development would be determined by the strategies of foreign firms and the policies set up to attract them to the Brazilian market. Indeed, existing explanations for the particular evolution of the Brazilian automotive industry often echo the more general debate between neoclassical and statist theorists. A large literature on foreign direct

[35] Douglass North's *Structure and Change in Economic History* (New York: W. W. Norton, 1981) is a variant of the new neoclassical approach with an important caveat: The state can have its own agenda. North paints the state as an autonomous vested interest group that seeks to maximize its own wealth, but at the expense of general economic welfare. As a result, there is a constant trade-off between economic efficiency and state power. Also, in Pranab K. Bardhan's *The Political Economy of Development in India* (Oxford: Basil Blackwell, 1984), which extends rent-seeking activity to the Indian state, the government itself may enter the fray. In Bardhan's view, conflicts between bureaucrats and industrialists over appropriation of rents interact with India's traditional rural–urban disparities to perpetuate stagnation.

investment explains the entrance of transnational firms into countries like Brazil and the ultimate structure of industries by the behavioral characteristics of global oligopolies, discounting the importance of state policy.[36] In contrast, some analysts of the Brazilian auto industry have adopted a state-centric approach by crediting government policy and administrative reform for the industry's emergence. These authors give particular credit to the Executive Group for the Automotive Industry (Grupo Executivo da Indústria Automobilística [GEIA]), created by President Kubitschek, for serving an indispensable planning function.[37] In its focus on institutions, this literature downplays the degree to which international and domestic economic circumstances impose boundary conditions on state intervention.

The literature that portrays the terms of foreign investment as being determined through a bargaining process between the state and transnational corporations overcomes the limitations of extreme versions of these approaches and their extension to the case of Brazilian auto. On the one hand, it acknowledges structurally determined aspects of peripheral industrialization. Its analysis of these constraints on state policy goes beyond the neoclassical world of competitive markets by portraying the economic and political power of transnational firms. On the other hand, unlike much of the earlier dependency literature, which allowed little scope for public policy, the independent dynamics of foreign capital do not completely determine the pattern of foreign investment within this bargaining framework.[38]

[36] See Richard E. Caves, *Multinational Enterprise and Economic Analysis* (Cambridge: Cambridge University Press, 1982), for a general discussion; Stephen Hymer, *The International Operation of National Firms: A Study of Direct Foreign Investment* (Cambridge, Mass.: MIT Press, 1976), on the impetus behind direct foreign investment; and Frederick T. Knickerbocker, "Oligopolistic Reaction and Multinational Enterprise" (D.B.A. diss., Harvard University Graduate School of Business Administration, 1972), on the oligopolistic interdependence of firms.

[37] See Barbara Geddes, "Building State Autonomy in Brazil, 1930–1964," *Comparative Politics* 22, no. 2 (January 1990):217–34; and Celso Lafer, "The Planning Process and the Political System in Brazil: A Study of Kubitschek's Target Plan 1956–1961" (Ph.D. diss., Cornell University, 1970), on executive groups in general; see Wellington Moreira Franco, "Nacionalização de veículos no Brasil" (Master's thesis, University of São Paulo, n.d.), on GEIA in particular.

[38] See Evans et al., *Bringing the State Back In*. For case studies on various industries in Latin America, see Richard Newfarmer, ed., *Profits, Progress and Poverty: Case Studies of International Industries in Latin America* (Notre Dame: University of Notre Dame Press, 1985). For studies on the Latin American auto industries, see Bennett and Sharpe, *Transnational Corporations versus the State;* Eduardo Augusto de Almeida Guimarães, "Industry, Market Structure and the Growth of the Firm in the Brazilian Economy" (Ph.D. diss., University of London, 1980), and *Acumulação e crescimento*

This book aims to integrate the general insights of neoclassical and statist approaches into a detailed, context-sensitive analysis of the bargaining process between the Brazilian state and the foreign auto companies. It broadens the bargaining framework to incorporate strategic objectives of both the state and the firms that went beyond investment per se. For Kubitschek, the installation of manufacturing capacity was not simply an end in itself but a means to rapid industrialization and the maintenance of political support. The automobile industry was the only consumer good in his Target Plan, a state-sponsored industrialization program. Nevertheless, the automobile, the pinnacle of technological maturity, was a potent symbol of development and would become the barometer of the Target Plan's success. Firms, in contrast, tried to limit their initial commitment to make it easier to recoup their investments and to reduce potential exit costs.

The incentive structure was designed to ensure that firms made large, up-front commitments to the auto project rather than incremental investments. Because of the uncertain policy direction of the next administration and firms' potential efforts to delay investing in the hopes of a policy switch, Brazilian technocrats felt it necessary to develop the industry to the "point of no return." Once significant investments had been made and a network of domestic suppliers created, it would be difficult both economically and politically to dismantle the industry.

This strategy involved trade-offs. Attracting numerous firms into a small domestic market that could not technically support even one plant operating at full capacity was bound to create short-run efficiency problems. To minimize diseconomies of scale, the preferable strategy might have been to start with lower domestic-content requirements that gradually increased as the market grew. Gradualism did not appear to be a viable option given the uncertainty about future presidential administrations, chronic foreign-exchange constraints, and the strategies of foreign firms. Because of the economies of scale in the industry and the discrete, long-run nature of investment, firms preferred to export from existing facilities. If government policies could force firms to invest, it was unlikely that these investments would simply be viewed as sunk costs that a firm would easily write off. The

da firma (Rio de Janeiro: Editora Guanabara S.A., 1987); Rhys Owen Jenkins, *Transnational Corporations and the Latin American Automobile Industry* (Pittsburgh: University of Pittsburgh Press, 1987); and Kenneth S. Mericle, "The Political Economy of the Brazilian Motor Vehicle Industry," in Rich Kronish and Kenneth S. Mericle, eds., *The Political Economy of the Latin American Motor Vehicle Industry* (Cambridge, Mass.: MIT Press, 1984), pp. 1–40.

alternative to an industry inefficient in the short run appeared to be no industry at all.

Therefore, this book expands the bargaining parameters to include the form and timing of entry, which generally are not considered but which were as fundamental as entry itself. To account for these aspects of the entry process, it is necessary to look at government institutions and policies. It is also necessary to incorporate economic variables specific to the sector, country, and product when evaluating the conditions required for rent redistribution and successful import substitution.

The book argues that a combination of economic and political factors contributed to Brazil's success. The first set of economic factors relates to the nature of the Brazilian market and of the macroeconomic environment and to characteristics specific to motor vehicles. The size of the market made a domestic industry viable; the initial inefficiency and required resource transfer resulting from low levels of production were more easily absorbed than they would have been in a smaller, weaker economy. It is in this regard that the neoclassical concern with efficiency becomes relevant. In general, the probability is small that a newly established and highly inefficient industry – for example, one characterized by large scale economies in a small market – will become more efficient over time; ongoing resource transfers will be required. Below a minimum threshold level, subsidies are likely to accommodate an industry's inefficiency rather than to induce a dynamic growth process. The growth potential of Brazil's domestic market also provided the government with more bargaining power vis-à-vis the auto firms. In addition, the repressed demand from the postwar years, and the fact that automobiles as luxury goods were relatively inelastic with respect to price, allowed firms to pass along their high costs to consumers. This also allowed the government to impose a high tax incidence on vehicles without diminishing total revenues. The same results would not have obtained had the policy involved an intermediate good rather than a consumer durable. The cost of a tax or inefficiency for an important manufacturing input would have had much more negative economic ramifications. Finally, the sectoral plan was relatively consistent with macroeconomic policies. When these were not aligned – for example, when the industry could not fully meet its targets in the early 1960s because of an increasingly binding foreign-exchange constraint – problems emerged.

The second set of factors involves the strategies of transnational firms. Brazil's success in attracting foreign direct investment was due in part to the nature of oligopolistic competition in the industry at the time. The country restricted auto imports when competition for foreign markets was intensifying, particularly in Europe; firms responded by following each other to these new markets. Brazil would have had less bargaining power vis-à-vis the transnational firms had it faced the virtual duopoly of Ford and General Motors that prevailed before World War II.

Although the advantages inherent in being a large country helped Brazil's foray into import substitution, as did the strategies of transnational firms, they were not sufficient for success. Argentina, which instituted a similar plan in 1958, did not achieve the same results with respect to either consolidation or rent redistribution.[39] The third set of factors, therefore, concerns the institutional and administrative capacity of the Brazilian state and specific aspects of the policies used. GEIA, the administrative agency overseeing the auto industry, had few policy instruments at its disposal and was not completely insulated from clientelistic pressures. The state's internal divisions and contradictory tendencies had serious implications for administrative capacity. Nevertheless, GEIA had sufficient authority and coherence to make the threat of impending market closure and investment deadlines credible on the one hand, and to make it costly for firms not to participate according to schedule on the other. It was also able to block projects that did not meet the plan's specifications. The Brazilian state *as a whole* was not the "hard state"[40] of South Korea. The Kubitschek government was nevertheless successful in creating *parts* of an administrative apparatus that could effectively wield carrot-and-stick mechanisms to shape private-sector behavior. Based on the historical record as preserved in firm and government archives, and as retold in interviews with key actors, the book differs from the existing literature on the Brazilian industry about the degree to which the structure of government incentives influenced firm strategy and the extent to which the interests of the Brazilian state and transnational auto firms converged. In contrast to some who have applied the bar-

[39] Production in Argentina had reached only 219,000 by 1970 and was not as consolidated among firms, making economies of scale more difficult to attain. Moreover, the fiscal consequences of the industry were radically different. Taxes as a share of both current costs and sales *decreased* over time. In 1960, taxes as a percentage of current costs came to 23%, and as a percentage of sales, 21%. These had fallen respectively to 15% and 14% in 1965, 15% and 12% in 1970, and 6% and 6% in 1975. For more on the Argentine experience, see Juan V. Sourrouille, *Transnacionales en America Latina: El complejo automotor en Argentina* (Mexico D.F.: Editorial Nueva Imagen, 1980); and Rhys Owen Jenkins, *Dependent Industrialization in Latin America: The Automotive Industry in Argentina, Chile, and Mexico* (New York: Praeger, 1977).

[40] The term is used by Jones and Sakong in *Government, Business, and Entrepreneurship in Economic Development: The Korean Case.*

gaining framework to the case of Brazilian auto, this book argues that market closure alone would not have been sufficient to obtain the same results in the absence of the state's capacity to pose a credible threat and to provide subsidies to reduce firm risk.

Remarkably, this agenda was carried out by an elected, civilian government. The Brazilian state was not the passive favor dispenser of the rent-seeking literature. In the 1950s, officials attempted to insulate parts of the economic bureaucracy from interest-group pressure, but the state also created new interest groups by virtue of its interventions. If the state has some degree of autonomy, it need not resort to authoritarianism to eliminate rent-seeking activity, as neoclassical authors such as Deepak Lal suggest. Stable policy is another tool: If the government establishes credibility in its commitment to a particular policy line, rent-seeking activity in that area will be ineffective and tend to wane.

The Brazilian case demonstrates that successful policy outcomes are jointly determined by market and policy variables. Efficiency and efficacy are not dichotomous but complementary objectives. It can be argued that efficiency acts as a constraint upon, even though it may not be a prime objective of, public policy, which has a variety of motivations. The degree to which this constraint is binding depends on a country's economic capacity, the size of the inefficiency, and the means by which and by whom it is paid. Clearly, a society may not be able to organize itself politically to take full advantage of even the most favorable economic conditions. But weak economies or those confronting a recessive international economy are more constrained. Stronger underlying economic conditions provide more latitude for policy manipulation and, ultimately, for policy mistakes.

The nature of the inefficiency and the distribution of its cost are also important. An inefficiently produced productive input has different economic ramifications than a similar consumer good. Whether the state is able to pass along the cost of its subsidization to the private sector or to consumers is also important, particularly for a fiscally constrained state like Brazil. This latter point has direct bearing on the state's capacity to extract rents from a foreign-owned sector, which is the critical issue.

Abba Lerner once said, "Economics has gained the title of queen of the social sciences by choosing solved political problems as its domain."[11] Unfortunately, this remains the case. When economists finally discovered the state, they found it wanting and tried to reason

---

[11] Cited by Bowles and Eatwell, "Between Two Worlds: Interest Groups, Class Structure, and Capitalist Growth," p. 217.

it away. In the new neoclassical synthesis, economics and politics remain divorced. But the state cannot be dismissed so easily if our understanding of how administrative capacity can vary between and within state apparatuses and how successful policy implementation can vary across markets and sectors is to improve. It is necessary to bridge the intellectual divide and to analyze the interaction between the state and the private sector to explain how policy successfully translates into microlevel behavior of the private firm. This public–private interface is really at the heart of development in most less-developed economies where private, rather than state-owned, firms are the principal executors of state policy.[42]

The book's conceptual argument does not add up to simple policy prescriptions such as "get prices right" or "implement an administrative reform." Rather, it suggests that there are no bags of policy tricks that work regardless of context. This is perhaps a less elegant, but more useful, approach to the real world than are broad generalizations. It also suggests that much of the theory on the state and rent seeking that has evolved during the 1980s could be strengthened by more complex empirical analysis. For neoclassicists, this would include closer investigation of actual cases of rent-seeking opportunities; for statists, this would involve moving beyond overly broad comparisons or conclusions with respect to national development strategies to a consideration of more bounded cases of success or failure. Comparative analysis can help to explain why particular strategies perform well or poorly in particular countries at particular times, and how economic and political constraints affect a country's options.

---

[42] The framework of this debate is reminiscent of an earlier one on European mercantilism. The question of whether fiscalism built up national states at the expense of economic development was defined by E. F. Heckscher as a trade-off between "power versus plenty." A conflict of interest between the crown and merchant class was assumed. But as C. H. Wilson remarked: "It seems doubtful whether the controversy is a very fruitful one. For it becomes plain as soon as we try to define what 'mercantilists' meant by 'power' that they were thinking of a political system which rested on an economic base and had certain economic ends. Equally, 'plenty' was thought of in relation to politics and strategy. 'Wealth' was not merely an economic conception; it had to be a character that would coincide with and reinforce the strength of the nation and its capacity to defend itself.... 'Power' and 'Plenty,' that is to say, were not mutually exclusive conceptions but complementary conceptions." For Wilson, the question became what conditions generate the "fiscal desperation" of Spain, or the British fiscalism that "seemed to move in parallel with powerful private and public interests and was less evidently damaging to economic development." C. H. Wilson, "Trade, Society, and the State," in M. M. Postan and H. J. Habakkuk, eds., *Cambridge Economic History of Europe: Part IV* (Cambridge: Cambridge University Press, 1967), pp. 494–5, 521.

Organization of the Book

Chapter 2 analyzes the decision to produce automobiles in Brazil within the post–World War II political and economic context. After the war, Brazil confronted chronic balance-of-payments crises. Although the country had developed significant manufacturing capacity as a result of the economic shocks and policies of the 1930s and 1940s, resolving the foreign-exchange constraint through export-led growth models based on light manufactured goods was inconceivable to Brazilian politicians and technocrats who had witnessed the collapse of raw material prices and world trade in the 1930s. Trade expansion continued to look bleak in the mid-1950s when Europe was rebuilding and its currencies were not yet fully convertible. Moreover, in the Brazilian context, export-promotion policies would have favored agricultural exports.[43]

In response, postwar governments adopted import-substituting industrialization strategies, in which motor vehicles played a central role. The decision to produce motor vehicles was arrived at incrementally and reflected a growing consensus among policymakers, economists, and sectors of the military on Brazil's need to industrialize. Policies to promote a domestic industry first emerged in response to the country's postwar balance-of-payments problems. The country imported all its vehicles, first as built-up units and, after 1954, only as knocked-down kits to be locally assembled. The industry took on strategic implications, as it was expected to play the role of leading sector through its ability to attract foreign capital and technology and to generate production linkages. Plans for a domestic industry began to unfold during the administration of Getúlio Vargas (1951–4) and culminated with Juscelino Kubitschek, who bestowed on motor vehicles a privileged position in his development program. The chapter charts this process, describes Kubitschek's blueprint for the industry, and explains why alternative projects such as railroad transportation,

---

[43] To understand the motivations behind the choice of policies, it is important to keep these international and domestic constraints in mind, as well as the weight of Brazil's recent historical experience. Pointing out these motivations and constraints does not fully explain how dominant political coalitions came together around import-substitution policies. For a discussion of this aspect, see Haggard, *Pathways from the Periphery;* Robert R. Kaufman, "How Societies Change Development Models or Keep Them: Reflections on the Latin American Experience in the 1930s and the Postwar World," in Gereffi and Wyman, *Manufacturing Miracles,* pp. 110–39; and Kathryn Sikkink, *Ideas and Institutions: Developmentalism in Brazil and Argentina* (Ithaca: Cornell University Press, 1991).

state-owned enterprises, and tractor production were rejected. With
its emphasis on the underlying continuity of automotive policy, this
analysis gives less weight than others to the political and ideological
character of the Kubitschek administration in determining the direction of auto policy. Its portrayal of the automotive program as the
product of state initiative also distinguishes it from work that stresses
the role played by the private sector.

Chapter 3 examines the negotiating process between the state and
the transnational firms. It illustrates how the analytic separation of
economics and politics has been reproduced in the literature on the
Brazilian auto, and it presents a more complicated bargaining framework, which takes into account the strategic and political objectives
of state policy. The chapter reviews Brazil's pre-1956 negotiations
with transnational auto firms and discusses the strategic importance
of timing. The chapter then documents the general process of firm
entry into the industry, providing detailed accounts of Volkswagen
and Ford based on archival evidence and interviews. It evaluates the
role of subsidies, along with other policies, in determining firm entry
and industrial structure.

The chapter shows that no firm planned to manufacture vehicles
in Brazil in the absence of government intervention. It demonstrates
that neither Ford nor Volkswagen had any intention to build manufacturing capacity in Brazil prior to the government decrees and
that both tried to evade GEIA requirements once the plan was put
into effect. GEIA's performance was not as stellar as generally portrayed, and it was not able to entice Ford or General Motors, the two
most powerful firms, into the passenger car market in the 1950s; both
firms restricted their Brazilian manufacturing operations to trucks
until 1967, leaving the field to Volkswagen and smaller companies.
However, GEIA was able to resist efforts to sabotage its program and
to force compliance with domestic-content requirements; it repeatedly
rejected car proposals submitted by Ford during 1958–61. GEIA was
powerful enough to keep Ford from entering the market on Ford's
terms but, in the absence of General Motors or Chrysler, was not
strong enough to get Ford in on its own. Ford did gain entry under
the military regime. Most important, GEIA was successful in initiating
motor vehicle production on its own schedule and in kickstarting the
country's industrial development.

Yet GEIA can take little credit for the consolidation of the industry
in the mid-1960s. It is true that GEIA had predicted that after initial
years of government subsidies, a winnowing-out process would occur:
Fewer firms would survive, economies of scale would be attained, and

costs and prices would fall. The shakeout of the industry did not
result simply from price competition among firms, however, but from
the economic crisis of the mid-1960s. Furthermore, the end of repressed demand and the imposition of price controls meant that firms
could no longer pass along all of their costs to consumers. Firms
became more concerned with increased volume and market share,
and new forms of competition emerged.

Chapter 4 evaluates the industry's performance in terms of rent
distribution and linkage effects. It calculates the total subsidies provided to the firms, and it measures the taxes and private profits generated by the industry from data on tax rates, prices, costs, and profit
margins for the industry as a whole and for some individual firms.
The state's capacity to capture rents increased over time, as did the
industry's efficiency. The data reveal a form of *rent redistribution* usually found between peripheral states and transnational firms that mine
and export raw materials.[44]

Chapter 5 looks at the automotive parts sector. The establishment
of a Brazilian-owned parts sector was a critical component of the
industrial strategy. It was seen as a means of expanding the industrial
sector and of directing a portion of the rents accruing from protection
to domestic capital. The intrasectoral redistribution of resources between the transnational corporations and local firms was expected to
strengthen the Brazilian industrial sector and to create a basis for
further accumulation. The chapter documents how the policy was less
successful in this area, as the parts sector effectively came under foreign control, either through vertical integration by the terminal producers or through independent direct investment.

Finally, Chapter 6 compares Brazil's experience in the automotive
sector in the 1950s with its foray into computer-related products in
the 1980s. It discusses recent developments in Brazil's auto industry
and offers some conclusions about Brazil and the conditions under
which state intervention in general can be effective.

[44] For case studies, see Theodore H. Moran, *Multinational Corporations and the Politics
of Dependence: Copper in Chile* (Princeton: Princeton University Press, 1974); and
David G. Becker, *The New Bourgeoisie and the Limits of Dependency: Mining, Class, and
Power in "Revolutionary" Peru* (Princeton: Princeton University Press, 1983).

2

WHY AUTO?

Juscelino Kubitschek first met Admiral Lúcio Meira, a staunch advocate of the Brazilian automotive industry, in 1955 while campaigning for the presidency in the state of Bahia. Meira had directed a subcommission on motor vehicles during the 1951–4 Getúlio Vargas administration before he was "exiled" to this post in northeastern Brazil by then-President João Café Filho, Vargas's successor. Meira used the encounter as an opportunity to convince Kubitschek that automobiles should be included in his proposed Target Plan, a state-sponsored industrialization program. At a political rally later that same day, Kubitschek tested the idea by promising that, if elected, he would initiate production of a national automobile. The idea was received enthusiastically. Convinced of the project's political expediency, he quickly added automobiles to his list of developmental targets.[1] Despite the haphazard route by which Kubitschek came to include autos among his campaign pledges, the industry would become central to his industrialization program. After the elections, Meira returned to Rio de Janeiro, the capital, as Kubitschek's minister of transportation and public works, with supervisory responsibility for the formulation and implementation of the automobile program.

Meira's suggestion did not come out of the blue. It emerged from years of discussions on government policies toward this sector in which he had played a vital role. This chapter outlines how the decision to produce automobiles was arrived at in Brazil. It shows how the idea of a domestic auto program first emerged in response to the country's postwar balance-of-payments crises but soon took on more strategic significance. Local production of motor vehicles, a major item in the import bill, was expected to ease the foreign-exchange constraint,

[1] Based on interviews with Lúcio Meira and Sydney Latini conducted by Wellington Moreira Franco in August 1970, cited by Luciano Martins, *Pouvoir et développement économique: formation et evolution des structures politiques au brésil* (Paris: Editions Anthropos, 1976), p. 417.

28

solve the transportation bottleneck, and attract foreign capital and technology into the country. Officials within the Vargas administration began to see the auto industry as a centerpiece of an integrated industrial structure – as it was in the United States. Motor vehicles, with their extensive backward linkages, were expected to trigger the development of complementary industries. With this broader goal in mind, and with support from the incipient auto parts sector, the industry's promoters were able to increase gradually the domestic-content requirements of locally assembled vehicles and to silence any opposition by invoking the country's ongoing foreign-exchange constraint. These moves toward the creation of a domestic auto industry culminated with Kubitschek's auto plan and the creation of the Executive Group for the Automotive Industry (Grupo Executivo da Indústria Automobilística [GEIA]). The chapter ends with explanations for why railroads were not used to resolve the country's transportation bottleneck, why foreign transnational firms, as opposed to state-owned enterprises, were relied upon to build the industry, and why automobile manufacturing preceded tractor production.

The chapter presents Brazil's move into automobile production as an incremental process that reflected a growing consensus among policymakers, economists, and sectors of the military on the need to industrialize. Kubitschek's auto plan is depicted not as a new initiative, but rather as the culmination of the past, which was refined to fit the new exigencies of his presidential administration. It suggests that the pragmatic orientation of policymakers and politicians generated a marked degree of continuity across postwar administrations. Kubitschek's own automotive program would both build upon and be constrained by policy steps that had already been taken toward the industry and by what had been defined as feasible strategies.[2]

The Balance of Payments

At the end of World War II, Brazilians went on an international spending spree. The pent-up demand for both industrial and consumer goods was enormous. The country had managed to accumulate US$600 million in reserves as a result of wartime import controls and shortages, together with large exports of raw materials and even of

---

[2] For an analysis of Kubitschek's development program that places greater emphasis on the importance of ideas and the ideological consolidation of developmentalism during the Kubitschek administration, see Kathryn Sikkink, *Ideas and Institutions: Developmentalism in Brazil and Argentina* (Ithaca: Cornell University Press, 1991).

some industrial products to markets that had been temporarily abandoned by the major powers.[3] With such a breathing space from Brazil's chronic balance-of-payments crises, the government adopted a relatively unrestricted import policy.

During the immediate postwar years, a surprising item appeared at the top of the import bill. In 1946, 1947, and 1948, motor vehicles and parts surpassed even the traditionally dominant imports of petroleum and wheat (see Table 2.1). Brazil's vehicle stock had suffered severely when imports were cut off during the war. In 1942–5, virtually no passenger cars, and only a trickle of commercial vehicles, came in (see Tables 2.2 and 2.3). Although Ford and General Motors (GM) had been assembling cars and trucks in Brazil since the 1920s, the industry remained completely dependent on imported "completely knocked-down kits" (CKDs) and "semi–knocked-down kits" (SKDs), primarily from Detroit.[4] This war-induced shortage generated a postwar scramble to refurbish the aging fleet of trucks, buses, and private cars. Between 1945 and 1948, automotive products as a share of total imports rose from 2.0 to 11.4 percent, growing at an even faster rate than the rapidly expanding aggregate import bill.[5]

But this import bonanza was short-lived. Balance-of-trade deficits reappeared by mid-1947. The problem lay not simply in the import boom. Exchange reserves and trade surpluses had come largely in inconvertible European currencies, whereas U.S. dollars were required for most imports. This fact, in combination with an overvalued cruzeiro, made the easy import policy unsustainable as dollar reserves dropped rapidly. In an attempt to block the drainage, the government imposed a full licensing scheme in February 1948 that allocated foreign exchange to five categories of diminishing priority. The plan

---

[3]   Albert Fishlow, "Foreign Trade Regimes and Economic Development: Brazil" (Unpublished manuscript, 1976), p. 17. Pedro Malan, "Política econômica e teorias de balanço de pagamentos: relações internacionais de Brasil no período 1946–1979" (Master's thesis, Federal University of Rio de Janeiro, 1981), arrives at the alternative figure of US$730 million.

[4]   Ford was the first to build an assembly plant in 1919, followed by GM in 1925. Assembling imported CKDs or SKDs allowed these firms to save on the higher transportation costs associated with finished vehicles. For more information on this early period, see José Almeida, *A implantação da indústria automobilística no Brasil* (Rio de Janeiro: Fundação Getúlio Vargas, 1972); and Benedicto Heloiz Nascimento, "Política e desenvolvimento industrial numa economia dependente – formação da indústria automobilística brasileira" (Ph.D. diss., University of São Paulo, 1972).

[5]   Eduardo Augusto de Almeida Guimarães, "Industry, Market Structure and the Growth of the Firm in the Brazilian Economy" (Ph.D. diss., University of London, 1980), p. 155.

Table 2.1. *Brazilian Imports, 1945-1955*

Year	Wheat and derivatives		Oil and derivatives		Automotive products		Total imports
	US$ thousands	% of total	US$ thousands	% of total	US$ thousands	% of total	US$ thousands
1945	73,322	16.76	28,273	6.43	20,414	4.67	437,354
1946	47,046	7.22	40,915	6.28	51,160	7.85	651,437
1947	124,478	10.92	74,568	6.54	147,231	12.92	1,139,465
1948	124,613	11.87	108,970	10.38	146,901	14.00	1,049,244
1949	115,741	11.21	107,454	10.41	104,884	10.16	1,032,404
1950	102,269	10.07	131,254	12.92	139,577	13.74	1,015,671
1951	129,504	6.96	198,129	10.63	276,523	14.87	1,859,917
1952	137,223	7.38	227,282	12.22	261,411	14.06	1,858,931
1953	185,745	14.08	242,151	18.44	64,675	4.90	1,318,667
1954	154,807	9.48	268,802	16.46	89,027	5.45	1,633,539
1955	161,683	12.37	259,374	19.85	51,765	3.96	1,306,855
Averages							
1945-52	106,775	9.45	114,606	10.14	142,388	12.59	1,130,552
1945-55	122,312	10.2	153,370	12.68	126,601	10.11	1,209,405

Source: Presidência da República, Conselho do Desenvolvimento, *Indústrias de Base*, vol.1 (Rio de Janeiro, 1958).

discriminated against "nonessential" consumer durables while favoring intermediate and capital goods considered essential for the rehabilitation of Brazil's industrial capacity.[6]

In 1949, as a result of deep cuts in total imports, Brazil showed a trade surplus in the dollar account. The licensing authorities had imposed particularly strict limits on automotive imports, which no longer topped the import list. Coffee prices rose in that year and soared in 1950, making the dollar deficit appear less critical. The outbreak of the Korean War in 1950 generated fears of yet another import shortage. These events induced the licensing authorities to ease import restrictions in order to stockpile industrial goods. After his inauguration to the presidency in January 1951, Vargas also liberalized certain imports to launch a more vigorous industrial program.[7] During this temporary respite from balance-of-payments concerns, the authorities loosened restrictions on motor vehicle imports more than the average, and their share in total imports rose from 7.0 to 10.3 percent between 1950 and 1952. Vehicle imports also regained their position at the top of the import bill.[8] By 1952, a huge deficit appeared in the current account. As a result, the licensing scheme was abandoned in 1953.[9] During these years, the foreign-

---

[6] The reasons why the Brazilians resorted to a licensing scheme rather than to a general currency devaluation are complex. The overvalued exchange rate itself was partly responsible for the balance-of-payments crisis, but was maintained in the effort to contain inflationary pressures and to discourage the expansion of the coffee sector. Furthermore, it was a powerful instrument with which to subsidize import-substituting industries. See Joel Bergsman, *Brazil: Industrialization and Trade Policies* (Oxford: Oxford University Press, 1970); Fishlow, "Foreign Trade Regimes"; and Pedro Malan, Regis Bonelli, Marcelo de P. Abreu, and José Eduardo de C. Pereira, *Política econômica externa e industrialização no Brasil 1939/52* (Rio de Janeiro: Instituto de Planejamento Econômico e Social [IPEA], 1980).

[7] Caio Prado Jr., *História econômica do Brasil* (São Paulo: Editora Brasiliense, 1962), p. 308.

[8] Guimarães, "Industry, Market Structure and the Growth of the Firm," p. 155.

[9] The licensing scheme failed to allocate foreign exchange adequately for other reasons as well. The lack of interagency coordination was partly responsible. The Bank of Brazil's Import and Export Bureau (CEXIM) conceded import licenses based on its evaluation of national interest, but did so independently of the foreign-exchange budget elaborated by the bank's Foreign Exchange Bureau. Licenses were therefore granted without foreign-exchange backing so that they often wound up in commercial arrears. Furthermore, license recipients could legally wait until the following year to import, making it difficult to control foreign-exchange expenditure in any given year. This occurred frequently between 1951 and 1952. See Pedro A. C. Lago, "A SUMOC como embrião do Banco Central: sua influência na condução da política economia 1945/65" (Master's thesis, Catholic University, [PUC], Rio de Janeiro, 1982).

exchange administrators had attempted to alter the import mix in favor of commercial vehicles by imposing more severe restrictions on passenger cars, but they met with limited success. In the import-relaxed environment after 1949, it was politically inadvisable to maintain severe import controls on automobiles. Car imports more than tripled in number from 1950 to 1951, and commercial vehicle imports almost doubled. The share of cars in vehicle imports, 43 percent in 1946–8, remained at 40 percent in 1949–52 (see Tables 2.2 and 2.3).

Early policy initiatives directed toward the automotive sector were motivated by these balance-of-payments concerns and relied exclusively on foreign-exchange–related instruments to reduce imports. The first was Advisory 288, issued by the Bank of Brazil's Import and Export Bureau (Carteira de Exportação e Importação [CEXIM]), on August 19, 1952. This decree prohibited the importation of some 104 groups of automotive parts that were produced domestically. Advisory 311, issued on April 28, 1953, by the Bank of Brazil's new Foreign Trade Bureau (Carteira de Comércio Exterior [CACEX]), went a step further by prohibiting the importation of assembled cars, effective July 1, 1953. After this edict, all vehicles had to be imported as CKDs and SKDs. As of January 1, 1954, this restriction tightened so that only CKDs stripped of those parts for which a domestically produced counterpart existed, and which therefore came under Advisory 288, could be imported.

An additional disincentive on automotive imports was imposed through a foreign-exchange auction system, which replaced the licensing scheme in 1953. Foreign exchange was allocated to five categories of diminishing economic priority. A minimum premium was set for each, with the ultimate price established through auction. Passenger cars occupied the fifth category; commercial vehicles were in the third.

The foreign-exchange constraint remained paramount during these years, despite the emergence of other arguments in support of the complete nationalization of the industry. Perhaps more important, it provided industry advocates the trump card with which to silence the opposition. Those opposed to a domestic industry correctly understood that although the motivation behind these policies may have been balance-of-payments pressures, their *consequence* was a mandated increase in the domestic-content level of motor vehicle production, that is, the first step toward a deliberate industrialization policy for the sector. In fact, the campaign against restrictions on imported auto parts actually was a component of the larger debate on industriali-

Table 2.2. *Composition of Automotive Imports, 1945-1955 (US$ thousands)*

	1945	1946	1947	1948	1949	1950	1951	1952	1953	1954	1955
Passenger cars, including "bagagem"	106	11,104	46,188	53,114	35,232	20,385	72,444	55,706	15,533	12,495	4,627
Trucks, buses, miscellaneous	1,113	4,443	20,810	25,026	20,896	23,491	57,238	59,322	23,573	30,704	9,216
Jeeps[a]	--	--	--	--	--	--	--	7,893	5,395	6,904	2,118
Chassis for trucks and cars	7,619	20,306	41,009	40,938	20,551	27,445	67,118	68,222	7,372	29,313	21,130
Tires	98	402	5,456	1,056	721	635	8,345	9,628	219	620	529
Accessories	11,478	14,905	33,768	26,767	27,484	67,621	71,378	60,640	12,583	13,891	14,145
Total	20,414	51,160	147,231	146,901	104,884	139,577	276,523	261,411	64,675	89,027	51,765

[a] Jeeps were included with trucks until 1952.

Source: Presidência da República, Conselho do Desenvolvimento, *Indústrias de Base,* vol. 1 (Rio de Janeiro, 1958).

Table 2.3. *Motor Vehicle Imports, 1925-1959 (units)*

Year	Passenger cars	Commercial vehicles	Jeeps
1925	28,600	15,100	
1926	26,000	7,000	
1927	16,500	13,100	
1928	27,900	17,500	
1929	29,400	24,500	
1930	1,700	300	
1931	2,900	1,600	
1932	1,200	1,400	
1933	5,100	3,700	
1934	7,800	7,400	
1935	9,600	7,900	
1936	9,900	9,000	
1937	14,400	9,100	
1938	11,800	11,100	
1939	12,000	9,700	
1940	13,900	9,600	
1941	12,800	12,400	
1942	2,700	5,100	
1943	0	700	
1944	0	2,100	
1945	100	7,800	
1946	9,637	18,732	
1947	28,794	37,035	
1948	31,751	36,148	
1949	21,390	19,503	
1950	15,717	33,010	
1951	47,274	62,228	
1952	30,494	49,625	5,755[a]
1953	6,363	6,719	3,823
1954	4,226	26,312	6,236
1955	1,536	9,318	1,744
1956	997	15,152	2,394
1957	2,617	31,853	9,292
1958	8,580	28,996	10,447
1959	27,087	53,926	10,870

[a] Previously with trucks.

Source: Eduardo Augusto de Almeida Guimarães, "Industry, Market Structure and the Growth of the Firm in the Brazilian Economy" (Ph.D. diss., University of London, 1980).

zation. Eros Orosco, the first secretary of GEIA, later observed with respect to this period:

> However much the official orthodoxy was opposed to the idea of restricting imports similar to local production, the exchange contingency wound up generating restrictions on these foreign purchases, so that, even if irregularly complied with at times, a global system

emerged during the years 1949–50 and after 1951 that was actually effective in protecting the local industry.[10]

The Subcommission on Jeep, Tractor, Truck and Car Manufacture, established by President Vargas in 1952, and in which Orosco participated, often resorted to this argument.[11] For example, minutes of the subcommission's meetings reveal that Lucas Lopes, then president of CEXIM, was against Advisory 288 because he feared it would discriminate against small producers and violate outstanding trade agreements with other countries. Critics in the Congress and the press similarly argued that the policy protected Ford and General Motors because they had assembly lines already in place. Small importers, on the other hand, did not, and could not economically construct them because of their small market share. Nevertheless, CEXIM was ultimately forced to accept the passage of Advisory 288 because "the Brazilian exchange situation is so tense."[12]

The shortage of foreign exchange was also used by the subcommission to deflect arguments from CEXIM and the manufacturers that the Brazilian parts sector was unable to produce an adequate supply. In response to the prediction by the president of the Union of Retail Trade of Cars and Accessories of shortages and Brazilian incapacity to produce certain parts (including those mentioned in Advisory 288), Admiral Lúcio Meira, director of the subcommission, said, "We have to start from the consideration that we are confronted by a *de facto* situation – scarcity of foreign exchange."[13] For Meira, the only long-

---

[10] Eros Orosco, *A indústria automobilística brasileira* (Rio de Janeiro: Consultec, 1961), p. 37. This effect was not unique to the automotive sector. Although the external bottleneck determined the direction of policy during these pre-Kubitschek years, and the instruments used were those related to foreign exchange, the consequence was a market reserve policy that furthered the general import-substitution process.

[11] The subcommission was under the Commission on Industrial Development (Comissão de Desenvolvimento Industrial [CDI]), whose purpose was to study and propose general norms for industrialization. As a result of the foreign exchange requirements imposed by imports, the subcommission was assigned the task of formulating an industrialization strategy for motor vehicles. It was the first institutionalized response to, and centralized discussion of, the problem. Negotiations among the various actors involved in the industry came under its aegis.

[12] Orosco, June 11, 1952, as quoted in Wellington Moreira Franco, "A nacionalização de veículos no Brasil" (Master's thesis, University of São Paulo, n.d.), Appendix 1, "Sinopse das Atas de Reunião da Subcomissão de Jeeps, Tratores, Caminhoões a Automóveis da Comissão de Desenvolvimento Industrial (hereafter referred to as 'Subcommission Minutes'). Unless otherwise indicated, all direct translations of written sources and interviews are by the author.

[13] Meira as quoted in Subcommission Minutes, January 7, 1953.

run solution was national production; despite inevitable problems and shortages in the short run, the first step had to be taken.

Although the country had developed significant manufacturing capacity in response to the economic shocks and policies of the 1930s and 1940s, resolving the foreign-exchange constraint through an export-led growth strategy was inconceivable to Brazilian politicians and technocrats who had witnessed the collapse of raw material prices and world trade during the 1930s and World War II. The Korean War rekindled fears of being cut off from critical imports, and trade expansion continued to look bleak in the mid-1950s.

Brazil's experience in the 1930s had also convinced policymakers that a devaluation would shift the terms of trade against them. Brazil was the major world supplier of coffee at the time and set the international price, but it appeared that coffee demand was inelastic with respect to price. A devaluation would have reduced total export earnings. In the days of coffee hegemony, the cruzeiro was often devalued to maintain the sector's cruzeiro income. In the mid-1950s, the government strove to maximize total exchange earnings.[14]

The power of the export sector also precluded the use of direct export taxes to transfer resources to the industrial sector. Although the second-best alternative of exchange-rate subsidies for the manufacturing sector had a similar economic impact, presumed economic rationality on the part of exporters did not necessarily translate into political action. As a Joint United States–Brazil Development Commission stated regarding the coffee sector in 1953: "While exporters were resigned to the continuation of a legally established exchange policy, even though it had effects similar to those of an export tax, their political resistance against the imposition of outright export taxes and the utilization of their proceeds for the subsidization of other sectors of the economy would have been much greater."[15]

It was in this context of export pessimism (combined with Brazil's abundance of natural resources) that import-substitution policies in general and auto policy in particular emerged. The foreign-exchange

[14] See Antônio Delfim Netto, *O problema do café no Brasil* (Rio de Janeiro: Fundação Getúlio Vargas, 1979); and Stephen D. Krasner, "Manipulating International Commodity Markets: Brazilian Coffee Policy 1906–1962," *Public Policy* 21 (Fall 1973):493–523.

[15] Joint Brazil–United States Economic Development Commission, *The Development of Brazil: Report of the Joint Brazil–United States Economic Development Commission* (Washington, D.C.: Institute of Inter-American Affairs Foreign Operations Administration, 1953), p. 67 (hereafter referred to as Joint Brazil–United States Commission Report).

constraint and the need to shift the economy structurally from exports to production for the domestic market would continue to provide the rationale and the underlying motivation for the automobile program.[16]

Transportation Bottleneck

Brazil's inadequate and dilapidated transportation network provided another argument in favor of a domestic automotive sector. For example, sectors of the military began to tout motor vehicles as a national security need after the war. The Brazilian railroad network had been built to service the export sector. A mountain shelf extending along the Atlantic coast prevents most of the major rivers from reaching the sea, so railroads were built to penetrate the interior. In this way, pairs of independent centers and hinterlands were created, exchanging goods with one another and, in turn, linked to the rest of the world by sea. Because of its export orientation, the system fostered regional, rather than national, integration. Almost all trade between the south and northeast, and even that between close neighbors, was conducted by sea. During the war, German attacks off the Brazilian coast isolated the major coastal cities from one another and demonstrated the vulnerability of the country's supply routes. Connecting the individual islands of the "Brazilian archipelago," as Lúcio Meira put it, and ending dependence on foreign vehicles thus became military concerns.[17]

Second, various elite groups during the Vargas administration and especially by Kubitschek's presidency had reached a consensus that Brazil had to industrialize because the coffee sector could no longer generate internal growth. Development based on the internal market, rather than on exports, made paramount the internal integration of the country. To meet the changing needs of the economy, therefore,

---

[16] Pointing out these motivations and constraints does not fully explain how dominant political coalitions came together around import-substitution policies. For a discussion of this point, see Stephan Haggard, *Pathways from the Periphery: The Politics of Growth in the Newly Industrializing Countries* (Ithaca: Cornell University Press, 1990); Robert R. Kaufman, "How Societies Change Development Models or Keep Them: Reflections on the Latin American Experience in the 1930s and the Postwar World," in Gary Gereffi and Donald L. Wyman, eds., *Manufacturing Miracles: Paths of Industrialization in Latin America and East Asia* (Princeton: Princeton University Press, 1990), pp. 110–39; and Sikkink, *Ideas and Institutions.*

[17] Interview with Lúcio Meira, April 1985, Rio de Janeiro.

it was not enough to repair the existing, dilapidated transportation system – it had to be completely redesigned.

The various technical commissions that studied Brazil's transport needs correctly placed primary emphasis on renovating the railroad and shipping networks.[18] They were critical of the already growing emphasis on road construction, made possible by the National Road Fund of 1945, which was financed by a special tax on the consumption of petroleum products. There is no question that motor vehicles were unduly favored at the expense of alternative modes of transportation. However, it is equally clear that even if Brazil had adopted a more comprehensive approach to the transportation problem that included railroads and shipping, the demand for road transportation would have continued to grow. Further industrialization promised both to increase the volume of transport and to alter its distribution among the available alternatives. The flexibility and door-to-door capability of road transport would become more important as the country moved away from its concentration on the bulk transport of unprocessed raw materials and agricultural products.

Linkages

During Lúcio Meira's first trip to the United States in 1930, he learned that one in eight American jobs was connected to auto production. He concluded that auto had the characteristics of a leading sector that could similarly transform Brazil. In this sense, the experience of the United States was explicitly used as the model that the Brazilians hoped to duplicate, albeit in a more condensed chronological and technological time frame. As Meira stated, "As in the highly industrialized countries, the automotive industry in Brazil is becoming and will be without doubt the leading sector of the entire economy, by force of its magnitude, complexity, and dynamism."[19]

Brazilian planners anticipated Albert Hirschman's idea of inducement mechanisms by arguing that the auto industry's demand for significant amounts of intermediate inputs would create pressures to develop other sectors in the economy. They expected that the automotive industry would serve as the hub of an integrated industrial structure by triggering the domestic production and technological advance of steel, machine tools, components, and other complemen-

---

[18] A full discussion of this issue is presented later in this chapter.
[19] Lúcio Meira, "A propagação dos efeitos promocionais da indústria automobilística," *Economia Brasileira* 4 (1958): 57.

tary industries. The emergence of input–output tables, which quantified linkage effects, provided additional theoretical justification for Brazil's foray into the world of high-technology consumer durables. The discovery that most industrialized economies displayed similar patterns of sectoral interdependence led to the assumption that these would be replicated in less-developed countries. Targeting high-linkage industries became the logical development strategy.

Brazil had already built domestic manufacturing capacity in steel. The state-owned National Steel Company (Companhia Siderúrgica Nacional [CSN]) was founded in 1941 during the authoritarian Estado Nôvo regime of Getúlio Vargas (1937–45). According to Benedicto Nascimento, the National Steel Commission had a domestic motor vehicle industry in mind when it founded the CSN, and it considered the steel sheet requirements of vehicles when choosing among alternative technologies. A motor vehicle industry would make use of Brazil's steel capacity. Although the existence of domestic steel capacity made the idea of a domestic automotive industry viable, it is not clear what role, if any, the state-owned National Steel Company played in the postwar debate on the subject.[20]

As the first and most direct private beneficiary of protective legislation and as the industry's most extensive backward linkage, the emergent parts sector lobbied hard for the nationalization of production. Protective legislation would force firms to substitute domestically produced automotive parts and components for imports. Motor vehicle producers are those firms that engage in the major tasks of assembly, stamping, and building engines and transmissions; in most national industries, many of a vehicle's 15,000-odd parts are produced and subassembled by independent parts producers. Simple parts had been produced in Brazil since the construction of the original assembly lines, but this sector really emerged only during the war, in response to the demand for replacement parts. The number of registered firms grew from eleven in 1940 to thirty-eight in 1945.[21] Discounting transnational firms like General Motors, which substantially increased the scale and scope of parts production during these years, almost all of these firms were Brazilian-owned. They would more accurately be characterized as small artisanal shops. Nevertheless, by 1944 they were

[20] Nascimento, "Política e desenvolvimento industrial numa economia dependente." For more on the early Brazilian steel industry, see Werner Baer, *The Development of the Brazilian Steel Industry* (Nashville: Vanderbilt University Press, 1969).

[21] Ramiz Gattás, *A indústria automobilística e a segunda revolução industrial: origens e perspectivas* (São Paulo: Prelo, 1981), appendix 1.

producing approximately two thousand different parts, including radiators, pistons, and springs.[22]

When the war ended, these newly established firms lost orders that were then redirected to foreign suppliers. One survey estimates that the number of firms fell from thirty in 1946 to twenty in 1948.[23] According to Ramiz Gattás, the first secretary of the Professional Association of the Automotive Parts and Similars Industry,[24] the remaining firms were able to survive until the 1948 licensing scheme because major U.S. and European suppliers needed time to convert their war-oriented factories back to peacetime production. Moreover, the foreign firms' first priority was to satisfy their own domestic markets. This phenomenon, coupled with the shortage of dollars, forced Brazilians to import more "exotic" vehicles (i.e., from Eastern Europe) that required new types of replacement parts. The scarcity of U.S. and European parts preserved some market space for national producers.[25]

Under the limited protection provided by licensing, the number of firms and the value of production in the parts sector continued to grow after 1948. The overall relaxation of imports after 1950, however, allowed a flood of imported parts. Fearing extinction, the sector's representatives lobbied for tariff protection and for what was to become Advisory 288. The Professional Association of the Automotive Parts and Similars Industry was founded on October 25, 1951, and formally registered with the Ministry of Labor on August 28, 1952, with 122 associated firms. This organization supplied CEXIM and the Vargas subcommission with data on the sector and participated in subcommission discussions on viable strategies for the nationalization of the automotive industry. It tried to document the sector's capacity to furnish quality parts in the amounts required. It realized that the

[22] Warren Dean, *A industrialização de São Paulo* (São Paulo and Rio de Janeiro: Difel, 1971), pp. 243–4. The parts sector as commonly defined does not include tire producers. Foreign-owned subsidiaries of B. F. Goodrich, Goodyear, Dunlop, Firestone, and Pirelli began producing tires in Brazil even before the war. Vivianne Ventura Dias, "The Motor Vehicle Industry in Brazil: A Case of Sectoral Planning" (Master's thesis, University of California Berkeley, 1975), p. 62.

[23] Nascimento, "Política e desenvolvimento industrial em uma economia dependente," p. 27. Among the various sources, there is a great deal of inconsistency with respect to firm and production numbers in this early stage of the parts industry. The mechanisms for gathering accurate statistics were virtually nonexistent.

[24] This association preceded the Union for the Automotive Parts and Similars Industry (Sindicato da Indústria de Peças para Veículos e Similares [SINDIPEÇAS]), which was founded in the state of São Paulo in 1953.

[25] Gattás, *A indústria automobilística*, p. 42.

absence of protection might spell the sector's disappearance. As Vicente Mammana Netto, the first treasurer of the association, said to the subcommission: "The goodwill of the assemblers is directly related to the difficulties they have with foreign exchange. It is a thermometer. If they had unlimited amounts of foreign exchange, the national parts industry would not have the conditions to survive."[26]

That the sector's existence could be used as proof of Advisory 288's viability was more important to these industry promoters than its lobbying efforts, particularly given its small size. In April 1952, the association supplied CEXIM with a survey indicating that 250 firms produced eight thousand different types of auto parts.[27] Though the data were suspect, CEXIM evidently accepted this estimate of Brazil's productive capacity without independent verification because of the exchange crisis.[28] It understood that the tiny sector would have short-run difficulties supplying even the items listed by Advisory 288, but it nevertheless provided a springboard from which to begin. And by 1956, when the GEIA plan came into existence, this industrial base would be even broader after the years of protection provided by the various advisories. In 1955, 900 parts firms were registered, and the average domestic-content level for an assembled vehicle was 30 percent.[29]

Technology and Capital

The authors of the Target Plan often characterized its purpose with the phrase *quemar etapas* ("to burn stages"). With the goal of shifting

[26] Subcommission Minutes, May 7, 1952.
[27] Gattás, *A indústria automobilística*, pp. 74–5. He cites 275 firms in his subcommission testimony.
[28] Orosco in Subcommission Minutes, May 28, 1952.
[29] Maria Fernanda Gadelha, "Estrutura industrial e padrão de competição no setor de autopeças – um estudo de caso" (Master's thesis, State University of Campinas, 1984), p. 13. Gattás, *A indústria automobilística*, p. 213, lists the growth in the number of parts manufacturers as follows: 1941, 12 manufacturers; 1946, 39; 1948, 66; 1951, 106; 1952, 250; 1953, 300; 1954, 360; 1955, 520; 1956, 700. This characterization of the parts sector as still dependent on the state's tutelage and initiative, despite its growing organizational strength and participation in state decision making, concurs with that of Martins. As he points out, plans for the industry came to a virtual halt after Vargas's suicide in 1954. Martins, *Pouvoir et développement économique*, p. 417. Furthermore, in contrast to its role in the subcommission, the private sector had no formal or informal representation in GEIA and did not participate in its proceedings. For an alternative view of the role of private capital and its representational organizations, see M. Antonieta P. Leopoldi, "Industrial Associations and Politics in Contemporary Brazil" (Ph.D. diss., Oxford University, 1984).

the economy away from raw materials toward manufacturing, they saw no reason to move through those stages that distinguished the development of the more-industrialized countries. Rather, Brazil could take advantage of being a Gerschenkronian "latecomer" and move immediately into capital-intensive, high-technology sectors like auto. The "immediate assimilation of technology accumulated over more than 60 years ... associated with a large volume of capital from the exterior" was expected to give an enormous boost to national productivity and income.[30]

The technological base established in the automotive industry was expected to have corollary effects in other sectors. The quality requirements for motor vehicles would force technological improvements in related supply industries ranging from basic steel to auto parts. An improvement was also foreseen in the quality and production costs of goods based on similar production processes. For example, bathtubs would conceivably move from artisanal construction to the mass-produced stamping methods used in auto-body production. Besides generating employment, the sector would provide technical training to the work force, thereby raising labor's productivity. To the extent that resources shifted from other sectors to automotive-related industries, it was assumed that the transition would be from lower to higher productivity investment.

Vargas's subcommission and Kubitschek's GEIA both concluded that direct investment by transnational auto companies would be the only means by which to transfer the required technology and capital. The Brazilian private sector was considered too weak to satisfy the capital and technological requirements of auto. Auto parts producers had made it clear to Vargas's subcommission that they were unable to finance such an undertaking, even if the government were to provide the original financing. The lack of a strong capital market in Brazil made it impossible to tap financial sources outside the sector. In addition, neither Ford nor General Motors, with whom the Brazilians had the most experience, had licensed technology to or formed joint ventures with foreign partners elsewhere. Even if domestic firms could have found other licensors, they would have had to import capital goods and pay for the technology, which would have necessitated large foreign-exchange expenditures.[31]

---

[30] Meira, "A propagação dos efeitos promocionais da indústria automobilística," p. 58.
[31] It is important to keep in mind that, at the time, no other peripheral country had successfully built up a domestic industry on the basis of "national champions." Although Japanese auto firms had developed and survived in the 1930s thanks to

State ownership was also ruled out as an alternative strategy, partly because the Brazilian state's fiscal capacity was extremely limited. This was both a historical problem for the state, which had few instruments by which to accumulate resources, and a reflection of the nature of Kubitschek's political compromise, which precluded any fundamental reform of the financial system. The budget remained under congressional control. Moreover, the budgetary process was a long and convoluted one that introduced an added element of uncertainty in Brazil's inflationary environment. The normal budgetary process was thus inadequate for long-run development finance. Kubitschek resorted to inflationary finance and the use of earmarked funds as a means of financing the Target Plan and of transferring resources to industrial capital.

Nevertheless, the fiscal constraint contributed, but was not paramount, to Kubitschek's decision to restrict the state's direct participation in building the automobile industry. The role of the state under Kubitschek was prescribed to the coordination and subsidization of private investment. State enterprise was restricted to infrastructure and some basic industries, for which financing was arranged. Venturing into the industrial sector was politically out of bounds, except in certain cases where foreign or domestic private investment was not forthcoming and the state entered as a last resort.

Yet, even Vargas, whose posture toward foreign capital was more antagonistic than Kubitschek's, had assumed that the auto sector would have to be built in conjunction with foreign capital. Although a state-owned vehicle plant was already in operation, Meira had convinced Vargas that it could not be used as a basis for a domestic auto industry. The National Motor Factory (Fábrica Nacional de Motores [FNM]), established during the war to produce airplane engines, was producing a small number of diesel trucks under license from Alfa

protectionist government policies (which also drove Ford and GM out of the country), the industry was still in disarray in the 1950s. Given Brazil's economic and political constraints, however, this strategy was not feasible. South Korea was only assembling imported built-up vehicles in the early 1960s, and moved to integrated manufacturing only after the 1973 oil shock. For more on the Japanese and Korean industries, see Michael Cusumano, *The Japanese Automobile Industry* (Cambridge, Mass.: Harvard University Press, 1985); Chuk Kyo Kim and Chul Hee Lee, "The Growth of the Automotive Industry," in Chong Kee Park, ed., *Macroeconomic and Industrial Development in Korea* (Seoul: Korea Development Institute, 1980), pp. 277–311; and Alice Amsden and Linsu Kim, "The Role of Transnational Corporations in the Production and Exports of the Korean Automobile Industry," in Dong-Ki Kim and Linsu Kim, eds., *Management Behind Industrialization: Readings in Korean Business* (Seoul: Korea University Press, 1989).

Romeo.[32] Vargas had established several other precedents for state
enterprises during his Estado Nôvo regime with the creation of the
National Steel Company in 1941, the Companhia Vale do Rio Doce
for mining in 1942, and, during his 1951–4 administration, Petrobrás
in oil. These had emerged under particular conditions that were not
applicable to motor vehicles.[33] The state went into steel only by default
after negotiations with U.S. Steel collapsed, and it benefited from U.S.
Eximbank loans. The experience of many of the technocrats in the
Vargas administration would also color their attitudes to the possibility
of proceeding without the assistance of foreign capital. The potential
veto power of the International Monetary Fund (IMF) and the World
Bank on the one hand and the difficulty of rationalizing the state in
the face of congressional opposition and clientelism on the other made
state-led development projects appear risky in more technologically
complex sectors.[34] In general, the production and organizational
capabilities required for auto production seemed to preclude state
enterprises, which had proved effective in raw materials and infrastructure but not in complex manufacturing.[35]

Therefore, in contrast to Vargas's general model for industrialization, public enterprise was not to be the stimulus or growth pole

[32] See discussion of the National Motor Factory later in this chapter.
[33] As Draibe put it, "The international conjuncture, the disinterest of the big multinational firms in investing in heavy industry, and Vargas's skill in carrying out the
'double game' between the Axis and the Allied powers were conditions which, at
most, explain why steel was obtained and furthermore, why it was not possible to
go beyond it, advancing the complex of projects from the installation of basic industries." Sônia Draibe, *Rumos e metamorfoses: estado e industrialização no Brasil 1930/
1960* (Rio de Janeiro: Paz e Terra, 1985), p. 128. For additional discussion on the
steel industry, see Baer, *The Development of the Brazilian Steel Industry;* and Martins,
Pouvoir et développement économique.
[34] Lourdes Sola, "The Political and Ideological Constraints to Economic Management
in Brazil, 1945–1963" (Ph.D. diss., Oxford University, 1982), p. 101.
[35] The Brazilians hoped that foreign firms would provide them with all the advantages
that Alfred Chandler attributes to the modern, large-scale enterprise, including
access to capital, technology, managerial expertise, the ability to realize economies
of scale and scope, and ultimately, faster growth. Because of constraints on capital
and entrepreneurship in LDCs such as Brazil, state-owned enterprises or transnational firms assumed the role that private, indigenous large-scale enterprises did in
the nineteenth-century developers on which Chandler's work focuses. See Alfred
D. Chandler, Jr., *The Visible Hand: The Managerial Revolution in American Business*
(Cambridge, Mass.: Belknap Press of Harvard University Press, 1977), and *Scale and
Scope: The Dynamics of Industrial Capitalism* (Cambridge, Mass.: Harvard University
Press, 1990). For a review of Chandler's work in the LDC context, see Albert Fishlow,
"Developing Countries and the Modern Firm," *Business History Review* 64, no. 4
(Winter 1990):726–9.

for private investment in the industry. What was the exception to Vargas's development agenda, however, would become the prototype of the Target Plan – foreign capital was to play the dominant role.

By the time Kubitschek took office in 1956, potential savings in foreign exchange was touted as only one of many benefits of a Brazilian automotive industry. The sector had come to symbolize the country's industrial potential. It would be the driving force behind the economy's structural shift out of raw material exports into industrialization for internal use. As Orosco put it:

> From the moment in which a sufficiently wide vision of the problem was acquired, with all its implications, a nonexplicit principle of action began to be considered, according to which the creation of the automotive industry in the country should become *not an objective in itself of government and national efforts, but a pretext or basis for more extensive acquisitions and a more profound repercussion on national life.*[36]

Kubitschek's Blueprint

Plans for the automotive industry were reactivated upon Lúcio Meira's return to Rio de Janeiro after President Juscelino Kubitschek's inauguration in January 1956. Under Meira's direction as minister of transportation and public works, the Working Group on the Automotive Industry was formed on April 27, 1956, and given thirty days to present a report.

Although Café Filho, considered to be more economically liberal than either Vargas or Kubitschek, had not implemented the recommendations of Vargas's subcommission, he did not dismantle the protectionist policies already in place. Moreover, tightened overall import restrictions reduced the number of imported vehicles but also stimulated domestic parts purchases. During his administration, personnel in CACEX continued to formulate policies for the industry. On March 6, 1956, the Monetary Authority (Superintendência da Moeda e do Crédito [SUMOC]) issued Instructions 127 and 128, which anticipated Kubitschek's auto decrees.[37] These instructions required firms to increase gradually levels of domestic content in return for favorable exchange rates for parts that were still imported. Although they were

---

[36] Orosco, *A indústria automobilística brasileira*, p. 11.

[37] These instructions required firms to increase gradually levels of domestic content in return for favorable exchange rates for parts that were still imported. Although they were not part of a comprehensive sectoral strategy, firms did begin to plan increases in domestic content and applied for foreign-exchange allocations.

not part of a comprehensive sectoral strategy, firms did begin to plan increases in domestic content and applied for foreign-exchange allocations.[38]

The fact that Meira's group was not starting from scratch provided both constraints and opportunities. Certain limitations were imposed by the policies that had already been taken toward the industry, as well as by the negotiations that had begun with the foreign firms. The group also benefited from the technical expertise accumulated during this postwar period. Many of Meira's personnel had worked with him in Vargas's subcommission and had written its final document, the "National Incentive Plan for Production by the Automotive Parts Industry and the Gradual Implantation of the Automotive Industry." This report had been approved by Vargas in October 1952 but was shelved after his suicide and Café Filho's inauguration in August 1954. It provided the basis of the working group's final document, which was written in only six hours and instituted by executive decree on June 16, 1956.[39]

Vargas's auto plan was also adapted to fit Kubitschek's own economic and political objectives, as well as the policy instruments available. Kubitschek had taken office amidst a polarized elite and military. Under the campaign slogan of "50 years [of development] in 5," he unified those associated with international capital and the mobilized urban masses into a populist alliance. Rapid growth would be fundamental to maintaining the political support of these constituencies. Kubitschek, like the Economic Commission on Latin America (ECLA), came to define Brazil's economic problem as one of growth, not of stability.[40]

Although classified as a "basic industry," the automotive industry was the only consumer good in the Target Plan. All others were related to power generation, other forms of transportation, and similar types

[38] Instruction 127 required firms to reach domestic-content levels of 90% by weight and 80% by value for jeeps, and 80% by weight and 70% by value for all other vehicles by July 1959.

[39] Orosco, *A indústria automobilística brasileira*, p. 56. The group's members were Lúcio Meira as president, Roberto Campos, Ignácio Tosta Filho, Guilherme Augusto Pegurier, Américo Cury, and Eros Orosco.

[40] For general accounts of the Kubitschek regime, see Sergio Abranches, "The Divided Leviathan: State and Economic Policy Formation in Authoritarian Brazil" (Ph.D. diss., Cornell University, 1978); Maria Victoria de Mesquita Benevides, *O Governo Kubitschek* (Rio de Janeiro: Paz e Terra, 1979); Draibe, *Rumos e metamorfoses;* Helio Jaguaribe, *Economic and Political Development: A Theoretical Approach and a Brazilian Case Study* (Cambridge, Mass.: Harvard University Press, 1968); and Sola, "The Political and Ideological Constraints to Economic Management in Brazil, 1945–1963."

of infrastructural investment. But the automobile, the pinnacle of technological maturity, was a potent symbol of development. More than any other sector, it would become the barometer of the Target Plan's success for the general public. For Kubitschek, it was most critical that the auto production target be reached.

It was also a method by which to garner middle-class support. The Target Plan was presented to the middle class not only as a means to bring Brazil into the twentieth century, but also as the only way to guarantee the future supply of automobiles. As discussed previously, car imports had been rationed in one way or another for fifteen years. During World War II, imports nearly ceased. Foreign-exchange controls operated thereafter. Consumers imported jeeps, vans, virtually anything with four wheels, as substitutes for scarce passenger cars. When convertible currencies – that is, dollars – were not available, they even imported unknown brands from Eastern Europe. With this experience in mind, and the perception that the foreign-exchange constraint was chronic, the Brazilian consumers accurately perceived that the alternative model to Kubitschek's auto program would not be unlimited imports at world prices. A more open economic model in the Brazilian context would still have included high tariffs on autos, and also, given the historical erosion of tariffs through inflation, some form of quantity rationing of foreign exchange, as they had experienced. They had no reason to change this expectation. What Kubitschek promised, therefore, was more cars than would otherwise have been available. Domestic production was seen as a solution superior to the limited open economy that Brazil otherwise would have had. Moreover, since the U.S. and European transnational firms would be building the domestic plants, Brazilians would be able to satisfy their preferences and drive the same cars as before, but now with a "Made in Brazil" label. Kubitschek could appeal to their developmental nationalism without sacrificing tailfins. Nationalism, therefore, was not only costless but advantageous – more cars would be available and at a cheaper cruzeiro cost than comparable imports.

The Executive Group for the Automotive Industry

Overseeing Kubitschek's plan was the Executive Group for the Automotive Industry, or GEIA, which came to be seen as the primary institutional innovation of the Target Plan.[41] Later generalized to

[41] In fact, a similar institution was approved by President Vargas in June 1954, only to be aborted upon his suicide in August of that year. The Executive Commission

other targeted sectors, this institutional reform was an attempt both to streamline bureaucratic decision making and to insulate the plan's administration from clientelistic pressures.

Represented in GEIA were all of the agencies that, by virtue of their policy jurisdictions, would necessarily be involved in the plan.[42] Meira, as minister of transportation and public works, acted as president. By joining the directors in one unit, GEIA allowed decisions to be made without members having to report back to their respective agencies, whose bureaucratic tangle and redundant technical studies inevitably caused delays. Each director would have responsibility to ensure that his agency would follow through as necessary. This approach was also intended to bypass intra-agency jurisdictional disputes and avoid the need to lobby each one. Granted the power of executive decree, GEIA could implement its program independent of the fragmented policy-making authority dispersed among the agencies involved. Furthermore, its location in the executive branch meant that its decision-making process was, at least in theory, insulated from congressional politicking. Thus, the technocrats would have a degree of autonomy that they had lacked in previous administrations. GEIA was granted a life span of five years – equal to the implementation phase of the industry. It was responsible for fixing nationalization and production targets and for accepting individual investment projects and monitoring their progress.

The Plan

The plan's general guidelines were revealed in various executive decrees.[43] The basic approach, adopted from Vargas's subcommission

for the Automotive Material Industries (CEIMA) was to be established within the Ministry of Finance and composed of representatives from the Foreign Trade Bureau (CACEX), the National Bank for Economic Development (BNDE), the Technology Institute, importers of automotive materials, the auto parts industry, and the steel industry. It was to elaborate and oversee plans for the industry, coordinate tariff and exchange policies, approve individual projects, etc.

[42] These included the minister of transportation and public works, who acted as president, the directors of the Foreign Exchange Bureau ("Carteira de Câmbio") and CACEX of the Bank of Brazil, the executive director of the Monetary Authority (SUMOC), and the director-superintendent of the BNDE. Representatives of the following institutions were included subsequently: the War Ministry in mid-1957; the newly formed Council on Tariff Policy (CPA) in August 1957; and the Agricultural Ministry in December 1959. It is noteworthy that representatives of the industry itself, though frequently consulted, were not formally included.

[43] Decree No. 39.412, June 16, 1956, establishing the overall plan and GEIA; Decree

Table 2.4. *Domestic-Content Requirements*

Deadline	Trucks (%)	Jeeps (%)	Utility Vehicles[a] (%)	Cars (%)
Dec. 31, 1956	35	50	40	–
July 1, 1957	40	60	50	50
July 1, 1958	65	75	65	65
July 1, 1959	75	85	75	85
July 1, 1960	90	95	90	95

[a]Utility vehicles are defined as mixed-service vehicles, used for either passengers or cargo, and include vans, station wagons, and pickups.

report, was effectively to close the market to imports and to force firms to increase the level of domestic content in exchange for a standard set of financial incentives. The plan instituted under Kubitschek sped up the process. Firms had to meet the following domestic-content schedules, measured by weight,[44] to continue receiving financial benefits (see Table 2.4).

The method by which domestic-content levels were increased was left to each firm's discretion, and detailed plans had to be submitted and approved. However, as I shall discuss, subsidies were structured to encourage the rapid domestic production of engines.[45]

As a consequence of political and economic constraints, GEIA resorted to the use of indirect incentives to attract foreign investment into motor vehicle production. In general, the Kubitschek government, like its predecessors, relied on differential exchange rates on exports and imports to transfer resources to the industrial sector. Five types of incentives were provided to those firms whose projects were approved by December 31, 1957.

No. 39.568, July 12, 1956, for trucks; Decree No. 39.569, July 12, 1956, for jeeps; Decree No. 39.676, July 30, 1956, for utility vehicles; and Decree No. 41.018, February 26, 1957, for passenger cars.

[44] GEIA thought it would be easier to regulate domestic-content levels by weight rather than by value. A value estimate for each part would have required complicated accounting and conversion procedures. Moreover, because transnational firms were more familiar with their components and often supplied them internally, value assessments were more subject to manipulation. Preliminary studies indicated that, given the stages by which most firms increased domestic content, the difference between value and weight was not significant. The short-term nature of the plan further minimized the potential impact of this differential.

[45] It should be noted that firms were not starting from scratch. Many had already reached levels of 30% due to "hang-on" parts, and due to earlier restrictions on importing parts for which there were domestic similars.

Table 2.5. *Exchange Rates (cruzeiro/U.S. dollar)*

Category	1956	1957 Jan.-Aug.	Sept.-Dec.	1958	1959	1960	1961
I	73.76	58.29					
II	81.29	74.51					
III	103.15	100.60					
IV	115.46	138.03					
V	222.36	299.07					
General import rate	--	--	80.29	148.45	199.45	233.00	--
Cost of exchange (custo de câmbio)	43.82	43.82	43.82	54.84	78.49	100.00	200
Free rate	73.60	75.67	75.67	130.06	156.60	189.73	255
Bergsman's "Free trade rate"	71.00	81.00	81.00	95.00	160.00	210.00	350

Note: Rates equal to official rate (1956-8: 18.82; 1959-61: 18.92) plus agio.
Source: All from Superintendência da Moeda e do Crédito (SUMOC), *Relatório do Exercício* (Rio de Janeiro, various years), except cost of exchange. 1957 from Albert Fishlow, "Foreign Trade Regimes and Economic Development: Brazil" (unpublished manuscript, 1976); 1958-61 from José Almeida, "A indústria automobilística brasileira " (unpublished manuscript; Rio de Janeiro: Fundaçáo Getúlio Vargas, Instituto de Economia, Centro de Estudos Industriais, 1969); and from Joel Bergsman, *Brazil: Industrialization and Trade Policies* (London: Oxford University Press, 1970).

1. Instruction 113

Between 1953 and 1957, foreign exchange was allocated through an auction system in Brazil. Foreign-exchange quotas were allocated to five categories of diminishing importance, with the final exchange rate in each determined by auction (see Table 2.5). Therefore, a hybrid system – part market-determined, part quota – was created. The difference between the import and export rates accrued to the state so that foreign-exchange operations became a major instrument of state finance.

Foreign auto firms were made eligible for the benefits provided by Instruction 113, a policy instrument issued by SUMOC in 1955 that allowed all equipment entering the country as direct foreign investment to be imported without exchange cover.[46] Firms could therefore

[46] Although Instruction 113 was issued by the Minister of Finance Eugênio Gudin before Kubitschek took office, it came to be a widely used policy instrument only during the latter's administration. Its benefits were not exclusive to the automotive industry. Interestingly, a policy instrument introduced by an economically liberal finance minister came to be a critical component of Kubitschek's import-substitution strategy.

bypass the auction system and avoid the implicit tax involved in exchange transactions. The subsidy was the difference between the higher, third-category cruzeiro–dollar exchange rate at which capital goods would otherwise have been imported and the free rate, at which the investment was valued and on which profit remittances were calculated. The government sacrificed what it would have earned in this foreign-exchange transaction. (After the exchange reform of August 1957, the number of categories was reduced to two – a general and a special rate.)

It was clear to the plan's authors that this policy discriminated against Brazilian investors, because they were unlikely to take advantage of Instruction 113. For the policymakers, the exchange crisis warranted such action. As stated in the *Relatório,* the official planning document:

> The difference in treatment provided to foreign and legitimate Brazilian entrepreneurs is justified by the simple reason that the former have available funds in foreign currency, while the latter, only in cruzeiros. Thus, the foreigners would effectively be able to make liquid capital investment in the country, importing equipment without foreign-exchange payment, and the Brazilians would need exchange cover, which the existing legislation permits under special exchange rates when the imports are financed.[47]

2. Financing at the "Cost of Exchange"

For equipment that was not imported as direct investment but required foreign financing, loans proportional to effective Brazilian capital, with interest rates no greater than 8 percent and with a minimum term of five years, could be repaid at the favorable *custo de câmbio* ("cost-of-exchange") rate. The implicit subsidy was the difference between the third-category exchange rate, which is what firms would otherwise have paid for the foreign financing, and the cost-of-exchange rate, which is what they did pay. The difference between these two rates was even greater than the subsidy offered by Instruction 113, because the cost-of-exchange rate was substantially lower than the free rate.

3. Exchange Quotas for Imported Parts

In the process of attaining 90 to 95 percent domestic-content levels, firms had to import those parts not yet locally produced. Quotas of

---

[47] Presidência da República, Conselho do Desenvolvimento, *Relatório do Grupo de Trabalho sobre a Indústria Automobilística* (Rio de Janeiro, 1956), p. 56 (hereafter referred to as *Relatório*).

foreign exchange within the overall foreign-exchange budget were reserved to import parts for high-priority vehicles such as trucks and jeeps during the transition period. These quotas were made available outside the normal exchange auctions at very beneficial rates: the average agio of the last three exchange auctions for the second category. To encourage rapid domestic production of the engine, considered the technological heart of the vehicle, parts for trucks and jeeps moved to the first category once 60 percent of their engines was locally produced. Although the import rates for passenger cars and utility vehicles were not as attractive, they nonetheless represented a subsidy. Parts could be imported in the third category through normal exchange auctions up to the limit allowed in each auction. There was no additional subsidy once engine production began. Rather, to continue receiving these exchange benefits after July 1, 1959, firms were required to reach 60 percent domestic content for engines. With the reform in the exchange regime in August 1957, parts could be imported on the basis of the average exchange-auction rate in the general category.[48]

4. Fiscal Benefits

Motor vehicle producers were exempt from import duties and sales tax on equipment and machines. Also, trucks, jeeps, and utility vehicles were exempt from sales taxes.

5. National Bank for Economic Development Financing and Loan Guarantees

Article 11 of Decree No. 39.412 of June 16, 1956, which established GEIA and provided the general outline of the plan, included motor vehicles among "basic industries."[49] This categorization made firms eligible for credits and financial guarantees from official banking institutions. The personnel of the National Bank for Economic Development (Banco Nacional de Desenvolvimento Econômico [BNDE])

---

[48] SUMOC's Instruction No. 143 of January 11, 1957, provided the criteria for parts imports: Only those parts not yet domestically produced could be imported with these benefits. Instruction No. 145 of February 1957 extended these guidelines and included in the fifth import category some one hundred parts and accessories for which domestic production satisfied demand.

[49] Basic industries included intermediate inputs such as steel, cement, and fertilizers, as well as capital goods industries such as shipbuilding, metal transforming, and heavy electrical.

interpreted this article as being directed at them, because the bank was clearly the only agency capable of fulfilling this role.[50]

The BNDE was founded in 1952 to finance long-run development projects. Its charter did not preclude it from lending to domestic or foreign private firms.[51] Before 1956, however, lending to private capital was not a significant issue for the bank, as 90 percent of its loans and guarantees went to railroad transportation and electrical energy projects. With the exception of some privately owned and foreign-owned firms in electrical power, most of these projects were public. With Kubitschek's Target Plan, t*he bank's focus shifted to electrical energy and basic industries. Between 1957 and 1960, basic industries absorbed 43 percent of the bank's national currency operations and 59 percent of its foreign loan guarantees.[52] Although most BNDE assistance still went to the public sector, the bank's involvement with these new industries meant an increased share of funds for private firms. The auto industry was to be built primarily by foreign firms, which, in theory, had greater access than did domestic firms to foreign finance, through either internal resources or contacts with foreign banks. As will be shown, this would become an issue for the bank.

Vehicle Types

Commercial vehicles were GEIA's top priority given the share of cargo transported by truck in Brazil. Furthermore, GEIA viewed truck production as less problematic than automobiles because scale economies were not as stringent or quality standards as high. The market was also more defined and secure. Therefore, GEIA personnel expected the auto firms to be less reticent about investing in truck production and that segment of the industry to have less trouble with capacity utilization. Car production was to be the final stage of the plan. The relevant decree was issued last – seven months after that for trucks – and its high domestic-content requirements (which would necessitate large initial investment) were expected to delay production. Postponing automobile production in this way was also expected to build up repressed demand, so that in the short run, the industry would face a larger market than it would have otherwise. However, production

[50]   BNDE, *Exposição sobre o Programa de Reaparelhamento Econômico, Exercício de 1956* (Rio de Janeiro, 1956); and internal BNDE memo from Jõao de Mesquita Lara, chief of Project Division, to Dr. Américo Cury, Acting Chief of the Economic Department, November 16, 1956.

[51]   BNDE, *Exposição...*, *Exercício de 1953* (Rio de Janeiro, 1953), pp. 35–6.

[52]   BNDE, *Relatório do BNDE* Relatório do BNDE (Rio de Janeiro, various years).

could not be postponed indefinitely. Passenger cars, not trucks, were the true symbol of advanced industrialization. Any motor vehicle program without them would appear second-rate. Moreover, the demand for automobiles implied continual pressure on the balance of payments.

Industry Structure

GEIA's understanding of the industry led it to expect a nonvertically integrated industrial structure, leaving the parts sector as a natural preserve for Brazilian capital. Local firms did not view the massive entry of foreign capital as a threat, but rather as creating new investment opportunities. Given its desire to generate backward linkages, which were used to legitimate foreign capital's dominance, GEIA specified that it would encourage nonvertically integrated projects. As stated in the *Relatório,*

> Despite the knowledge that in industrialized countries, especially in the United States, the automotive industry tends toward a superficial structural organization, it would not seem reasonable to intend that in its implantation in Brazil, this same industry is going to work based on schemes of vertical integration.... Thus, an excellent opportunity would remain for national investors to operate, possibly on a more economical basis, specializing in the supply of parts and components to various or all aforementioned 'manufacturers' ... recognizing therefore the advantage in a horizontal industrial structure, from which emerge two types of producers: manufacturers, primarily foreign, and subcontractors, predominantly national.[53]

No concrete policies were adopted to prevent vertical integration. GEIA assumed that transnational firms would be forced to rely on domestic parts producers to satisfy domestic-content requirements. GEIA also thought that an independent parts sector would be more efficient because of the specialization and the economies of scale attainable by supplying more than one manufacturer. Technological efficiency, therefore, would generate the preferred industrial structure; rigid policies were not required.

Discarded Alternatives

The reasons why Kubitschek rejected alternative strategies either for solving the transportation bottleneck or for creating a motor vehicle industry merit special comment.

[53] Presidência da República, Conselho do Desenvolvimento, *Relatório,* pp. 17–18.

Railroads

The Target Plan's program for revitalizing the nation's rail system was not a comprehensive one. Road transport had definitely emerged as the system of choice. Rightly, the plan has been criticized for lacking an integrated approach to the problem of transportation. Costly long-run consequences have since unfolded from this early emphasis on motor vehicles at the expense of all other modes of transportation.[54] A variety of factors explains the thrust toward motor vehicles.

As described previously, the Brazilian railroad network had been built to service the export sector. The railroad system of the postwar period continued to reflect this trading pattern: In 1952, 90 percent of the existing railroads had been laid down by the end of the nineteenth century.[55] Much of the system was in disrepair. Even during the years of export orientation, relatively little capital, either foreign or domestic, had been invested in the railroads compared with the amount invested in production. As a result, the lines were not well maintained except for those in the new, more prosperous agricultural areas in the center-south.

This situation was not remedied after the war. While vast sums were being spent on motor vehicles, investment in rolling stock amounted to only Cr$775 million from 1944 to 1952, or 160 locomotives and 3,650 freight cars, equivalent to 4 and 7 percent, respectively, of existing stock. By 1953, 59 percent of broad-gauge and 63 percent of meter-gauge locomotives were over thirty years old. One-third of all freight cars were obsolete for heavy cargoes.[56] Together, the amount of replaced track and crossties and the number of new locomotives did not cover the minimum requirements of reposition. The quick pace of obsolescence resulted in a real decapitalization of the system and a reduction of effective capacity by 20 to 30 percent from the early 1930s to 1950.[57]

With increasing urbanization and industrialization, it was to be expected that road transportation would become more central to the Brazilian economy. But the poor quality and unreliability of the rail-

---

[54] See Richard Darbera and Remy Prud'homme, *Transports urbains et développement économique du brésil* (Paris: Ed. Economica, 1983).

[55] Joint Brazil–United States Commission Report, p. 83.

[56] Ibid., p. 85.

[57] Grupo Misto BNDE-Cepal, *Esboço de um programa de desenvolvimento para a economia brasileira 1955–62* (Anexo 1 – Atividades fiscais do setor público; Anexo II – Transportes, segunda redação), May 1955, pp. 57–8.

road lines, already strained beyond capacity, generated unusually intensive road usage. Construction of new urban centers and industries depended on the timely delivery of building materials. These bulk commodities would normally have been more cheaply transported by railroad or ship. Despite higher rates, the relative speed and security of road transport meant that, as roads were built, they were used not only for trafficking high-value products but for bulk commodities as well.

The overvalued exchange rate, which lowered the relative price of imported motor vehicles and fuel, provided an additional incentive to use road transport. Gasoline and oil could be imported with relatively few restrictions in the postwar years, and taxes did not rise significantly. Therefore, the unitary costs of truck cargo transport rose only 53 percent from 1946 to 1952, while general prices rose by 84 percent. Even though railroad rates were regulated and did not keep up with costs that rose by as much as 85 percent, trucking prices remained competitive in regions that still had railroad capacity.[58] The rate structure, therefore, combined with poor transport alternatives, contributed to the surge in demand for vehicles.

All these factors fostered competition, rather than complementarity, among alternative modes of transportation, even in areas where railroads and shipping had inherent cost advantages. Given the condition of the railroad system, the introduction of road transport in Brazil had very different consequences than it had in more-industrialized countries. Competition did not encourage increased specialization and greater efficiency in the transport system as a whole but instead resulted in the continuing deterioration of both shipping and railroads. The share of road transport in total cargo rose from 25 to 48 percent between 1948 and 1953.[59] The relative growth rates of alternative transport are demonstrated in Table 2.6.

To address these deficiencies, a massive overhaul of the existing railroad network would have been required. Such an undertaking would have entailed enormous public investment and upheaval in a bloated administrative apparatus that included a multiplicity of regulatory agencies. Moreover, the system was not physically unified, because the individual railway lines were originally built by different foreign nationals.

---

[58] Joint Brazil–United States Commission Report.
[59] Economic Commission on Latin America (Carlos Lessa), "Fifteen Years of Economic Policy in Brazil," *Economic Bulletin for Latin America* 9, no. 2 (1964):169.

Table 2.6. *Index of Real Output of Transportation (1939 = 100)*

	1939	1943	1945	1948	1951
Railroads	100	108	111	119	130
Tramways	100	123	123	125	115
Motor vehicles	100	83	86	152	300
Coastal shipping	100	116	151	136	220
Airways (1946 = 100)[a]				146	295
Weighted Total	100	103	112	136	212

[a]To avoid distortion of the overall measure of transportation services, the base index for air transport, which grew at an exponential rate, was set at 1946. On the basis of 1939 = 100, it had reached 320 by 1943 and 510 by 1945.

Source: *The Development of Brazil*: Joint Brazil–United States Economic Development Commission, *Report of the Joint Brazil-United States Economic Development Commission* (Washington, D.C.: Institute of Inter-American Affairs Foreign Operations Administration, 1953), p. 33.

It appears that Vargas originally may have been interested in promoting railroads – not to the exclusion of motor vehicles, but to a greater extent than ultimately occurred. According to Sônia Draibe, state investment in railroads was a priority for the Vargas administration.[60] It identified railroads as a bottleneck to development, and their extension was expected to save foreign exchange. Vargas also assumed that such an initiative would receive financial assistance from the United States.

As recompense for supporting the Allies during World War II, Brazil expected special assistance from the United States. During the war, the Taub Mission in 1942 and the Cooke Mission in 1943 – both sent from the United States – proposed large investment programs to foster the industrialization of the country. As Pedro Malan points out, however, U.S. interest in Brazilian industrialization was a function of the war effort and would end with it, though it did raise Brazilian expectations.[61] In 1948, the U.S.–sponsored Abbink Mission marked a return to traditional American advocacy of reliance on internal resources and private capital flows rather than government-to-government funding.

The Joint Brazil–United States Commission, formed as a provision to the Act of International Development passed in 1950, signaled a return to the previous approach by focusing on the "elaboration of concrete and well-formulated projects, admitting of immediate ap-

[60] Draibe, *Rumos e metamorfoses*, pp. 188–9.
[61] Malan, "Política econômica e teorias de balanço de pagamentos," p. 16.

preciación by financial institutions such as Eximbank or the World Bank."[62] The commission was formed in response to the cold war and Latin America's disaffection for American preoccupation with Europe. It was also part of the U.S. effort to engender support for the war in Korea. It offered new support for industrialization attempts and focused on bottlenecks in development for which public investment would be critical. The viability of the commission's projects was predicated on the availability of foreign assistance. The World Bank was to be the primary source of finance.

The commission carried out an exhaustive study of Brazil's transportation system and outlined a proposal for the rehabilitation of railroads and shipping. The entire transportation program called for a total investment of US$219.6 million and Cr$8.8 billion, US$146 million and Cr$7.7 billion of which was to go toward railroads. It was one of the projects that Brazilians expected would benefit from a US$500 million World Bank loan.[63]

For a variety of reasons, this assistance was not forthcoming. Vargas, facing a balance-of-payments crisis and publicly sounding increasingly hostile to foreign capital, unilaterally imposed restrictions on profit remittances and returns to capital in 1952. The U.S. State Department and the World Bank protested. The bank in particular threatened to withhold financing of the Joint Commission's projects until a satisfactory solution could be found with regard to remittances. None was found. World Bank and Eximbank credits to Brazil totaled US$170,690,000 between 1952 and 1955.[64] Except for one loan in 1958, the World Bank offered no assistance whatsoever from 1955 to 1965.[65] Furthermore, the end of the Korean War and Dwight D. Eisenhower's inauguration in 1953 spelled a decline in U.S. interest in aiding Latin American development. Most of the Joint Commission's projects, railroads included, were scrapped for lack of funds.[66]

The bank's decision may have influenced railroad policy. Given the nature of railroad construction and the political and economic reality

---

[62] Ibid., p. 33.
[63] Joint Brazil–United States Commission Report, p. 107; and BNDE, *Exposição . . . Exercício de 1961* (Rio de Janeiro, 1961), p. 15.
[64] Ibid.
[65] Malan et al., *Política econômica externa*, p. 35. After Brazil broke with the IMF in 1958, all credit lines with international agencies were cut until 1960. See A. C. Sochaczewski, "Financial and Economic Development of Brazil, 1952–1968" (Ph.D. diss., University of London, 1980), p. 183.
[66] A major exception was the creation of the BNDE in 1952. The BNDE lent much of its funds to railroad projects in the 1950s and tried, unsuccessfully, to rationalize ownership of the lines by creating a holding company.

in Brazil, however, it is not at all obvious that railroads would have become more central had the loan come through. Even the Joint Commission's program was not a program of national integration, which would have cost a fortune.

Moreover, the underlying conditions that had propelled road construction at the expense of the railway system until that point remained unchanged. A transportation network centered on roads and vehicles was less taxing on the state's fiscal capacity. Road construction required much less cash outlay by the state and, in contrast to the large, immediate investment needed for railroads, could be financed incrementally. It could begin with dirt, to be followed by concrete and asphalt as traffic warranted. More important, a large part of the expense would be incurred by individuals because vehicles are privately financed.

Furthermore, the financing of road construction came from funds earmarked for that purpose. No new public funds had to be appropriated once the 1945 National Road Fund imposed a consumption tax on petroleum products. The conditions that prompted the following conclusion of the Joint Brazil–United States Commission in 1952 remained in effect:

> The combined result [of incentives such as cheap imported vehicles and available highway funds] was a powerful drive for highway expansion which won wide psychological acceptance and which created serious resistance to the establishment of an overall control of investments in transport. Efforts for coordination have not infrequently been interpreted as a measure dictated by vested railroad interests and by a lack of comprehension of the dynamic potentiality of the country, rather than as a requirement of sound economic planning.[67]

A circle was thus created: "virtuous" for automotive transport, "vicious" for rail. Roads and poor rail services led to greater reliance on trucking, which in turn led to more oil consumption and higher tax revenues, which were used to finance increased road construction.

In theory, the revenues derived from petroleum taxes could have been used for railroad construction, but this transfer could not have been accomplished with the existing political constituencies. Although the federal government had inherited a railroad system plagued by deficits, raising rates was politically difficult. It was not feasible to

---

[67] Joint Brazil–United States Commission Report, p. 96.

incur greater expenses by investing in the system. As pointed out by Alan Abouchar, even though financing railroad deficits represented as significant a resource transfer as the subsidies offered to road transport, the former was covered by resources from the national treasury but the latter by indirect oil taxes. The costs of the railroad subsidy were therefore much more obvious.[68]

Roads, on the other hand, were the classic pork barrel. In the 1920s, Washington Luiz Pereira de Sousa, who served as president of the state of São Paulo and then as president of the Republic, pronounced, "Governar é abrir estradas" (To govern is to build roads).[69] Vargas, too, used highway funds as political capital and is himself quoted as having said that the biggest national party was the Partido Rodoviário (Highway party).[70] State government leaders knew that roads were considered synonymous with development and, as a result, vigorously competed for highway funds.

The perception that identified motor vehicles with development is only one of what Josef Barat has called the "subjective" factors that contributed to the demise of railroads.[71] By the 1950s, railroads had lost their glamour worldwide – they were no longer perceived as a basis of industrialization. The Brazilian urban middle classes, who represented a large part of Kubitschek's constituency, were clamoring for automobiles.

Clearly, Kubitschek's policy toward foreign capital and the centrality of the auto industry to his Target Plan exacerbated these tendencies. Once in place, transnationals further encouraged the consumption of motor vehicles. Vargas's belief in the centrality of state investment might have led to a greater emphasis on railroads had he remained in office. But he would have had to confront the same economic and political pressures favoring road construction. Kubitschek's policies, which were more favorable to foreign capital and relied less on public investment, further destroyed the political and economic conditions under which a broad transport plan could have been developed.

Kubitschek's target for railroads was not very ambitious. Like the Joint Commission's program, it centered on rehabilitating rather than augmenting the existing system. The plan was to purchase 440 diesel-

---

[68] Alan Abouchar, *A política dos transportes e a inflação no Brasil* (Rio de Janeiro: EPEA, 1967), cited in Josef Barat, "Crise do petróleo e reformulação da política de transportes," *Pesquisa e Planejamento Econômico* 5 (1975):484.
[69] Nascimento, "Política e desenvolvimento industrial numa economia dependente," p. 15.
[70] Barat, "Crise do petróleo," p. 482.
[71] Ibid.

electric engines and 12,000 passenger carriages and goods wagons, to lay 791,000 tons of rail, and to buy 6,770 sleepers and 15 million cubic meters of ballast. By 1960, only 7,052 coaches and wagons had been purchased; 80 percent of the repair of existing lines had been carried out, but the length of the network was extended by only 3.2 percent.[72]

The National Motor Factory (*Fábrica Nacional de Motores*)

As described previously, the idea of a "national champion" was discarded because of limits on state intervention and the financial and technological requirements of the automotive industry. Nevertheless, the existence of the National Motor Factory (FNM), a state-owned enterprise established during World War II, could conceivably have served as a basis for a national industry and moved the debate beyond the realm of theory. Its history, however, though not causing the decision to rely on foreign capital, did nothing to discourage it.

For security purposes during World War II, the United States sought to diversify the production locations for airplane engines. As an ally, the Brazilian federal government established the FNM in June 1942. Financed under the Lend-Lease Program, the firm was to produce 450-horsepower Wright engines.

The decision to produce airplane engines, according to Túlio de Alencar Araripe, who served as industrial director and president of the FNM, can be ascribed only to either stupidity or bad faith.[73] By the time the first finished engine left the factory, the war had ended and the United States immediately lost interest. More important, the Wright engine was already obsolete. Airplane engine technology is highly advanced and changes rapidly. (Even when Brazil began to export commercial and fighter planes to Europe and the United States in the 1970s, it still imported the engines.) The potential market for Wright engines had evaporated, except for replacement demand and possibly some government purchases for military training purposes. Rather than mothball the plant, the directors used its equipment to produce a variety of other products, such as refrigerators.

By 1948, the firm had been incorporated with 99 percent of its stock under the federal government's control and was producing trucks under license from the Italian firm Isotta-Franschini. On De-

[72] Economic Commission on Latin America (Carlos Lessa), "Fifteen Years of Economic Policy in Brazil," p. 165.
[73] Interview with Túlio de Alencar Araripe, February 1985, São Paulo.

cember 31, 1949, fifty trucks came off the line with 30 percent domestic content. Of the more than four hundred machines inherited from the original factory, only ten were not adapted to truck production. Although this strategy may not have created the most efficient plant, it minimized investment costs, and the small output levels made it possible. The truck cabins at this time were handmade.[74] In 1951, Isotta went out of business. The Italian government arranged a similar contract with Alfa Romeo, of which it was a sponsor. The product line of the FNM, heavy diesel trucks, began with 35 percent national content. Because Alfa picked up the deal, Isotta's failure was probably a blessing: Its truck model dated back to the Abyssinian War.[75] As Araripe once said, "Thank God it failed."[76]

Even though a comprehensive auto manufacturing program had not yet been introduced, the FNM gradually increased domestic-content levels. The firm actively sought parts producers and is given credit for stimulating the parts industry. By 1956, the FNM was producing trucks with 70 percent domestic content, a level at least twice as high as the transnationals.[77]

From the earliest government planning discussions, the possibility that the FNM would play a large role in the industry was never considered. In 1951, before creating the subcommission, Vargas asked Meira to study the firm's potential. Meira's ultimate report discussed the FNM only in passing[78] and apparently convinced Vargas that the industry's development could not be dependent on it. As a result of its history and its hodgepodge production process, the firm's reputation was questionable. It was viewed as a holdover from the war and was not taken seriously. Until 1954 when, to the surprise of a skeptical public, its trucks were already on the streets, Meira reportedly never even visited the plant, though it was nearby on the outskirts of Rio.[79] He recommended selling it off to the private sector, which Vargas opposed.[80] Nevertheless, Vargas approved the subcommission's final program, which gave foreign capital a predominant, and

[74] Ibid.
[75] "Entre fé e descrença, vinte anos de história," *Visão*, November 22, 1976, p. 151.
[76] Interview with Túlio de Alencar Araripe, February 1985, São Paulo.
[77] Nascimento, "Política e desenvolvimento industrial numa economia dependente," p. 73; and Presidência da República, Conselho de Desenvolvimento, *Relatório*, p. 28.
[78] Nascimento, "Política e desenvolvimento industrial numa economia dependente," p. 33.
[79] Interview with Túlio de Alencar Araripe, February 1985, São Paulo.
[80] Moreira Franco interview with Lúcio Meira, cited in Martins, *Pouvoir et développement économique*.

the FNM only a negligible, role. Even Túlio de Alencar Araripe did not think a state-owned industry was feasible, although he supported the FNM and believed it had an important role to play in providing utility vehicles and in controlling prices by providing a yardstick.[81] The FNM's location also made the firm less viable as a base for the industry, because the bulk of assembly and parts production was concentrated around São Paulo.

Even when the subcommission was discussing direct state intervention as an alternative strategy for the industry, the FNM was not considered a serious contender. In the face of both foreign and domestic private capital's unwillingness or inability to invest, Meira himself proposed that the government finance a motor vehicle plant that could later be sold to private Brazilian capital. He once suggested that resources derived from exchange agios could finance a fund for the establishment of the industry.[82] The parts producers repeatedly made it clear, however, that they did not have the resources for such an enterprise.[83]

Views toward the FNM provide a small indication of the differences between Vargas and Kubitschek. The subcommission agreed to maintain the FNM, but in the report establishing GEIA and its program, in keeping with the emphasis on private enterprise, the firm was definitely to be sold.[84] As Meira put it, GEIA was "radically" against the socialization of the industry.[85]

It would be incorrect to conclude from these events that the FNM was responsible for the privatization of the industry. Nevertheless, it is fair to say that the firm's poor prestige paved the way for the internationalization of the industry. Had the FNM been more efficient, it may have been politically more difficult to argue for the necessity of foreign capital and ultimately to sabotage the firm. It could also have given the sector of the military who controlled the firm and who argued that motor vehicles were an issue of national security, greater leverage in the discussions. Instead, the FNM's weak performance raised serious doubts about the capacity of state enterprises to manufacture motor vehicles. The other state-owned initiatives in steel and mining were successful in comparison, which may

---

[81] Interview with Túlio de Alencar Araripe, February 1985, São Paulo.
[82] Subcommission Minutes, August 27, 1952.
[83] Subcommission Minutes, May 7, 1952.
[84] Presidência da República, Conselho do Desenvolvimento, *Relatório*, p. 18.
[85] Interview with Lúcio Meira, April 1985, Rio de Janeiro.

have convinced some people that the state could be effective in raw materials and basic industries, as opposed to manufacturing.

Nevertheless, although the FNM was marginal to GEIA's program, it was not sold until 1967. The military, which continued to control the firm, was reluctant to give it up. According to Sydney Latini, Orosco's successor as secretary of GEIA, the military resisted GEIA's authority, arguing that the FNM predated GEIA and that as a national security issue, the plant should be directly under the president's authority.[86] It is also unclear whether there were any serious buyers. Furthermore, GEIA was aware of the ideological function of the FNM, particularly as foreign dominance in the industry became more and more apparent. As Meira stated, "Imagine what the Communists would have said if it [the industry] was 100 percent foreign."[87]

As a result of this legacy, the plant continued to operate without clear direction. Its use for political objectives and patronage not only added yet another constituency behind its survival, but also guaranteed that it would live up to its unfavorable reputation.

Tractors

A national plan for tractors was not approved until December 1959, three and a half years after the establishment of GEIA. The delay in domestic tractor production is noteworthy given Brazil's attempts to mechanize agriculture during this period and tractors' technological affinity with motor vehicles. The reasons for the delay included the political strength of the Brazilian agricultural producers, the nature of the technology, and the characteristics of the international tractor industry. These impediments were more serious to tractor production than were similar obstacles to the production of trucks and passenger cars.

During World War II, Brazil imported tractors, farm implements, and fertilizers directly through the Agricultural Ministry's Resale Commission, which then resold these items to the agricultural sector. After the war, the commission was preserved. It continued to import and sell tractors at cheap prices by taking advantage of an overvalued exchange rate, special financing, and tax exemptions. According to Latini, it was also easily manipulated by special interests and plagued by corruption. Too many tractors of too many brands were imported.

[86] Interview with Sydney Latini, December 1984, Rio de Janeiro.
[87] Interview with Lúcio Meira, April 1985, Rio de Janeiro.

If a tractor broke down, it was easier to buy a new one than to repair the old. Imported parts were hard to obtain and relatively not as cheap as a new tractor. Local replacement parts were scarce because the market was atomized among some 130 different brands. Moveover, machine shops had to be brought into the countryside, whereas cars could be taken to the machine shop. As a result, 80 percent of the existing tractor fleet was nonfunctional.[88]

If one uses imports as an indicator, the market for tractors was small in the postwar years, much smaller than that for motor vehicles. The 1962 market for tractors was estimated at fifteen thousand units.[89] As a reflection of market size and the nature of competition in the international tractor industry, Brazil continued to import the finished product. Transnationals did not begin significant assembly operations there or in any less-developed country until the 1960s, when the Green Revolution augmented markets and government production plans took effect. The Argentine Deere plant, the first North American tractor subsidiary outside Western Europe, was established only in 1959.[90]

Therefore, an industrial springboard based on existing assembly installations and parts manufacturers did not exist for tractors as it had for motor vehicles. Nor had a constituency evolved to support domestic manufacture. Instead, a politically powerful coalition composed of the Ministry of Agriculture, landowners, and U.S. tractor manufacturers emerged to defend the status quo. This group was able to block protective legislation necessary for the feasibility of domestic tractor production.

Despite the foreign-exchange crisis, tractor importers were given an added incentive of special exchange rates. This was a reflection not simply of the landowners' political clout, but also of the perception of tractors as productive agricultural inputs. Government policymakers worried about the negative effects of higher tractor costs on agricultural production prices.

Thus, there was a peculiar conflict inherent in the domestic pro-

[88] Interview with Sydney Latini, April 1985, Rio de Janeiro.
[89] Orosco, *A indústria automobilística brasileira*, p. 76. The value of tractor imports during these years was (in US$1,000): 1953, 20,758; 1954, 52,568; 1955, 18,737; 1956, 14,867. ANFAVEA (National Association of Motor Vehicle Manufacturers), *Indústria automobilística brasileira* (São Paulo: ANFAVEA, 1963).
[90] See Rhys Owen Jenkins and Peter J. West, "The International Tractor Industry and Its Impact in Latin America," in Richard Newfarmer, ed., *Profits, Progress and Poverty: Case Studies of International Industries in Latin America* (Notre Dame: University of Notre Dame Press, 1985), pp. 299–342.

duction of tractors that was absent for motor vehicles. On the one hand, because of its potential significance to agricultural costs, the short-run impact of increased prices was worrisome. On the other hand, tractors were considered essential to national development.[91]

As a result, some halfhearted attempts were made to produce a national tractor. President Eurico Dutra (1946–51) issued a presidential decree in January 1946 that ordered the FNM to produce tractors. At that time, the FNM was a likely candidate because it was state-owned and was still searching for an alternative to the Wright airplane engine. According to this tractor program, production was to begin with the assembly of imported kits and gradually increase the level of domestic content over a period of four to five years. The plan authorized the Ministry of Agriculture to purchase ten thousand units.[92] After a prototype was produced, Dutra changed his mind and opted for producing trucks under contract with Isotta-Franschini. Dutra also recanted because licensing negotiations with Mack broke down. That firm would license tractor assembly only in exchange for control of the operation.[93]

Vargas also initiated tractor production. The FNM conducted a study to document how it could manufacture tractors with the same machines used in truck production. It ultimately did produce seven hundred tractors before that plan was also aborted.[94]

When Kubitschek took office, he assigned the problem of tractor production to the Working Group for the Mechanization of Agriculture. It issued regulations for importing agricultural machinery that maintained favorable exchange treatment. A complete industrialization program, however, was not forthcoming.

In 1958, GEIA set up a subgroup that devised a tractor program and ultimately drafted a decree that authorized its implementation. However, it was not officially issued until late 1959. According to Latini, the timing was inopportune for two reasons: The auto parts sector was already stretched beyond capacity from the motor vehicle industry's orders; and there was difficulty in "reconciling the industrialization plans with the exchange subsidy regime for tractor im-

---

[91] The cost effect of domestic truck production on transport prices or consumer response was not considered critical.

[92] Nascimento, "Política e desenvolvimento industrial numa economia dependente," p. 28.

[93] Eurico Andrade, "Morte e vida feneme. Entrevista com o Major S. Martins, director da fábrica," *Quatro Rodas*, March 1966.

[94] Interview with Túlio de Alencar Araripe, February 1985, São Paulo.

ports."[95] GEIA did not have the power to counter the Ministry of Agriculture and interests associated with it.

GEIA personnel apparently believed that an established motor vehicle industry would both technologically and politically facilitate the initiation of tractor production. Tractor components – motors, axles, transmissions, and gear shifts – were also the most technologically advanced motor vehicle parts. Their production required large investments and came last in manufacturers' nationalization schedules. GEIA thought that after the productive capacity for these components was established in motor vehicles, it could successfully lobby for the necessary protection against tractor imports. At the same time, scale economies would make it possible to produce a more reasonably priced tractor.[96] As Meira stated, "GEIA did not have the conditions to struggle with this force [agricultural associations, importers, and agriculture's political power], which was so well organized. Once the 'point of no return' was reached in the case of trucks and cars, we returned to tractors. The first task was to convince the national farmer that tractor production was important for him."[97]

The tractor plan was finally approved in December 1959, and the Resale Commission and import subsidies were terminated. The agricultural sector was still able to make its political power felt, however. Unlike motor vehicle buyers, landowners, with transnational tractor producers' support, won subsidies for the increased cost of domestic tractor production. To substitute for the old exchange benefits, GEIA successfully negotiated with the Bank of Brazil for financial subsidies.

Brazil's postwar policies toward the auto industry are noteworthy for their high degree of continuity. Policymakers responded pragmatically to the constraints and opportunities presented by the domestic and international political economy. The foreign-exchange

---

[95] Sydney A. Latini, *SUMA Automobilística*, vol. 1 (Rio de Janeiro: Editora Tama, 1984), p. 56.

[96] Interview with Sydney Latini, April 1985, Rio de Janeiro. An implicit assumption behind this argument is that the same facilities that produced these parts for motor vehicles would produce for tractors. For reasons involving technological sophistication and economies of scale, Latini claims that the FNM's earlier forays into tractor production were misguided. Although the issue of technological sophistication may be warranted, the economy-of-scale argument is more dubious. The market for tractors was small, but economies of scale are even harder to achieve in automobile production. Furthermore, the most restrictive stage of auto production is not machining parts that compose tractors (although they may be the most technologically sophisticated) but stamping metal sheets.

[97] "Um almirante pé na tábua," entrevista com Lúcio Meira, *Quatro Rodas*, January 1966, p. 54.

constraint was paramount in their minds. This historical experience shaped GEIA's perception of the possible, as it adopted the general strategy of Vargas's subcommission.

From the vantage point of Brazilian policymakers in the 1950s, the world did not look hospitable to export-led growth strategies. A political coalition emerged to support import substitution in response to the volatility of coffee prices and the legacy of coffee hegemony. Import-substituting industrialization came to be portrayed not as a choice but as a necessity in the face of what appeared to be Brazil's chronic foreign-exchange constraint.

It was not inevitable that import substitution be spearheaded by motor vehicles. Tractors, or even railroads, were conceivable alternatives, but technical, economic, and political factors favored automobiles. Auto assembly had a long history in Brazil, and a constituency of parts producers had arisen around it. The total automotive import bill was costly, and the higher costs of domestically produced vehicles were dispersed among middle-class consumers. In contrast, tractor imports had less impact on the balance of payments, consumers were more concentrated and had powerful backing, and a complementary parts sector had not yet arisen. Finally, neither tractors nor railroads had the panache of motor vehicles. If Brazil was to follow in the footsteps of the United States, where the automobile had become the symbol of industrial might, it would have to develop its own industry. Its success in this pursuit would depend on the response of transnational auto firms to the GEIA proposals, which is the focus of Chapter 3.

3

THE DETERMINANTS OF
FIRM ENTRY

Brazil's first attempts to convince transnational auto firms to shift from assembly to full manufacture were met with resistance. In the early 1950s, representatives of the Ford Motor Company told Brazilian planners that the idea of building a domestic automobile industry was "utopian" and that engines could not be produced in the tropics. These protests notwithstanding, Ford, accompanied by most of the major players in the international automotive industry, participated in Brazil's five-year auto program. Of the eleven firms that initiated vehicle production, three (WillysOverland, Vemag, and the National Motor Factory) were controlled by Brazilian capital, two (Mercedes-Benz and Simca) were fifty–fifty joint ventures between Brazilian and foreign capital, and six—Ford, General Motors (GM), International Harvester, Scania Vabis, Volkswagen (VW), and Toyota – were controlled by or were wholly owned subsidiaries of foreign firms. US\$156 million of imported manufacturing equipment was invested in the terminal sector of the industry by 1961, not to mention investment in local currency. In that year, vehicle production reached 145,000 units, with an average domestic-content share of 93 percent by weight and 87 percent by value.[1] By 1968, the industry had consolidated, and three foreign firms – Ford, GM, and VW – were responsible for 89 percent of all vehicles produced. Subsequently, the industry led the Brazilian economic "miracle" with annual growth rates of over 20 percent.

Given foreign firms' initial resistance to local manufacture, what accounts for this turnabout? Various explanations for firm entry into the Brazilian market have been suggested, and they mirror the more general debate between neoclassical and statist theorists. These frameworks can be categorized by their relative emphasis on economic versus political variables or on forces internal or external to Brazil. On one side are those that emphasize the role of government policies and

---

[1] For details on production, investment, and domestic content, see Appendix A.

institutional innovation in attracting foreign investment. At the other extreme are those that portray firm entry and market fragmentation as resulting from the oligopolistically competitive strategies of foreign firms.

This chapter argues that the underlying model behind these approaches is misspecified. It documents how both the state and foreign firms had strategic objectives beyond the investment itself, so that the *form* and *timing* of entry, which these approaches neither consider nor explain, were as fundamental as entry per se. For Kubitschek, the installation of an auto industry was a means to develop rapidly the manufacturing sector as a whole and to maintain political support. Firms, however, preferred to limit their initial investments to reduce risk, make it easier to recoup their investments, and reduce potential exit costs. The incentive structure was designed to ensure that firms made large, up-front commitments to the auto project, rather than incremental investments. Because of the uncertain policy direction of the next administration and firms' potential efforts to delay investing in the hopes of a policy switch, Brazilian technocrats felt it necessary to develop the industry to the "point of no return." Once significant investments had been made and a network of domestic suppliers created, it would be difficult both economically and politically to dismantle the industry.

Attracting numerous firms into a small domestic market that could not technically support even one plant operating at full capacity was bound to create short-run efficiency problems. To minimize diseconomies of scale, the preferable strategy might have been to start with lower domestic-content requirements that gradually increased as the market grew, so that those production processes characterized by highscale economies, such as metal stamping, could be added last. Gradualism did not appear to be a viable option given the uncertainty about future presidential administrations, chronic foreign-exchange constraints, and the strategies of foreign firms. On the one hand, because of the economies of scale in the industry and the long-run nature of investment, firms preferred to export from existing facilities. On the other hand, if government policies could force firms to invest, it was unlikely that these investments would simply be viewed as sunk costs that a firm would easily abandon. The alternative to an industry that would be inefficient in the short run appeared to be no industry at all.

In this context, the *credibility* of impending market closure was fundamental, particularly since Brazil was setting a precedent in the region. Firms had to be convinced that they could not evade the program's requirements and that the market would remain closed to imports. Therefore, it is important to look at the government policies and institutions that made the threat of market closure and deadlines credible and placed high costs on firms' failure to participate on schedule.

The chapter documents how firms resisted GEIA's high domestic-content requirements and sought ways to reduce their investment costs. They were reluctant to commit significant resources to Brazil because of the country's political and economic uncertainty, and they worried about repatriating profits in the future. Some preferred to continue exporting to Brazil in order to operate existing plants at full capacity. GEIA was not flawless but proved strong enough to resist attempts to sabotage the plan. The foreign-exchange constraint continued to serve as a potent weapon for the government in its negotiations with foreign firms. Moreover, the program's subsidies reduced firm risk and put late entrants at a competitive disadvantage, forcing firms to invest within a short time period and thereby to accelerate Brazil's industrialization process.

The chapter begins with a review of Brazil's pre-1956 experience in negotiating with the transnational corporations (TNCs) in the auto industry. It then discusses the strategic importance of speed and the logic of the incentive structure. Next, it documents the general process of firm entry into commercial vehicle and passenger car production. The chapter then provides detailed accounts of Volkswagen and Ford strategies and the companies' negotiations with the Brazilian government. Finally, it evaluates the role of subsidies, along with other factors, in determining firm entry and industrial structure and compares these findings to conventional explanations of the Brazilian experience.

Foreign Capital

As discussed in Chapter 2, the immediate postwar import bonanza was cut short by balance-of-trade deficits that reappeared by mid-1947. The problem lay not simply in the import boom. Exchange reserves and trade surpluses had accumulated largely in inconvertible European currencies, whereas U.S. dollars were required for most imports. As a result of the dollar scarcity and foreign-exchange rationing, European imports gained a foothold in the market. Although absolute sales did not fluctuate greatly, their relative market share did increase at the expense of U.S. imports, which varied with the availability of dollars.

As seen in Table 3.1, U.S. firms continued to dominate the market

Table 3.1. *Brazilian Motor Vehicle Imports by Exporting Countries, 1946-1959 (%)*

	Passenger cars					Commercial vehicles					Jeeps[a]	
Year	United States	Germany	United Kingdom	France	Total (units)	United States	Germany	United Kingdom	Italy	Total (units)	United States	Total (units)
1946	89.5	--	6.2	2.7	9,637	92.8	--	4.7	0.2	18,732	--	--
1947	76.3	--	8.6	11.0	28,794	93.8	--	3.1	0.3	37,035	--	--
1948	59.0	--	23.0	13.9	31,751	95.1	--	3.0	0.3	36,148	--	--
1949	43.8	--	41.6	8.5	21,390	87.3	--	7.8	2.0	19,503	--	--
1950	27.1	2.5	55.1	6.8	15,717	81.2	3.0	11.7	1.9	33,010	--	--
1951	63.5	5.1	22.1	5.1	47,274	82.4	7.2	5.9	2.0	62,228	--	--
1952	59.4	6.5	28.0	4.2	30,494	77.4	10.2	5.8	2.4	49,625	86.8	5,755
1953	50.1	32.8	5.1	8.6	6,363	74.3	7.6	--	--	6,719	99.6	3,823
1954	34.1	49.8	0.0	7.3	4,226	75.9	11.8	--	0.0	26,312	98.9	6,236
1955	65.8	16.9	1.5	8.3	1,536	50.0	12.8	9.6	23.2	9,313	80.8	1,744
1956	54.8	7.8	0.5	0.3	997	52.5	17.0	3.3	21.9	15,152	91.4	2,394
1957	61.1	23.4	0.6	2.1	2,617	56.1	29.7	1.0	11.1	31,853	97.3	9,292
1958	29.9	65.2	0.2	0.8	8,580	61.6	27.9	0.1	8.3	28,996	89.9	10,447
1959	20.4	68.1	0.1	10.9	27,087	74.2	18.0	--	6.3	53,926	71.2	10,870

[a] Jeeps were included with trucks until 1952.

Source: Eduardo Augusto de Almeida Guimarães, "Industry, Market Structure, and the Growth of the Firm in the Brazilian Economy" (Ph.D. diss., University of London, 1980).

during most of these years; American cars remained the most sought after and had the most extensive sales and service networks. The United Kingdom and Germany were the main European exporters to Brazil. This reflected a global pattern, whereby the dollar shortage and Germany's slow recovery boosted the United Kingdom to the position of largest vehicle exporter by 1950. By 1956, German exports surpassed the British (in part because of Australian import restrictions) and Germany remained the world's largest exporter until 1973.[2]

The increase in European imports also reflected pressure by the firms' home governments to export as much as possible, despite unmet domestic demand. These countries, too, faced foreign-exchange constraints and domestic supply bottlenecks, especially in steel. Many European governments provided their recovering auto industries with a variety of financial incentives and privileged access to imported raw materials to promote exports. French auto companies, for example, received indirect subsidies on unassembled vehicle exports until mid-1957. In Italy, the government refunded 5 percent of a vehicle's export price as relief on the turnover tax, and reduced duties on imported raw materials. Germany provided a tax rebate of 3.85 percent on exports until the end of 1955.[3] In that year, exports represented 45 percent of domestic production in Germany, 41 percent in the United Kingdom, 30 percent in Italy, and 24 percent in France. In contrast, the U.S. industry, which was not dependent on imported raw materials and which supplied European markets primarily from local subsidiaries, exported only 3 percent of domestic production.[4]

[2] George Maxcy and Aubrey Silberston, *The Motor Industry* (London: George Allen and Unwin, 1959), pp. 16–18. The aggregate import figures by country of origin mask firm nationality and hence exaggerate the inroads made by European-owned companies. Ford, unable to source its assembly plants with imports from the United States, shifted its export base to its European subsidiaries. The large increase in British imports in the late 1940s came in large part from the Ford subsidiary at Dagenham, which began exporting to Brazil in 1946. Later, French and Canadian subsidiaries were also used, depending on foreign-exchange availability. Ford also engaged in barter deals, exporting Brazilian raw materials for imported vehicles (Manager's Monthly Letters, Ford Motor Company-Brazil, March 1, 1946, March 1, 1948, and January 28, 1953. ID CF Storage B-38 119A, Mira Wilkins Personal File, Florida International University, North Miami, Florida). It should be noted that some European currencies became fully convertible only in 1959. For historical treatments of the industry, see also Gerald Bloomfield, *The World Automotive Industry* (Newton Abbot, London: David and Charles, 1978); and Daniel Roos and Alan Altshuler, codirectors, *The Future of the Automobile* (Cambridge, Mass.: MIT Press, 1984).
[3] Maxcy and Silberston, *The Motor Industry*, p. 144, n3.
[4] Eduardo Augusto de Almeida Guimarães, *Acumulação e crescimento da firma* (Rio de Janeiro: Editora Guanabara, S.A., 1987), p. 136.

The emphasis on exports also reflected new patterns of international competition among large auto manufacturers. In the late 1940s and early 1950s, both U.S. and European companies faced sellers' markets at home as a result of the repressed demand that had accumulated during the war. By the mid-1950s, however, when most of this demand had been satisfied, particularly in the United States, domestic and international competition intensified. As various countries began erecting tariff barriers to auto imports, countries such as the United Kingdom were also losing the benefits of imperial preference.

Profits on domestic operations fell. Firms in the United States and Europe placed greater emphasis on overseas expansion, either by exporting, expanding existing subsidiaries, or creating new ones. In the United States, changing market conditions bankrupted the independents, leaving GM, Ford, and Chrysler in control of 95 percent of the car market by 1955.[5] In Europe, the creation of the European Economic Community and the gradual reduction of tariffs on imported vehicles created additional pressures; the volume of intraregional trade in motor vehicles nearly quadrupled between 1958 and 1965. Although national markets still remained remarkably segmented, with imports accounting for a small share of total sales, this period witnessed the first cross-penetration of producer-country markets; before the war, most exports had gone to nonproducing countries.[6] The protected, relatively faster growing European market also became more significant for U.S. firms, which had invested in local manufacturing capacity in the 1920s and 1930s, when European countries established tariffs to protect their national automotive industries. Ford and GM had particularly aggressive expansion plans. European firms were therefore confronting new types of competition but were also becoming larger and more efficient as a result of domestic market growth, exports, and the promotion of mergers and national champions by home governments.

---

[5] Rhys Owen Jenkins, *Transnational Corporations and the Latin American Automobile Industry* (Pittsburgh: University of Pittsburgh Press, 1987), p. 29.

[6] Tariffs on passenger cars had fallen slightly after the war but still averaged over 30% in 1960 except in Germany, where they were 13–16%. By 1968, tariffs within the EEC were eliminated, and they had fallen to 17.6% in the U.K. Vehicle trade among the major auto-producing countries in Europe was 6% of production in 1950, 7% in 1960, and 12.3% in 1970. Trade within Western Europe as a whole was 18.1, 18.8, and 25.8% of production for those same years. Roos and Altshuler, *The Future of the Automobile*, pp. 17, 22. European companies had not penetrated each others' markets prior to this time, but the U.S. firms – particularly Ford and GM – had done so through direct investment.

The recovery of the European industry also led to increased competition in the U.S. market. Imports jumped from less than 1 percent of sales in 1955 to 10 percent in 1959. This increase was due to reduced productivity differentials and to European firms' ability to fill the small car market niche vacated by the independents. Volkswagen was particularly aggressive in this regard.[7]

Brazil's restrictions on auto imports in the early 1950s thus came at a time when competition for foreign markets was intensifying and when the dominance of U.S. firms was being challenged. The country represented the largest market in Latin America, accounting for 25 percent of the 2.7 million vehicles in circulation in 1955.[8] After Brazil prohibited the importation of built-up vehicles in 1953, firms such as Volkswagen, Mercedes-Benz, and Willys Overland[9] began to export completely and semi–knocked-down kits (CKDs and SKDs) for local assembly. The new assembly operations that were set up by the companies themselves or by Brazilian importers joined the long-established facilities of Ford and GM.

Nevertheless, despite these changing global conditions, despite chronic foreign-exchange shortages that provoked tighter and tighter regulation of auto imports, and despite government blueprints for a domestic industry, no firm was, to use Frederick Knickerbocker's phrase, "stealing a march" on its competitors and plunging voluntarily into full-scale local production to garner any first-mover advantages.[10] The threat of complete market closure was not taken seriously. Although highly profitable, the Brazilian market was still seen as too small to accommodate the industry's economies of scale and as too economically and politically volatile.

For example, Ford, the first auto company to assemble in Brazil, had no intention of producing motor vehicles in the country. Before World War II, the company dominated passenger car sales; between 1935 and 1940, annual exports from Ford's U.S. and Canadian op-

---

[7] Ibid., p. 25. Europe's import share declined when the Big Three introduced their own compact models in the early 1960s but bounced back to 10% by 1970.

[8] Eduardo Augusto de Almeida Guimarães, "Industry, Market Structure and the Growth of the Firm in the Brazilian Economy" (Ph.D. diss., University of London, 1980), p. 173. The next-largest countries – Argentina, Mexico, and Venezuela – each had only 200,000 vehicles in circulation.

[9] Willys Overland had been a successful jeep and small truck producer in the United States and merged with Kaiser-Frazer in 1953 after establishing an assembly plant in Brazil.

[10] Frederick T. Knickerbocker, "Oligopolistic Reaction and Multinational Enterprise" (D.B.A. diss., Harvard University Graduate School of Business Administration, 1972).

erations averaged 42 percent of wholesale deliveries into Brazil. Because of Ford's historic contribution to the automotive sector and its market dominance, the Brazilians went out of their way to elicit the company's cooperation. Ford's local management had also tried to impress on Dearborn the seriousness of Brazilian intentions. The Manager's Monthly Report of April 19, 1951, mentioned that, in an address to the Federation of Industries, a top official of the Bank of Brazil made it clear that companies that insisted on importing would soon be out of business. At the same time, the government asked Ford-Brazil for a report on how Brazil might develop a local industry, and Humberto Monteiro, then assistant manager, complied.[11]

Ford-Dearborn adopted an intransigent position from which it hardly deviated in coming years. According to Monteiro, he was heavily criticized for supplying such a report to the Brazilian government without prior authorization and was told: "We are not going to lead; we are going to be led."[12] Whereas Chrysler and GM began local manufacture of truck bodies and cabs even before the GEIA decrees, Ford took the lead in attempting to thwart Brazil's manufacturing ambitions. The company took credit for preventing the Vargas subcommission from rushing directly into full-scale manufacture in 1951 and for convincing it to start by assembling CKDs with increasing amounts of domestic content.[13]

In February 1953, Lúcio Meira, then director of President Vargas's subcommission on motor vehicles, led a Brazilian delegation to Ford's facilities in Dearborn, Michigan, at the company's invitation. Upon their arrival, Ford did everything possible to convince them that producing trucks in Brazil made no sense because of the country's small market and lack of infrastructure. Arthur J. Wieland, vice-president of Ford International in New York, who organized the Brazilians' trip, wrote to his colleagues in Dearborn requesting their "help and cooperation in giving them a good indoctrination of the problems of automotive manufacture." In a separate communication, he also sug-

---

[11] Memo from G. K. Howard to Appropriations Committee, February 3, 1950, Acc. 106, Box 26; and Manager's Monthly Report, April 19, 1951, Wilkins Personal File.
[12] Mira Wilkins interview with Humberto Monteiro, November 8, 1961, Wilkins Personal File. According to Branco Ribeiro, this phrase was often repeated by Walter McKee, Ford's vice-president for Latin America, as well. Ford-Brazil had to convince Dearborn that there was no alternative to manufacturing, which Dearborn thought was not financially viable. Interview with Ribeiro, August 4, 1988, São Paulo.
[13] Executive communication to Henry Ford II et al. from Arthur J. Wieland, vice-president, Ford International, January 23, 1953, Acc. AR-67-6, Box 2, Ford Industrial Archives, Redford, Michigan.

gested that "when making such arrangements, it is suggested that some of our largest suppliers, from the point of view of physical facilities, be included to impress on the Committee the importance of the outside supplier to our business."[14] At the time, the company had plans to increase marginally domestic-content levels but had no intention of moving to completely integrated manufacturing. Meira returned to Brazil disappointed but undeterred.[15] The firm also protested strongly when Brazil banned the importation of parts with domestic counterparts in that year. Monteiro, closer to the scene, understood that the Brazilian industry was a fait accompli, and he thought that Ford would be better positioned if the company helped shape the program rather than resisted it.

Volkswagen conceivably could have built upon its market niche created through exports after World War II and seized on Brazil as an opportunity to capture a market previously dominated by U.S. firms. Although VW predated the war, full-scale production at its facilities in Wolfsburg began only after peace returned. As mentioned, the German government promoted auto exports, and the company itself engaged in an aggressive export strategy to gain footholds in new markets and to realize scale economies. VW began to export in 1948; in 1951 it was exporting one-third, and by 1960, one-half of its output, mostly to Europe and North America.[16] When Brazil banned the importation of assembled cars in 1953, VW turned to Brasmotor, a Brazilian company, to assemble its knocked-down vehicles. The possibility of building a manufacturing plant was considered and rejected and, at the time of the GEIA decrees in 1956, VW had no plans to move beyond building its own assembly plant. Still concentrating on expanding capacity in Germany, the firm was reluctant to move into vehicle production in Brazil.

In an approved news bulletin in July 1953, VW announced its plans to build a manufacturing plant in Brazil that would go beyond simple assembly. The company expressed high hopes for the future Brazilian market and planned to use the country as an export base to the rest of South and Central America. At the time, VW had not yet invested

[14] Arthur J. Wieland vice-president, Ford International, executive communication to Henry Ford II et al., January 23, 1953; and executive communication to I. A. Duffy, January 26, 1953, Acc. AR-67-6, Box 2, Ford Industrial Archives. Ford International moved from New York to Dearborn in 1956.

[15] Interview with Lúcio Meira, April 1985, Rio de Janeiro.

[16] Steven Tolliday, "Rethinking the German Miracle: Volkswagen in Prosperity and Crisis, 1939–1992" (Paper presented at the Business History Seminar, Harvard Business School, November 4, 1991).

in any foreign assembly or manufacturing operation. However, the *Aufsichtsrat*, VW's supervisory board, had approved funds only for assembly, and a year later the company clarified that it would build an assembly, rather than a full manufacturing, facility. Further production plans would be contingent on long-term economic and political developments in Brazil. Thus, in 1956 VW still had no plans to move beyond building its own assembly plant. Concentrating on expanding capacity in Germany, the firm was reluctant to go into vehicle production at that time, although, when dealing with Brazilian authorities, VW tried to emphasize that the manufacturing project was only on hold and not canceled.[17]

Like their counterparts in Dearborn, VW executives in Wolfsburg were nervous about moving too quickly in Brazil, even if Mercedes-Benz appeared to be going ahead with a truck program. As was the case with Ford, the VW personnel on site in Brazil pushed for more aggressive plans. F. W. Schultz-Wenk, the director of VW do Brasil, wrote to VW president Heinrich Nordhoff recommending that the company participate in an industry fair for public relations purposes, noting that companies such as Ford and GM had registered. Nordhoff rejected the idea as too expensive and only a moneymaking scheme for the organizers.[18] Schultz-Wenk also complained to Nordhoff that the export types in Wolfsburg did not really understand the financial or political context in Brazil and were using inappropriate criteria to assess the company's plans.[19]

The strongest advocate of an integrated manufacturing facility was Olavo de Souza Aranha. As vice-president of VW do Brasil, he rep-

[17] VWD Frankfurt a. Main, no. 171, "Director Nordhoff Concerning the VW Factory in Brazil," July 27, 1953, Volkswagen Archives, Wolfsburg. As of July 1954, the *Aufsichtsrat* had approved DM5 million for only assembly and machining equipment in Brazil (letter from the head of the *Aufsichtsrat* to VW, July 4, 1954). According to a report on the minutes of an *Aufsichtsrat* meeting on August 27, 1954, the board clarified that the payment to VW do Brasil was for the sole objective of starting an assembly plant, not a manufacturing facility. VW President Heinrich Nordhoff informed O. E. de Souza Aranha, VW's Brazilian partner and a vice-president of VW do Brasil, of the supervisory board's decision in a letter dated August 30, 1954, adding that building a complete factory would be put on hold to await further developments in Brazil. On convincing the Brazilians that the project had not been canceled, see the letter from Heinrich Nordhoff to F. W. Schultz-Wenk, October 30, 1954, Volkswagen Archives.

[18] Personal correspondence, F. W. Schultz-Wenk to Heinrich Nordhoff, May 27, 1954; and official correspondence, Heinrich Nordhoff to F. W. Schultz-Wenk, June 22, 1954, Volkswagen Archives.

[19] Letter from Schultz-Wenk to Nordhoff, November 19, 1954, Volkswagen Archives.

resented the Monteiro-Aranha holding company's 20 percent share of VW do Brasil. In a series of letters in the mid-1950s, he pushed Wolfsburg to go ahead with the manufacturing plan.[20] Nordhoff and others repeatedly warned Aranha that they did not share his optimism about Brazil and that the company had no immediate intention of going beyond assembly.[21]

VW's personnel in Brazil pushed Wolfsburg to commit itself to build a factory in Brazil after the Monetary Authority (Superintendência da Moeda e do Crédito [SUMOC]) issued Instructions 127 and 128 in March 1956, shortly after President Juscelino Kubitschek took office. These instructions required firms to increase domestic-content levels in return for favorable exchange rates for imported parts, putting firms that did not move toward integrated manufacturing at a competitive disadvantage. VW do Brasil executives also noted that Kubitschek intended to define his own auto program, as indicated by the formation of his Working Group for the Automotive Industry in April. Nevertheless, in April and May of 1956, shortly before the passage of Kubitschek's first automotive decrees in June and July, Nordhoff warned Schultz-Wenk not to spread unrealistic expectations about VW's plans for Brazil. He emphasized that agreement had been reached in the company only about the *future possibility* of producing cars in Brazil, and that in no way had any decision yet been taken about moving ahead with engine production. The supervisory board had shown no willingness to go ahead with such plans.[22] Nordhoff insisted that the timing of VW's investment and production decisions would be determined by VW and not by Brazil. Moreover, since the company, unlike the Brazilian government, would not go back on a promise, the project had to be thoroughly researched. He cautioned

[20] Letter from O. E. de Souza Aranha to Heinrich Nordhoff, September 27, 1954; letter from F. W. Schultz-Wenk to Nordhoff, November 29, 1954, relating Aranha's position; letter from Aranha to directors of VW-Wolfsburg, April 26, 1955, Volkswagen Archives.

[21] Letters from Nordhoff to Aranha, October 12, 1954, and December 13, 1954. In a May 24, 1955, letter to Aranha, Nordhoff explained that Wolfsburg did not share Aranha's optimism about Brazil, that they planned to wait until the next elections before moving ahead, and that future manufacturing plans would be contingent on how things went with the assembly plant. In a May 26, 1955, letter to Schultz-Wenk, Nordoff repeated that, in contrast to Aranha, people outside Brazil did not judge the situation to be very good and that VW would begin with an assembly plant, which could later be transformed into a car body shop if necessary. Volkswagen Archives.

[22] Letter from Nordhoff to Schultz-Wenk, April 20, 1956, Volkswagen Archives.

his colleague not to confuse optimistic newspaper articles and political promises with Brazilian economic reality.[23]

The Brazilian planners' skepticism about transnational corporations' interest in the plan and their view of TNCs' preference for extending production runs at existing facilities and exporting seemed borne out. After years of fruitless negotiations, Brazilian planners concluded that TNC cooperation would not be forthcoming unless firms were given no alternative. As Lúcio Meira complained:

> We always had the consideration to question the firms' representatives about their plans, about what incentives they needed from the Government in order to launch the automotive industry in Brazil. We made it a point to emphasize that the government's objective was to install this industry or launch it and questioned what kind of collaboration we could expect from these firms. The answers were the same: almost none. I have the impression that no foreign automobile company has an interest in producing 100 percent in our country and only will do it when compelled.[24]

The automotive plan, issued soon after President Juscelino Kubitschek took office in 1956, was designed to provide that necessary compulsion.

The Importance of Timing

As discussed in the previous chapter, firms had to meet an extremely ambitious domestic-content schedule to be eligible for the full range of financial subsidies. Each year, their vehicles had to contain an increased percentage of domestically purchased components. By July 1, 1960, trucks and utility vehicles were to contain 90 percent domestic content and jeeps and cars, 95 percent.

[23] Letter from Nordhoff to Schultz-Wenk, April 30, 1956, Volkswagen Archives.
[24] Lúcio Meira, as quoted in Wellington Moreira Franco, "A nacionalização de veículos no Brasil" (Master's thesis, University of São Paulo, n.d.), Appendix 1, "Sinopse das Atas de Reunião da Subcomissão de Jeeps, Tratores, Caminhões e Automóveis da Comissão de Desenvolvimento Industrial" (hereafter referred to as Subcommission Minutes), May 14–15, 1952. Despite some interest shown by Mercedes-Benz and General Motors in the early 1950s in gradually beginning domestic manufacture, no major investments had come through. In an executive communication, Arthur J. Wieland, vice-president of Ford International, suggested that GM retreated in response to Vargas's 1952 restrictions on profit remittances. Executive communication to Henry Ford II et al. from Arthur J. Wieland, vice-president, Ford International, January 23, 1953, Acc. AR-67-6, Box 2, Ford Industrial Archives.

Just as each firm's conduct in Brazil must be understood as part of its international strategy, the auto plan must be viewed within the prism of the state's larger objectives and context. The program's fast pace was at once a method to achieve these general goals and a response to political and economic constraints faced by Kubitschek. GEIA personnel typically explained the five-year time frame as a reflection of Kubitschek's political ambition and of the pressure he faced to end his five-year term with a Brazilian automobile on the road. He had taken office amid a polarized elite and military, and he succeeded an administration that had been economically liberal in orientation. In fact, the debate over whether Brazil would further industrialize or continue to finance much of its manufacturing needs through coffee exports was still unresolved. Lacking full congressional support, Kubitschek implemented his Target Plan through the power of executive decree. Also, the uncertain policy direction of the next administration and potential efforts by TNCs to delay their investments made it necessary to develop the industry to "the point of no return"[25] and virtually impossible to dismantle.

The strategic implications of the auto industry, which went beyond the sector itself, were the most important reasons behind this race against time. The industry was expected to play the role of leading sector through its ability to attract foreign capital and technology and to generate production linkages. Therefore, delaying its starting date would have had serious implications for the development of the manufacturing sector as a whole. The basis of Kubitschek's political power and coalition was fast growth. Furthermore, GEIA expected the foreign-exchange constraint to become increasingly binding. In the short run, the industry required foreign currency to import components and to finance capital equipment that did not enter under Instruction 113, but in five years the industry was expected to become self-sufficient. GEIA was skeptical about whether the strategy would be feasible, economically or politically, over the long run.[26]

---

[25] Interview with Lúcio Meira, April 1985, Rio de Janeiro. Sydney Latini, a secretary of GEIA, also used this term: "We have no time to lose. We must reach the target in the fixed time period. We must get beyond the 'point of no returning.' Afterward, we will have the rest of our lives to discuss." Sydney Latini, *SUMA Automobilística*, vol. 1 (Rio de Janeiro: Editora Tama, 1984), p. 13.

[26] Brazil was not unique in its concern with speed. Mexican policymakers also attempted to install the industry during the course of one presidential term, or the *sexenio*. See Douglas C. Bennett and Kenneth E. Sharpe, *Transnational Corporations versus the*

When speed is included as one of the plan's primary objectives, the significance and logic of the incentive structure become clear. Policies were designed to ensure that the TNCs made large, up-front commitments to the project, rather than incremental investments. Having to reach 90–95 percent domestic-content levels in five years, for example, meant that the major investments required for metal stamping or engine blocks could not be postponed. Furthermore, policies that made it costly not to participate on schedule had to be devised. By offering the financial incentives for only a limited period, the plan would put laggardly entrants at a competitive disadvantage. GEIA's high discount rate created a bias toward offering extremely attractive incentives to maximize the probability of immediate firm entry into domestic manufacture. An investment commitment today was worth much more than one five years later. Whether firms would have entered the market on their own ten years later, a possibility that others have raised to minimize the importance of GEIA and government subsidies, was irrelevant.

However, policies alone were not sufficient. To induce the desired investment behavior, the threat that foreign exchange would be withheld from those firms that failed to meet the domestic-content schedules, as well as the commitment to end subsidies after a certain date, had to be credible. That the Brazilian authorities would display the will or the means to implement this plan was by no means obvious. There was also enormous uncertainty about how firms would respond. As the first in Latin America to attempt domestic production, Brazil could not benefit from the experience of neighboring countries. The threat of market closure was less credible than it would later be in Argentina and Mexico, which followed Brazil's example.[27]

Furthermore, in the mid-1950s, Brazil was not a country in which systematic rules always applied. A great deal of arbitrariness prevailed, and political connections could often be relied upon to gain exceptional treatment. The planning and administrative capacity of the

---

State: The Political Economy of the Mexican Auto Industry (Princeton: Princeton University Press, 1985), pp. 128–9.

[27] For example, Ford's behavior was markedly different in Argentina and Mexico, where it took the lead in beginning domestic manufacture (Mira Wilkins interview with J. Sundelson, May 11, 1960, Wilkins Personal File). See also Douglas C. Bennett and Kenneth E. Sharpe, "The World Automobile Industry and Its Implications," in Richard Newfarmer, ed., *Profits, Progress and Poverty: Case Studies of International Industries in Latin America* (Notre Dame: University of Notre Dame Press, 1985), p. 214.

state, with its unwieldy bureaucracy and discordant government branches, was also dubious.

Kubitschek created GEIA, with its legal norms and centralized decision making, to revise these expectations and to signal the seriousness of his intentions. Convinced of the industry's long-run profitability, GEIA attributed firms' reluctance to invest to the insecure environment and the fear of discriminatory treatment. GEIA's effectiveness would be necessary not only to coordinate and enhance the credibility of the program, but also to reduce the risk for those firms that did participate.[28]

Entry Process

Eighteen firms submitted projects to GEIA. All were accepted, but only eleven implemented their plans (see Appendix A). Most firms manufactured more than one type of vehicle; six firms produced trucks, three produced utility vehicles, three produced jeeps, and five produced passenger cars. A total vehicle market predicted to reach 130,000 by 1962 clearly could not technically support so many manufacturers.[29] In the 1950s and 1960s, estimates for the optimum scale of an integrated auto plant, or the point at which additional cost savings from increased production taper off, ranged from 300,000 to 500,000 units a year. The optimum varied among processes, with the largest economies of scale in stamping metal exteriors (which therefore set the optimum for an integrated plant), followed by forging and machining engines.[30] In itself, this degree of fragmentation

[28] The TNCs were not formally involved in drafting the Brazilian plan and, along with Brazilian private capital, were excluded from formal GEIA deliberations. The official decrees were issued soon after completion of the original report so that no real bargaining occurred between the TNCs and the government over the plan as such. In contrast, the Mexicans waited two years between the publication of the original plan and the final official decrees, during which time changes were made. On the other hand, the Brazilian decrees were much vaguer than the Mexican. See Bennett and Sharpe, *Transnational Corporations versus the State*, pp. 94–116.

[29] Several estimates of market demand were calculated to justify the feasibility of domestic motor vehicle production. They were generally unsophisticated and arbitrary, which was partly the result of poor data. The original demand estimates for 1960 were for 56,000 trucks and about 15,000 cars and jeeps. This was revised to 130,000 vehicles by 1962. Original figures cited in Presidência da República, Conselho do Desenvolvimento, *Relatório do Grupo de Trabalho sobre a Indústria Automobilística*, (Rio de Janeiro, 1956), pp. 2–13; later figure cited in Eros Orosco, *A indústria automobilística brasileira* (Rio de Janeiro: Consultec, 1961), p. 35.

[30] Relevant estimates for optimum plant size vary. Bain estimated 300,000 (Joseph Bain, *Industrial Organization* [New York: John Wiley, 1968], pp. 284–7). Baranson

seems to lend credence to the claim that the nature of firm entry was a response to oligopolistic competition. The bunched investments appear as defensive maneuvers rather as than a response to short-term profits and, therefore, to financial incentives or subsidies.

Although the competitive strategies of oligopolistic firms are clearly a large part of the story, they are not the entire story. These general figures mask the underlying dynamic of the entry process. A disaggregated portrayal reveals different forms of firm entry, which reflected variations in firm strategy and policy impact.[31] Variations between U.S. and European firms are especially noteworthy. Moreover, GEIA had a much harder time eliciting proposals for cars than for trucks; the threat of market closure was not sufficient to attract an acceptable car project from any of Detroit's Big Three. Finally, the program was not entirely insulated from political pressures, which firms tried to use to their advantage; they did not take market closure and the new rules of the game lying down.

General Entry Guidelines

The formulators of Brazil's automotive program were familiar with the U.S. and European industries and were aware of the scale economies inherent in motor vehicle production. They assumed that the

showed production costs per unit leveling off at 120,000 for assembly, 240,000 for engines and other power-train parts, and 600,000 for body stampings (Jack Baranson, *Automotive Industries in Developing Countries*, World Bank Occasional Staff Papers, no. 8 [Washington, D.C.: The World Bank, 1969]). Maxcy and Silberston (*The Motor Industry*, pp. 75–98) estimated optimum capacity at 100,000 for assembly, 100,000 for casting, 400,000 for machining engines, and up to 1,000,000 for body pressings, even though the rate of cost savings decreased as volumes grew. The economies of scale available to an individual firm differ from an individual plant. A firm can spread preproduction costs across plants and products, and a multi-product mix allows some interchange of components. Measurement is difficult because of the nonhomogeneity of product and the variety of cost allocation methods used by firms. Maxcy and Silberston estimated that technical economies were exhausted at 1,000,000 units, and that most of the substantive gains were made at the 400,000 mark. Optimum production for the industry as a whole would take into account the economies of scale available to suppliers as overall auto production increases. These estimates are all related to automobile production of the 1950s and 1960s. As a result of technological and organizational innovations, similar calculations for the industry in the 1990s would differ.

[31] For a similar attempt to identify the impact of firm-specific variables on host country–transnational firm bargaining at a later stage of the Brazilian auto industry, see Barbara C. Samuels II, *Managing Risk in Developing Countries* (Princeton: Princeton University Press, 1990).

Brazilian industry would ultimately take on an oligopolistic structure as the U.S. industry had, a process they viewed as fundamental to reaching cost-efficient levels of production. The *Relatório,* the planning document for the sector, and the executive decrees establishing the industry's guidelines explicitly stipulated that, although any company was theoretically acceptable, those that duplicated installed capacity would be less desirable. The planners reasoned that favoring those firms already producing in Brazil was warranted to take advantage of existing installations and networks of commercial agents and technical assistance.

Despite this vague guideline, GEIA was not empowered to take more directive steps to limit the number of entrants. It perceived its role as restricted to selecting firms according to standardized criteria and verifying that the plan's guidelines, especially those concerning domestic content, were met. It expected an industrial shakeout to reduce the number of firms, as it had in the U.S. automobile industry. Rather than arbitrarily picking the "winners" of this competitive struggle at the outset, GEIA hoped to fabricate neutral market conditions in which the transnational firms would fight it out. It assumed that, in this way, the transnational firms would bear all the risks and costs associated with making large investments in a relatively small market.

GEIA also presumed that limiting entry from the outset would promote monopolistic pricing. It realized that a certain degree of concentration was inevitable but hoped to lessen its extent and mitigate its impact. As Eros Orosco, GEIA's first secretary, stated in a GEIA meeting, "I think the only realistic price control is that which emerges from competition from equal bases."[32] Discussing the Toyota jeep proposal, José Fernandes de Luna, the director of the Foreign Exchange Bureau, concurred: "The Foreign Exchange Bureau is always in favor of increasing the number of projects with the object of lowering the price of the vehicle."[33] These statements reveal strong implicit assumptions about the nature of competition in the industry. GEIA expected that price competition would prevail over other forms of oligopolistic competition, even in a protected market with rationed foreign exchange.

In addition, GEIA's preference for particular companies made it impossible for it to accept proposals simply on a first-come, first-served basis until market predictions were satisfied. It sought the participa-

[32] Minutes from GEIA meeting, December 4, 1956, GEIA Archives, Conselho do Desenvolvimento, Ministério de Indústria e Comércio, Rio de Janeiro.
[33] Minutes from GEIA meeting, December 26, 1956, GEIA Archives.

tion of the large, well-known firms that had already been serving the Brazilian market. This was especially true for passenger cars (as opposed to commercial vehicles). Orosco expressed this orientation clearly with respect to Ford:

> The fact that Ford is one of the most well known motor vehicle producers in the world (along with GM) would make it very difficult for the Brazilian Government to deny approval of its project if Ford were to be late relative to other interested, lesser-known parties....
>
> There would not be a way to reject other projects even if the estimated Brazilian market was saturated by projects presented earlier. Thus, if Ford presents itself, the alternative would be either to approve its project, with obvious oversaturation of the market or to reject it, which would be hard to carry out when facing the name Ford.[34]

Finally, it was important that GEIA not appear to favor any individual firm or nationality and especially not to seem partial to foreign capital. This was particularly true regarding proposals submitted by firms with substantial Brazilian participation. GEIA's approval of a jeep project by Vemag, a Brazilian-owned company whose production was licensed by Germany's Auto-Union, illustrates this concern. Willys's planned jeep production could have supplied the estimated market demand on its own. Nevertheless, GEIA approved jeep projects from Vemag and Rover, both firms with Brazilian participation, so that Willys would not have a monopoly.[35]

Commercial Vehicles

For about a year after its inception in June 1956, therefore, GEIA's operating principle was to accept any project that met the general requirements outlined in the decrees. Although it did try to estimate future demand and to weigh each project relative to existing ones, it

---

[34] Internal memo by Eros Orosco, February 8, 1957, attached to Ford truck project proposal, GEIA Resolution 16, File no. 217, GEIA Archives.

[35] Minutes from GEIA meeting, June 4, 1957, GEIA Archives; and interview with Lúcio Meira, April 1985, Rio de Janeiro. Originally, Vemag was solely owned by Grupo Financeiro Nôvo Mundo, a banking and importing organization that had imported vehicles into Brazil since 1945. In 1955, Vemag entered a licensing arrangement with Germany's Auto Union to assemble its models. The next year, the company took in Auto Union, Frits Mueller Pressefabrik, and August Laepple as minority shareholders, but retained 87% of Vemag's equity capital (Vivianne Ventura Dias, "The Motor Vehicle Industry in Brazil: A Case of Sectoral Planning" [Master's thesis, University of California, Berkeley, 1975], pp. 43–4).

felt that the market was large enough to accommodate many projects in the medium run. GEIA personnel also assumed that the resultant competition could have only positive consequences. Because most equipment was imported without exchange cover, the additional investment required no foreign-exchange expenditures. Therefore, in their view, they could costlessly accommodate the different objectives listed previously without sacrificing any one in particular.

In its second year of operation, however, GEIA's attitude toward the number of firms began to change. Once again, the foreign exchange situation helped sound the alarm (see Table 3.2). Predictions about the country's overall balance of payments were worse than expected, but more important, GEIA's approved commercial vehicle projects had cost more foreign exchange than anticipated. Fernandes de Luna of the Foreign Exchange Bureau noted that although they had planned to spend US$35 million in the first year of operation, they had actually spent close to US$70 million, without including investment financing.[36] These cost overruns appear to have arisen because a greater number of projects were implemented than originally planned; the subsequent higher production levels required more spare parts imports. Also, the value (as opposed to weight) estimates for these imported parts were higher than anticipated.

In addition, the already-approved projects of General Motors, Ford, Mercedes-Benz, and the FNM (National Motor Factory) could satisfy the predicted demand for trucks. Nevertheless, Krupp, Borgward do Brasil S.A., Rio Motores do Brasil S.A., Scania Vabis-Vemag S.A., International Harvester, and Mercedes-Benz had new projects pending. Volvo, Berliet, Saurer, and Isuzu were considering submitting truck proposals.[37] GEIA began to fear that additional installed capacity would flood the market.

Finally, GEIA was growing skeptical about the positive correlation between the number of firms and vehicle price. Pressure was mounting in Congress in response to the high price of Brazilian motor vehicles. Partly to address this criticism, GEIA commissioned the Economic Commission on Latin America (ECLA) to undertake a study of price formation in the industry in conjunction with the Development Council (Conselho do Desenvolvimento). In September 1957, during the commission's investigation, one of its participants told GEIA that the advantages from generating internal competition had

---

[36] Minutes from GEIA meeting, September 6, 1957, GEIA Archives.
[37] Minutes from GEIA meeting, August 28, 1957, GEIA Archives.

Table 3.2. *Balance of Payments, 1957-1961 (US$ millions)*

	1957	1958	1959	1960	1961
I. Trade balance (goods)	107	64	72	-24	111
a. Exports	1,392	1,243	1,282	1,269	1,403
b. Imports	-1,285	-1,179	-1,210	-1,293	-1,292
II. Services	-393	-326	-373	-470	-359
a. Receipts	200	167	159	176	121
b. Expenditures	-593	-493	-532	-646	-480
III. Trade and services	-286	-262	-301	-494	-248
IV. Transfers	-13	-4	-10	-14	7
V. Capital movements	470	455	336	482	214
a. Autonomous	290	202	182	52	270
1) Entry (inflow)	533	526	575	529	713
2) Exit (outflow)	-243	-324	-393	-477	-443
b. Compensatory[a]	180	253	154	430	-56
VI. Errors and omissions	-171	-189	-25	26	27

[a] Negative sign indicates surplus; positive values correspond to balance-of-payments deficits.

Source: Superintendência da Moeda e do Crédito (SUMOC), *Relatório do Exercício* (Rio de Janeiro, 1961).

already been attained.[38] In his view, low capacity utilization for the industry as a whole (67 percent as of May 1957) was one of the major factors behind high industrial costs and, therefore, high prices; entry by new firms would only exacerbate the problem.

According to minutes of GEIA meetings, a long debate ensued about limiting the number of truck proposals. In the meantime, new project approval was held up as GEIA tried to determine whether the exchange situation allowed further expansion and, if so, according to what criteria. In September 1957, GEIA issued a change in policy – Resolution 41 – to automotive companies.[39] In it, the group elaborated the reasons for the policy switch and enumerated new criteria that any future truck proposal would have to fulfill. These included limitations on foreign-exchange requirements, already having productive capacity in Brazil (i.e., assembly lines), and not duplicating previously approved vehicle types. GEIA acknowledged that the four approved truck programs had not been subject to these criteria but argued that new circumstances justified the change.

This attempt to establish new criteria marked a turning point for GEIA. It signified a change of the rules midstream. Although impelled by unforeseen circumstances, GEIA was nevertheless reneging on its commitment to treat all applicants alike, one of its touted virtues. Its actions also demonstrated flexibility, however, in the face of the realization that the decrees' guidelines were insufficient.

Judging from the projects that were later approved, this resolution apparently had little effect.[40] Four of the projects that were then under consideration – Mercedes-Benz, Scania-Vabis, International Harvester, and Krupp (considered separately) – were ultimately approved, even if they did not meet all the new criteria. GEIA does appear to have stopped the submission of additional truck proposals.

The inability to limit the number of firms reflected GEIA's inherent contradiction: its claim of impartiality and limited intervention versus its need to establish guidelines to fulfill stated objectives. These conflicting tendencies could not be reconciled within GEIA's narrowly defined purpose and administrative purview. As the plan progressed, GEIA's guarantee of equal treatment to any project that met the decrees' requirements became a noose around its neck.

GEIA was in the difficult position of having a minimal number of policy instruments for achieving a diverse array of targets. As a purely

---

[38] Stefan Podgorski, Minutes from GEIA meeting, September 4, 1957, GEIA Archives.
[39] Minutes from GEIA meeting, August 28, 1957, GEIA Archives.
[40] Minutes from later GEIA meetings were not available.

administrative body with little discretionary power – fiscal or otherwise – it did not have the means to intervene directly, to choose between competing projects, or to establish priorities if goals conflicted. No new policy instruments were devised, and GEIA had to rely on the indirect policy incentives, primarily related to the foreign-trade sector, that were available to its constituent agencies. Direct price control, for example, was not an alternative tool to limit monopoly pricing.

The personnel in GEIA understood this dilemma and perceived their sphere of action as circumscribed. In an early GEIA discussion on limiting truck projects, it was pointed out that applicants always used the decrees in their defense. Members discussed pointing to the scarcity of foreign exchange for importing spare parts as a reason for limiting the number of projects, thus placing the blame on the Foreign Exchange Bureau. In response, the director of that agency complained, "The Foreign Exchange Bureau will be stuck with the unsympathetic role." Then-secretary of GEIA Sydney Latini responded, "Does GEIA itself have the prerogative to refuse?"[41]

GEIA was also captive to and participated in the free-market rhetoric of the Kubitschek era. Planning was legitimate, but the extent of state intervention was limited by ideological disposition and budget constraints. Great efforts were being made to attract foreign direct investment in general to Brazil. GEIA personnel often characterized their activity as creating free market conditions as much as possible. As Latini explained years later:

> Therefore, in a regime of free enterprise it seemed that we should authorize all the producers that, through the projects submitted to GEIA, fulfilled the minimum requirements. In principle, we admitted that by definition, these manufacturers should know the market better than we did, should know more about automobiles and should take care with the money that they were going to invest because it was theirs.[42]

Some GEIA personnel questioned their ability as technocrats to determine what was best for the industry; they felt that the firms had the experience they lacked.[43]

[41] Minutes from GEIA meeting, June 4, 1957, GEIA Archives.
[42] Sydney Latini, Testimony before the Parliamentary Inquest Commission for the Verification of the Cost of the National Vehicle (Comissão Parlamentar de Inquérito Destinado a Verificar o Custo de Veículo Nacional), October 26, 1967, GEIA Archives.
[43] Mexico also had difficulty limiting the number of firms, even though, following the Brazilian experience, it made a more explicit attempt to do so. According to Bennett

The following commercial vehicle projects were approved and implemented: Ford and GM in light trucks; Ford, GM, and Mercedes-Benz in medium trucks; Mercedes, Scania Vabis, FNM, and International Harvester in heavy trucks; Mercedes in buses; Volkswagen, Vemag, and Willys Overland in utility vehicles; and Toyota, Vemag, and Willys in jeeps. (For a complete list of all approved projects, see Appendix A.)

Passenger Cars

The contradictions in the policy-making process and their consequences are starkly revealed in the experience with passenger cars. From the start, the automobile program, as compared with that for commercial vehicles, was much more subject to political forces beyond GEIA's control. It became the most controversial aspect of the plan.

Commercial vehicles were GEIA's top priority given the high share of cargo transported by truck in Brazil. Even though truck production was more complex than that of other durable goods produced in the country in the 1950s, GEIA viewed trucks as less problematic than automobiles. Scale economies were not as stringent, and the market was more defined and secure. Therefore, GEIA personnel expected that TNCs would be less reticent about investing in truck production. Although car production was to be the final stage of the plan, it could not be postponed indefinitely. Passenger cars, not trucks, were the true symbol of advanced industrialization. Any motor vehicle program without them would appear second-rate.

The car decree was issued last, on February 26, 1957, seven months after that for trucks. Its high domestic-content requirements were expected to force firms to produce many of their components in-house. This would necessitate large initial investments and delay production. Postponing automobile production was expected to build up repressed demand so that, in the short run, the industry would face a larger market than it would have otherwise. The delay would also reduce pressure on the balance of payments. Meanwhile, approved projects and construction activities, though not yet in operation, could be ceremoniously displayed to the public as tangible progress toward domestic automobile production.

Unfortunately, the car projects originally submitted were all prob-

and Sharpe (*Transnational Corporations versus the State*, pp. 111–12), pressure from the U.S. and Japanese governments, combined with the lack of internal cohesion within the executive branch, accounts for the failure.

lematic. To become eligible for financial incentives, proposals had to be presented to GEIA by December 1957. By the summer of that year, only one auto plan – a relatively small one by Vemag – had been approved; two others were under consideration. Fabral, a joint effort between Alfa Romeo and Matarazzo, its Brazilian partner and one of the country's original, family-owned conglomerates, proposed building relatively expensive Alfa Romeos. The French firm, Simca, in association with Brazilian partners, presented a project that did not meet general guidelines.

The major European and U.S. companies, however, were not actively pursuing car production.[44] Some European firms did submit project proposals but tried to negotiate better terms. Volkswagen, for example, tried to bend the rules of the National Bank for Economic Development (Banco Nacional do Desenvolvimento Econômico [BNDE]) (see subsequent discussion) and sought exemptions from domestic-content guidelines, arguing that its car had special engineering characteristics.[45] As late as September 1957, GEIA feared that VW would limit itself to producing vans. Mercedes and Borgward held their car projects hostage to pending truck proposals (which may explain why their truck plans were approved even after the change in guidelines).[46]

Most important, the Americans were not expressing any interest in producing automobiles. Before World War II, it would have been difficult to find a European car on the streets of Brazil. Large-engined, long-bodied Fords were the vehicles of choice. Although GEIA did not want to promote the production of large cars in Brazil, it was convinced of American engineering superiority and ability to produce cost-efficiently in Brazil. Yet, it appeared that Ford and GM would produce only trucks; Chrysler and American Motors were facing dif-

---

[44] Japanese firms also stayed out of Brazil's passenger car market. At the time of Brazil's automotive decrees, Japan was producing fewer than 200,000 cars a year and exporting very few; see Michael Cusumano, *The Japanese Automobile Industry* (Cambridge, Mass.: Harvard University Press, 1985), p. 4. Toyota submitted a small investment project to produce jeeps, which was accepted and implemented. As a result of Japanese firms' late arrival on the international scene and their reluctance to source major components from off-shore sites, they have avoided the Brazilian car market to this day.

[45] Memoranda attached to VW's auto project proposal, GEIA Resolution 63, File no. 39, GEIA Archives.

[46] Minutes from GEIA meetings, GEIA Archives. Mercedes's and Borgward's car plans were ultimately accepted but never implemented. It is not clear whether Borgward's truck proposal was rejected or withdrawn.

ficulties in the United States. As a representative of Chrysler told Meira, "How can we invest in Brazil when our own house is on fire?"[47]

Thus, as of September 1957, with the December deadline fast approaching, what was to be the showpiece of Kubitschek's program was not even off the ground. Only substandard projects were on line. From a public relations point of view, the absence of Ford and GM was a disaster.

Kubitschek let his concern be known, and GEIA was pressured to approve questionable projects. Over GEIA's initial objections, the Alfa Romeo was accepted. GEIA thought smaller, economy cars more appropriate for Brazil and criticized the project's large requirements of foreign and domestic financing. In a heated GEIA meeting, Meira defended the project on public relations grounds: "It [Fabral] is not ideal because they are going to make a vehicle that perhaps is not the most suitable for Brazil. We may need a more modest vehicle. At least, that is how we economists think. The general public does not think that way. The Brazilian is a bit of an exhibitionist." Asked how he could justify BNDE funding for Alfa Romeo when the bank at that time was denying financial support to priority vehicles like trucks, Meira responded that they already had enough truck projects. "But in the case of the automobile, we have no one. We have to establish the incentive and it can be financing, be it in foreign or national currency."[48] Also in response to questions about price and quality, Latini referred to GEIA's limited jurisdiction: "We must accept any project that fits the Decree. There is an aspect not mentioned in the Decree – the question of price."[49]

Although the Fabral plan was approved, Matarazzo, the Brazilian partner, backed out in 1958. Alfa Romeo approached the state-controlled FNM, in which it held a minority interest. The FNM produced only heavy trucks, and its directors were split on the advisability of producing expensive automobiles.[50] Given the prestige of the name, and substantial pressure from Kubitschek, the plan was ultimately accepted and the car was christened the "JK" in his honor.

Simca

Simca's interest in Brazil predated GEIA and was personally generated by Kubitschek. Between the presidential election in October 1955

[47] Interview with Lúcio Meira, April 1985, Rio de Janeiro.
[48] Minutes from GEIA meeting, May 17, 1957, GEIA Archives.
[49] Minutes from GEIA meeting, June 4, 1957, GEIA Archives.
[50] Interview with Túlio de Alencar Araripe, February 1985, São Paulo.

and his inauguration in January 1956, Kubitschek traveled to Europe. While in France, he toured the new Simca plant on a visit arranged by the president of Brazil's National Steel Company, a general whose daughter was married to one of the plant's engineers. Impressed by what he saw, Kubitschek invited Simca to participate in his automotive program and jokingly suggested that they locate the plant in his home state of Minas Gerais. Immediately after Kubitschek took office, Simca followed through on this initial encounter with a letter stating its intent to produce not only in Brazil but in Minas. On a visit to Minas soon after, Kubitschek publicly announced that Minas was to be the proud home of Brazil's first automobile plant.

In the meantime, GEIA was formed. Kubitschek passed on Simca's letter of intent to Lúcio Meira. Simca balked at GEIA's request for a complete project proposal as required by the decrees. The firm claimed that because its tentative proposal predated GEIA and had the president's support, it fell outside of GEIA's jurisdiction. Representatives of the National Steel Company (CSN) and a national bank, both Brazilian participants in the project, lobbied Orosco, Meira, and Kubitschek to exempt Simca from the normal requirements. They trusted their connection to the president as a guarantee of circumventing GEIA.

Simca also took its campaign directly to Minas. The plan was politically popular there, and the state legislature had quickly offered various incentives. In the press and elsewhere, Simca pointed to GEIA as the sole obstacle to construction. According to Latini, Kubitschek could not visit his home state without being harassed about GEIA's delay in approving Simca's project. Kubitschek urged GEIA to move quickly on the Simca proposal because it was becoming a political problem. GEIA insisted that Simca had to present a project like everyone else. Simca finally did present a weak project proposal that was nonetheless accepted with seventeen contingencies.[51]

---

[51] Interview with Sydney Latini, December 1984, Rio de Janeiro. Simca rented an old factory in São Paulo to start assembly and to fulfill the domestic-content guidelines. Although it did not meet the domestic-content requirements of the program's second stage, Simca assumed that GEIA would still allow it to import spare parts. GEIA refused to release its foreign-exchange allocation and production was halted for six months. The firm ultimately had to scrounge for Brazilian-made parts and earned a reputation for poor quality. Simca sent a high-level executive from France to reactivate the plant. Despite its original promises, the firm never did relocate from São Paulo to Minas Gerais. At one point, when it appeared that Simca would not be able to implement its project, Latini himself went to Turin to try to convince Fiat to substitute for Simca. Apparently, the families of the presidents of Fiat and Simca

According to a Ford observer, GEIA's consideration of Simca's project provoked Orosco's resignation as secretary:

> An interesting sidelight is the fact that the Simca proposal seems to have been the main factor behind Orosco's resignation from GEIA. Simca has some very strong backing from influential Brazilians (for instance, the head of the Volta Redonda Steel Works [CSN]) who have brought considerable pressure to bear on GEIA to reduce deletion percentages to match the Simca proposal. Supposedly, Mr. Orosco was the main stumbling block in this maneuver because he continually insisted that the decree percentages remain as originally fixed. He apparently resigned because he felt he was not getting support from Minister Meira and also to dramatize the fact that consideration was being given to a "special" deal for Simca.[52]

Bilac Pinto's Congressional Challenge

Increased political pressure heightened the sense of urgency in GEIA's deliberations. Congress was mounting its own attack on the auto program. Led by Deputy Bilac Pinto, Kubitschek's political opposition was anxious to capitalize on the scarce supply of automobiles and the inflationary impact of high prices.

Even before the formation of GEIA, Congress began debating legislation introduced by Pinto that would have allowed cars to be imported at the free exchange rate, with tariffs reduced in proportion to the vehicle's domestic-content level.[53] The primary rationale for the legislation was to stop illegal imports coming in through "Operation Immigrant": Because immigrants and tourists were allowed to bring cars into Brazil, an illegal market emerged in which individuals paid foreigners to enter Brazil with an automobile. How widespread this practice was is unknown, but Congress's Economic Commission was informed, according to Pinto, that the number of illegally imported cars surpassed the number of legal ones. Stopping the drain on foreign exchange and the criminal profiteering involved, the bill's supporters argued, would also make cars cheaper for the consumer and would allow the Treasury to get its share via import duties.[54]

---

were related through marriage (Latini, Testimony before the Parliamentary Inquest Commission for the Verification of the Cost of the National Vehicle).

[52] Memo from D. B. Kitterman on Simca's Brazilian Car Proposal to Walter McKee, May 2, 1957, AR-67-6, Box 2, Ford Industrial Archives.

[53] Project 997-A, introduced by Bilac Pinto, Fifty-eighth Session of Congress, June 12, 1956.

[54] Anais de Câmara dos Deputados (Congressional Record).

Pinto and his allies waged a very clever campaign against the motor vehicle program by presenting themselves as the protectors of Brazilian consumers against greedy TNCs that charged exorbitant prices after receiving government favors and protection. They accused the TNCs of making huge monopoly profits and forced GEIA to commission the previously mentioned Development Council study of the industry's cost structure. They also tried to distinguish GEIA from the politically popular president, implying that the executive group was not acting on Kubitschek's request.

The original Bilac Pinto bill did not pass the Senate, but Pinto ultimately was successful in adding a proviso to the General Tariff Reform of 1957. Known as Article 59, it extended import-duty exemptions and provided stable exchange rates to components and parts not produced in Brazil. Previously, these exemptions had been restricted to capital goods. Most important, Article 59 created a special two-year foreign-exchange auction for passenger-car imports. US$20 million was allocated to this auction: US$12 million the first year, US$8 million the second. In order to discourage luxury-car imports, only vehicles weighing up to sixteen hundred kilograms and costing under US$2,300 FOB were permitted.[55] Only 15 percent domestic content was required to participate, so that even assemblers of CKDs were eligible. Import duties on the imported components were reduced in proportion to domestic-content levels, however, and profits were controlled.

Article 59 provided breathing space for those manufacturers involved in the auto program by delaying domestic production and increasing imports in the short run. Ten passenger-car projects had been approved, six of which were implemented. These included cars produced by VW, Vemag, FNM, Simca, and Willys. Only firms with approved GEIA projects had access to the foreign-exchange auctions, and all except Vemag imported under this system.

Although it is an exaggeration to say, as Orosco did, that Article 59 derailed GEIA's automobile program, it did change the rules of the game.[56] Congress succeeded in creating uncertainty, which made firms wary. On the one hand, Article 59 reduced the requirements for auto production in the short run by changing the domestic-content target; on the other hand, it made market closure appear less certain.

---

[55] In 1957, the average factory list price for a standard-equipped U.S. automobile was US$2,749. The average price for a four-door sedan was US$2,644, and for a two-door sedan, US$2,046 (*Ward's Automotive Report*, February 18, 1957).

[56] Orosco, *A indústria automobilística brasileira*, p. 14.

On the eve of the bill's passage, Vemag representatives told GEIA of the increased difficulty they were having in securing foreign financial assistance for their jeep plan: "With the Bilac Pinto Law, what confidence can these foreign firms have in our firm and in the automotive industry in general?" They asked what would prevent the importation of jeeps at the same exchange rate as agricultural equipment or with an ad valorem rate of 4 percent (the rate assigned to tractors), which would make their product uncompetitive.[57] In fact, Pinto was attacking the high price of jeeps at this time. He argued that high prices made jeeps prohibitively expensive for the agricultural sector that depended on them, and he tried to exempt jeeps and trucks from consumption taxes.[58] Complaints from Vemag and others may have been simply a foil, but Article 59 gave them space to pressure GEIA and to procrastinate with their investment plans. Although GEIA was successful in mitigating the impact of the bill by limiting the auction to two years, this challenge to its authority, as well as other problems revealed in the following cases, raise questions about GEIA's effectiveness.

Volkswagen and the BNDE

In 1956, VW had no manufacturing facilities outside Germany and was financially constrained. Although as a special property of the German government it was forbidden from raising capital through public shares until 1959, it was also the recipient of various forms of state support.[59] The company was the market leader at home and was seeking new markets abroad – VW of America, Inc., was founded in 1956 to distribute cars in the United States. In Brazil, the company was in the process of building an assembly plant when the GEIA decrees for utility vehicles were issued in July 1956.

As mentioned previously, some VW managers were already concerned about responding to SUMOC Instructions 127 and 128 even before GEIA was formed. Olavo de Souza Aranha, a vice-president of VW do Brasil who represented VW's Brazilian shareholder, thought that the firm would be better positioned with Kubitschek's

---

[57] Minutes from GEIA meeting, June 14, 1957, GEIA Archives.

[58] Minutes of Congress, July 2 and July 12, 1957.

[59] The company was partially privatized in 1961, when 60% of its shares were sold to the public and the rest divided equally between state and federal governments. For more on VW's history, see Simon Reich, *The Fruits of Fascism* (Ithaca: Cornell University Press, 1990); for a more anecdotal account, see Henry Nelson, *Small Wonder* (Boston: Little, Brown and Company, 1965).

administration if it already had a project accepted by SUMOC.[60] Wolfsburg was reluctant to commit itself. VW president Heinrich Nordhoff doubted whether the Brazilian government could guarantee the importation of necessary components. From his experience, he was not convinced that anyone in Brazil could give such assurance or that even the president could be counted on.[61]

Ultimately, the potential loss of market access prompted VW to manufacture vans in Brazil. Yet, it was concerned about the implications of a new Brazilian facility for production levels in Wolfsburg. In August 1956, VW submitted a proposal for a Brazilian van factory to the German Economic Ministry. This proposal was formulated prior to GEIA's July decrees, as it was designed to respond to the slightly less rigorous domestic-content conditions of SUMOC's Instructions 127 and 128. In this proposal, the firm addressed concerns that German production would be negatively affected by such a move. It pointed out how Brazilian import restrictions were currently limiting VW's total annual exports to about 1,500 vehicles, whereas demand in a free market could reach 25,000. Brazilian domestic-content levels were to reach 80 percent by July 1959 (as compared with GEIA's requirement of 90 percent by July 1960), but 20 percent of each vehicle would still be imported. VW argued that at initial annual production rates of 5,000 vehicles, German production for the Brazilian market would therefore be at least equivalent to the 1,000 cars built and exported from Germany and, during the transition period, the import content would be even higher.[62]

When GEIA accepted VW's van proposal in November 1956, the firm had not yet submitted a proposal for passenger cars. Kubitschek and GEIA personnel started soliciting car projects from VW even before GEIA's car decree was issued in February 1957. While Heinz Maria Oeftering, the chair of the *Aufsichtsrat*, was visiting Brazil, Kubitschek surprised him by asking, "Without further ado, without putting any plans before me, will the VW passenger car be built or not? The VW is the ideal car for Brazilian streets." When Oeftering responded that they were going to start with the Kombi, as the van was called in Brazil, Kubitschek answered, "That's fine. But the Kombi doesn't interest me like the passenger car. Why can't you clarify at

---

[60] Letter from O. E. de Souza Aranha to O. W. Jensen, April 21, 1956, Volkswagen Archives.

[61] Internal communication from Heinrich Nordhoff to O. W. Jensen, June 15, 1956, Volkswagen Archives.

[62] Memorandum of the Planned Completion of VW Transporter in Brazil, submitted to the German Economic Ministry, August 1956, Volkswagen Archives.

what point VW will begin with its production of cars? Does it [the delay] have to do with financial matters? That should be no obstacle. I need your car."[63] Oeftering, along with the local VW management, was under the impression that VW would indeed produce cars in Brazil. But they were persuaded otherwise by Nordhoff's surprising response to a draft of Oeftering's letter to Kubitschek, which predicted that VW would produce cars during Kubitschek's presidency. In his response, Nordhoff insisted that producing cars in Brazil was out of the question in the foreseeable future, and Oeftering's final letter to Kubitschek contained a much more conditional and tentative statement about cars.[64]

Nordhoff continued to remind his personnel in Brazil that cars were not under discussion, although he was not always successful in stifling unauthorized initiatives.[65] He remained cautious even after the passenger-car decree was passed in February 1957. In April, he wrote to Schultz-Wenk that developments in Brazil did not look good. In his view, it was becoming clear that the government wanted a car company for political reasons and that VW was its favorite because, with few exceptions, all other companies were holding back. He added that his own reservations about the Brazilian government had increased, because it was exacting obligations from others without taking any upon itself and was doing little to resolve inflation. As long as the Kombi continued to be plagued with problems and profits were not being transferred, he thought it irrelevant even to consider passenger cars.[66]

[63] Letter from F. W. Schultz-Wenk to Heinrich Nordhoff, October 8, 1956, Volkswagen Archives. (All translations from German courtesy of Laura Hastings.)

[64] Draft of letter to Kubitschek from Oeftering attached to letter from Oeftering to Nordhoff, September 28, 1956; telegram from Nordhoff to Oeftering, October 10, 1956; letter from Schultz-Wenk to Nordhoff expressing surprise over his reaction to car production, October 11, 1956; letter from Oeftering to Kubitschek, December 13, 1956, all Volkswagen Archives.

[65] Letter from Nordhoff to Schultz-Wenk reiterating that cars were not under consideration, October 22, 1956. In a letter to O. W. Jensen in Wolfsburg, Aranha wrote that VW do Brasil had requested BNDE financing for its car project, which in principle had been approved by management. He mentioned that he was told that Kubitschek personally advised the BNDE to help VW with its car financing. At the top of the letter is an annotation written by Nordhoff, in which he expresses shock to see that a financing project was being discussed on VW do Brasil letterhead for something (i.e., cars) that had not yet been approved. Letter from O. E. de Souza Aranha to O. W. Jensen, December 3, 1956, Volkswagen Archives.

[66] Letter from Nordhoff to Schultz-Wenk, April 12, 1957, Volkswagen Archives.

Despite Nordhoff's skepticism, VW did submit a proposal for the Beetle in October 1957. Implementation of the project was not guaranteed, however, as complications arose regarding financing. After receiving GEIA's approval for its car project in December, Volkswagen applied to the BNDE for a guarantee on a foreign loan. The firm had already received a Cr$150 million loan from the bank to produce the Kombi.

The new BNDE request differed from the first in three significant ways. First, it was for automobiles rather than for utility vehicles, which GEIA had deemed more significant for development. The BNDE had already resolved this issue in theory. Because automobiles had been included in the Target Plan as a "basic industry" and granted the same financial incentives as trucks, car projects were technically eligible for bank assistance. In practice, however, as discussed already, few car projects had yet been submitted and approved. Vemag's request for cruzeiro funding, which must have been under consideration when VW submitted its proposal, was approved shortly thereafter in January 1958.

Second, the request was not for cruzeiro financing but for an aval (cosignature) on a foreign loan of DM10.8 million. By assumption, transnational firms were expected to have better access to foreign capital.

Third, the new proposal was not submitted by Volkswagen do Brasil, under whose name GEIA had approved the project, but by its Brazilian minority partner, Monteiro-Aranha, a multifaceted holding company. In order to maintain its 20 percent share in the company (the other 80 percent was held by Volkswagen GmbH), Monteiro-Aranha was required to supply 20 percent of total financing and, of that, 20 percent of the cost in foreign exchange corresponding to the DM50.4 million (US$12 million) to be invested as foreign equipment under Instruction 113. The Brazilian firm was negotiating with European banks for the loan but needed the guarantee of the BNDE. Originally, VW had planned to import all the necessary equipment under Instruction 113.[67] GEIA approved the switch to Monteiro-Aranha, but the BNDE had reservations. It was worried about duplicating investment with the Kombi project and about whether the required domestic-content levels for the van's engines would be

---

[67] VW had sent an earlier request for funding in its own name along with its van proposal in November 1956. Cruzeiro financing was provided for van construction; the car project was not followed up at that time.

reached. It was willing to leave these technical doubts to GEIA, but was still left with unresolved legal and financial questions about the project.

The legal question concerned whether Monteiro-Aranha could negotiate with the bank in its own name. Technically, the firm was neither a manufacturer of motor vehicle parts nor a subcontractor of a company whose project had been approved by GEIA and that produced parts for motor vehicles. This was how the decree had defined manufacturers eligible for benefits.

Moreover, in the opinion of the BNDE, VW was overvaluing its foreign investment by using an incorrect exchange rate. In 1958, for example, VW valued the deutsche mark at 71.48 cruzeiros. According to bank calculations, with a base of DM4.20 to the U.S. dollar, that cruzeiro–deutsche mark exchange rate corresponded to Cr$300 to the dollar, which was much higher than official exchange rates and higher even than Joel Bergsman's calculated shadow price or "free-trade rate" of 95 cruzeiros to the dollar.[68] This overvaluation in turn inflated the amount of resources Monteiro-Aranha had to provide to maintain its percentage share.

The BNDE argued that because the funding was basically required to maintain Monteiro-Aranha's financial position in Volkswagen do Brasil, and therefore resembled commercial credit, it fell outside the purview of an investment bank. The bank's guidelines forbade it from making loans that simply allowed a shareholder to increase its share of social capital in a firm implementing an industrial project. Moreover, this loan did not even increase Brazilian participation and could not be rationalized on the basis of preventing a foreign takeover. The bank also noted that the conversion at the high rate of exchange for deutsche marks favored only the Germans. To these technocrats, the scheme implied using foreign credit to maintain the German firm's position. Also, with this aval, Brazil would be losing an opportunity to obtain foreign capital, because VW had previously shown its willingness to import everything under Instruction 113. VW could have wanted the aval only to gain further credit. Furthermore, accepting the proposition meant implicitly accepting VW's valuation of the imported equipment.

The bank's technocrats also wondered why Monteiro-Aranha could not maintain its investment share with cruzeiros, or why the German

---

[68] Joel Bergsman, *Brazil: Industrialization and Trade Policies* (Oxford: Oxford University Press, 1970), p. 45. The deutsche mark did not reach full convertibility until 1959, which probably fostered the ambiguity surrounding the exchange rate.

partner could not finance the Brazilians without the bank's interference. They surmised that VW wanted the bank to be connected to the project because it was pessimistic about Monteiro-Aranha's financial standing. The bank's cosignature then could be used to justify future credit solicitations.

VW's motives in this case are ambiguous. Given the bank's predilection for assisting domestic firms, or only those foreign-controlled firms with domestic participation, VW may have assumed that its chances would have increased when a well-connected firm like Monteiro-Aranha made the request in its own name.[69] The argument for maintaining a constant domestic participation rate seemed to jibe with the bank's objectives. Especially since it had originally planned to import all the equipment directly under 113, VW may have judged slim its own chances of getting BNDE financial assistance. This assessment seems to have been correct, judging from internal BNDE memos. Moreover, VW was financially weak and experiencing foreign-exchange constraints at the time. The BNDE aval may in fact have given them better access to foreign finance, as the BNDE surmised.

It is likely that events unrelated to VW also influenced the BNDE's decision-making process in 1958.[70] The most noteworthy was Brazil's tightening foreign-exchange constraint. Coffee export revenues had fallen drastically, and the sector had to be subsidized. Short-term foreign debts were coming due. The threat of a cutoff in foreign credits forced Kubitschek to initiate discussions with the International Monetary Fund (IMF). A letter of intent was signed in 1958, but Kubitschek broke with the Fund in mid-1959. The bank's access to

[69] O. E. de Souza Aranha no doubt helped raise expectations that the Brazilian government would be sympathetic to VW's requests. He wrote O. W. Jensen of Volkswagen-Wolfsburg on April 16, 1956, that one of his best friends, Lúcio Meira, had been appointed minister of transportation. Volkswagen Archives.

[70] Considerations external to the case's particular merits were not mentioned in the internal files to which I had access. GEDOC, Processos de Financiamento, BNDES Archives on Volkswagen Funding Requests, Files R 641, F-171/56, and 172/56, Rio de Janeiro. Ongoing conflict between VW and Aranha may also have contributed to the confusion surrounding the request to the BNDE. VW and Aranha quarreled over the appropriate exchange rate to use for the deutsche mark. On one occasion when VW sent equipment to Brazil to be registered as direct investment, VW claimed that it was undervalued since Aranha had profited since VW had to contribute more liquid cash than it otherwise would have to maintain its 80% share. Aranha also used an unrealistic exchange rate, according to Wolfsburg, which gave an even lower value to the imported machinery in cruzeiro terms. Letter from O. W. Jensen to O. E. de Souza Aranha, August 22, 1958, Volkswagen Archives.

credit from international agencies was cut off and its resources were reduced. This also affected its capacity to grant avals.

According to Eliza Willis, in 1958 the BNDE "virtually excluded firms with majority foreign ownership from enjoying the benefits of Bank credit."[71] Exceptions were made only for firms producing goods deemed critical to national development or with the personal blessing of Kubitschek. Motor vehicles certainly were considered critical to development, and in the absence of car projects, Kubitschek had been pressuring GEIA, if not the BNDE, to expedite project approval and implementation. Nevertheless, VW was requesting an aval at a time when foreign exchange was scarce. The bank judged that its assistance was not fundamental to the plan's survival.

Furthermore, internal tensions were rising within the BNDE in general and with respect to foreign capital in particular. The compromise that had been established between the more nationalistic technocrats, found primarily in the technical staff, and the more internationalistic management, epitomized by the bank's president, Roberto Campos, began to unravel. This was partly a result of the "Roboré affair," in which concessions were granted for petroleum exploration in Bolivia to private firms tied to foreign capital, and of the handling of SANBRA, an Argentine food product company. That firm had applied for assistance in 1957 and received the personal support of Kubitschek. Despite the bank's internal review rejecting the request, which was accepted throughout the hierarchy, Campos argued in its favor, and it was passed by the directorate in a split decision.[72] Finally, Campos's central role in the IMF negotiations also helped exacerbate ideological differences within the bank. How these internal divisions affected the VW loan is unclear, but they certainly burdened the decision with political implications.

VW's request was not resolved until early 1959. In May, Monteiro-Aranha informed the BNDE that VW in Germany had provided the necessary DM2.4 million in financing to be applied to 20 percent of the imported equipment. The company proceeded with its plans to produce the Kombi and the Beetle.

Ford, O Cidadão Industrial ("The Industrial Citizen")[73]

As mentioned previously, Ford was the first auto company to assemble in Brazil and had dominated passenger-car sales. Why did Ford not

---

[71] Eliza Willis, "The State as Banker: The Expansion of the Public Sector in Brazil" (Ph.D. diss., University of Texas at Austin, 1986), p. 256.

[72] Ibid., pp. 289–93.

[73] John Goulden, general director of Ford of Brazil, referred to Ford in this way in

go in to protect its car market, which Francisco Salles Cesar, who headed sales in Porto Alegre for twenty years, called "the basis of the business"?[74]

It was not because the business was unprofitable. To the contrary, based on its original investment, Ford's assembly operations had been enormously remunerative. As of December 31, 1955, the Brazilian company's net worth was US$14.1 million, "developed from an original investment which amounted only to the cost of two or three hundred vehicles shipped to Brazil in the early 1920s." Over that time, profit remittances to the United States totaled US$27.8 million.[75]

It was by no means self-evident to Ford executives, however, that the company should even manufacture trucks in Brazil. In response to previous government policy initiatives toward the industry, the company planned to increase the domestic-content levels of its trucks to 30 percent but had no plans to move into integrated manufacturing. When the truck decree was issued on July 12, 1956, Ford executives were not convinced that they should stay in the market. Their first response was to try to figure out how to appear to be in compliance with the decree while investing as little as possible.[76] Predictions about profits were optimistic, but the foreign-exchange constraint made Ford worry about future repatriation controls.[77] Ford surveyed its

Testimony before the Parliamentary Inquest Commission for the Verification of the Cost of the National Vehicle, October 10, 1967, GEIA Archives.

[74] Mira Wilkins interview with Francisco Salles Cesar, November 16, 1961, Wilkins Personal File.

[75] In addition to profits earned locally in Brazil, from 1947 to 1955 the accounting profits earned by Ford–United States on exported units were estimated at US$18,541,000, and the economic profits at US$36,518,000; cited in background materials in the Presentation on the Brazil Truck Manufacturing Program made to the Executive Committee of Ford Motor Company, October 30, 1956, Acc. AR-67-6, Box 2, Ford Industrial Archives.

[76] In an October 3, 1956, letter to Chairman Ernest R. Breech, A. J. Wieland, vice-president of Ford International, wrote: "We wanted the (Executive) Committee to know the problem and the steps we were taking to try to keep our place in Brazil without following Government edicts which would have involved large sums of capital investment.... we must make some gestures to indicate to the Brazilian Government that we are interested in their problem and in their future growth. The plan that will be presented at the Executive Committee encompasses a probable investment of around $22,000,000, of which $14,000,000 would be in dollars and the balance in Brazilian currency. Obviously, we have no intention of recommending that we walk into Brazil with $14,000,000 as there are still a great many factors... that must be worked out." Acc. AR-67-6, Box 2, Ford Industrial Archives.

[77] Letter from J. S. Andrews, regional director for Latin America and the Orient, Ford International, to Tom Lilley, assistant general manager, Ford International, March 30, 1956. In anticipation of GEIA's automotive decrees, Andrews wrote, "In short, it would appear that the investment of dollar capital in Brazilian industry could well

operations in search of old, amortized equipment that could be shipped to Brazil and tried to convince its suppliers to invest. It also investigated alternative financing strategies.[78]

Ford also made its participation in the truck program completely contingent on GM's. In its presentation to the Executive Committee in October 1956, Ford's International Division recommended:

> In our judgement, the issuance of automotive industry decrees by the Brazilian Government would not of itself make Ford International recommend that Ford Motor Company necessarily participate in a vehicle manufacturing program in Brazil at this time, although it is our opinion that market and profit opportunities will make it desirable for us to do so in the future. However, G.M.'s expressed intention to manufacture trucks, with an engine program which could also comfortably support future passenger car manufacturing plans, makes it, in our opinion, important that Ford Motor Company maintain its competitive position in a market with Brazil's potential.[79]

Ford International's recommendation to go ahead with a truck program was subject to confirmation of GM's implementation of its own plan.

In the view of Ford International, Brazil's entire truck plan was not viable without the participation of a major company like GM. "If GM proceeds, it is reasonable to assume that the Brazilians can carry out their restrictions and succeed in barring imports from non-participants. Without the support of GM or other major U.S. producers, Brazil still plans to proceed with its program but the chances of success over the next several years will be significantly reduced."[80] A GM decision to go ahead with truck production would substantially increase the costs to Ford of not participating, as well as the possibility that it would not be allowed to enter the market on its own timetable in the future.

result in far more than an adequate return in cruzeiros, but that the outlook for remitting adequate return on the investment in dollars to the U.S. is limited and perhaps obscure." Acc. AR-67-6, Box 2, Ford Industrial Archives.

[78] In an October 24, 1956, memorandum to Mr. T. O. Yntema, Tom Lilley discussed various ways to reduce Ford's direct investment, which included getting financing from the Export–Import Bank and from the BNDE. "Our conversations in Brazil, however, have indicated that no such concessions will be granted and that to require them would be a way of rejecting the Brazilian plan." Acc. AR-67-6, Box 2, Ford Industrial Archives.

[79] Proposal for Truck Manufacturing Program, draft version, n.d., p. 25, Acc. AR-67-6, Box 2, Ford Industrial Archives.

[80] Memorandum from Tom Lilley to T. O. Yntema, October 24, 1956, Acc. AR-67-6, Box 2, Ford Industrial Archives.

Nevertheless, the Executive Committee was still not convinced by Ford International's formal presentation in October 1956 about the wisdom of investing in Brazil, no matter what GM planned to do. In his report on the presentation to Humberto Monteiro, the general manager of Ford-Brazil, J. S. Andrews, the regional director for Latin America and the Orient at Ford International, wrote: "The projected return on assets employed is low when compared to returns received on investments here in the United States, and the risks are considered to be much higher in Brazil."[81] The proposed truck program would have involved an equity investment of US$16.4 million and local expenditures of US$9.6 million in cruzeiros. The Executive Committee instructed Ford International to investigate all possible ways to increase local purchases in order to reduce investment in fixed assets, especially in stamping, and to try to get more BNDE financing. The company continued to scan Ford's global operations for surplus or obsolete equipment and even considered the joint use of facilities with GM and Chrysler. Toward this end, the Executive Committee agreed to help arrange meetings with GM, Chrysler, and International Harvester to explore areas of cooperation.[82] By December, the Executive Committee had still not approved the program, and Ford cabled Meira on December 10 promising that it would submit a truck proposal to ensure that GEIA would allocate enough foreign exchange for Ford's import needs in the coming year.

Ford may have assumed that GEIA could not afford its absence from the auto program and would therefore accept the company's conditions of entry. This expectation was no doubt bolstered by the visit of Brazilian Vice-President João Goulart to Dearborn in May 1956, when he promised concessions in exchange for Ford's participation. As chronicled by Tom Lilley of Ford International,

> [Goulart] stated that, speaking officially for his Government, he was in a position to promise that if Ford made a concrete proposal [for truck manufacture], we would be granted every possible accommodation and advantage.... With regard to timing, Mr. Goulart mentioned the various propositions which are being made to Brazil by European competitors, including Renault and the various German manufacturers. He indicated that he and his associates would clearly prefer to do business with Ford and they would be happy to make

[81] Confidential letter to Humberto Monteiro, general manager, Ford Motor Company, Exports, Inc., Brazil, from J. S. Andrews, October 31, 1956, Acc. AR-67-6, Box 2, Ford Industrial Archives.
[82] Notes from January 16, 1957, meeting at which Ford's International Division presented a revised truck proposal to Ford's Executive Committee (provided by J. C. Goulden to Mira Wilkins), Wilkins Personal File.

important concessions to get Ford in the program. He was quite candid regarding the political advantage to his Government of obtaining a Ford program for Brazil. He was also candid regarding the political difficulty of turning down various deals proposed by competitive manufacturers based on the hope, but not the certainty, that Ford would eventually submit a proposal.[83]

By late December, however, impatient with Ford's procrastination, the Brazilian authorities were no longer responding as charitably to the company. Nor were they obliged to. GM and Mercedes, among others, had submitted proposals for truck production, reducing GEIA's dependence on Ford. Ford's personnel in Brazil, who were not involved in formulating or presenting the truck proposal, tried to make Dearborn realize that the Brazilian negotiating position had hardened. In a December 21, 1956, letter to J. S. Andrews, Humberto Monteiro of Ford-Brazil, wrote:

> We must at this time advise you that we feel very strongly that unless the presentation [to GEIA] is patterned almost exactly after the requirements indicated for submitting a manufacturing plan that we will have practically no chance of securing approval of the plan. The chances that we can expect any concessions at this time are obviously minimized by the fact that the plans of our principal competitor [GM] have already been submitted and approved.... We can safely state that everyone in the Government and the public in general have been deeply disappointed with Ford's retarded action in connection with the presentation of a manufacturing program. Minister Meira has repeatedly told friends of ours that his great hope was that Ford would come in before GM. The truth of the matter is that, while we hope to regain some of the sympathy and prestige which we have lost, our attitude in presenting the program must be faced realistically.

Monteiro was particularly concerned that, if Ford did not present a proposal in January, its chances of getting sufficient foreign-exchange allocations for 1957 would be remote.[84]

GEIA's resistance, strengthened by the tightening foreign-exchange constraint and GM's entry into the Brazilian truck market, did force Ford to submit a truck proposal that met GEIA's requirements. The

---

[83] Memo from Tom Lilley to J. S. Andrews on Goulart's visit, May 14, 1956, Acc. AR-67-6, Box 2, Ford Industrial Archives.

[84] Letter from Humberto Monteiro, general manager, Ford Motor Company, Exports, Brazil, to J. S. Andrews, regional director, Latin America and the Orient, Ford International, December 21, 1956, Acc. AR-67-6, Box 2, Ford Industrial Archives.

Executive Committee, followed by GEIA on February 8, 1957, approved a project to produce light (F-100) and medium (F-600 and F-350) trucks. According to an executive communication by J. S. Bugas, head of the International Division, the program involved an equity investment of US$13 million and local currency expenditures of US$7 million plus an open credit account for eighteen months. From 1957 through 1960, the company earned additional profits of US$31 million after taxes in the form of profit and service-fee remittances, interest income, and economic profit on components. "Thus we have recovered almost double our equity investment for this program," Bugas wrote.[85]

Ford's Car Proposals

GEIA issued its decree for passenger cars on February 26, 1957, soon after it had approved Ford's truck plan. Although Ford did not begin to produce automobiles in Brazil until 1967, it submitted car proposals from 1958 until the end of Kubitschek's administration. GEIA rejected them all. As with trucks, Ford tried to minimize its investment and to evade GEIA's requirements. GEIA was powerful enough to keep Ford from entering the market on Ford's terms but, in the absence of GM or Chrysler, was not strong enough to get Ford in on its own.

Some prescient Ford executives worried about the European companies' inroads into the Brazilian market. As early as 1949, N. A. Bogdan, director of finance at Ford International, noted:

> As in all South American countries, there is in Brazil a noticeable trend toward smaller cars. It first started with bare necessity, in the absence of American products, but necessity is beginning to develop into taste and preference – and don't let us be ostrich-like in that respect! In addition, the suspension systems of the 1949 American models have proven unsuitable for the rough roads in the interior and one hears much praise of the smaller and possibly sturdier European units.[86]

[85] Executive communication from J. S. Bugas to Board of Directors, Brazil – Proposed Passenger Car Manufacturing and Facility Expansion Program, December 14, 1960, Acc. AR-67-14, Box 2, Ford Industrial Archives.

[86] N. A. Bogdan, director of finance, Ford International, confidential notes from a trip to Brazil, December 23, 1949. In these notes, Bogdan argued that Brazil was intent on industrializing and that people in the organization had to change their thinking "radically" in regard to local manufacturing. Acc. AR-65-71, Box 26, Ford Industrial Archives.

J. S. Andrews echoed these thoughts seven years later:

> Brazil, in common with the rest of Latin America, has traditionally been considered as essentially a market for United States source passenger cars. Much has been said about Brazil's preference for the styling, performance, size and comfort of United States source passenger cars, and it has been assumed that this preference would not only continue but also grow. It would appear to the writer that, as in the past, there will continue to exist a preference for United States type passenger cars among those purchasers with the ability to pay. However, it would also seem to the writer that we should profit from our experience in Europe, where before the war United States source passenger cars amounted to over perhaps 70 percent of the market but now account for only from 10 percent to 15 percent of the total passenger car market, having been displaced by small low-cost European source passenger cars. Judging from the relatively low per capita income in Brazil, the writer has a very strong suspicion that any passenger car manufacturing operations undertaken in Brazil must of necessity be predicated on small, European-type passenger cars, if any major volume is to be achieved. The entrance, although still in the planning stages of such European units as the DKW and the Volkswagen, could result in a literal monopoly of the Brazilian market by these and similar vehicles.[87]

Despite the opinions of people like Bogdan and Andrews, Ford initially expressed concern about matching the investments of its competitors only from the United States and not from Europe. At this time, Ford was not worried about Volkswagen and was not sure that it had a small car with which to compete in VW's market niche.[88] A potential Chrysler program did raise some concern, however. According to Walter McKee, regional director for Latin America, it motivated a Ford executive to approach Henry Ford II about investing US$10 million in a Brazilian car project. Ford replied that he did not think they wanted to make this additional commitment to Brazil, and the issue was closed.[89] In the meantime, Ford closely monitored the auto plan. Virtually every firm was having trouble meeting the do-

---

[87] Letter from J. S. Andrews to Tom Lilley, March 30, 1956, Acc. AR-67-6, Box 2, Ford Industrial Archives.

[88] In 1950, Ford and GM had also decided not to compete with VW's Beetle in Germany but to compete with each other for the midsize car market. Mira Wilkins and Frank Hill, *American Business Abroad: Ford on Six Continents* (Detroit: Wayne State University Press, 1964), p. 391.

[89] Mira Wilkins interview with Walter McKee, May 29, 1962, Wilkins Personal File. According to McKee, the Chrysler board rejected the car program and fired all of the people involved.

mestic-content requirements. Yet, the cheap imported components available under Article 59, along with the seller's market, generated profits for many of them.

Nevertheless, as locally manufactured European cars were about to appear on Brazilian roads, Ford's concern about preserving both dealer loyalty and its option to enter the car market at a later date grew. On December 16, 1958, assuming that the company was powerful enough to evade GEIA's domestic-content requirements, the Executive Committee agreed to submit an interim car manufacturing program that would begin with 30 percent local content and reach 73 percent by 1962. Ford planned to use some of the foreign exchange allocated for its truck program to import the necessary components. The vehicle to be produced was the 1959 Ford Custom 300, a mid-sized passenger car. This model was chosen because it used the same engine and many of the same components as Ford's Brazilian-made trucks, thus reducing new investment requirements. GEIA rejected the proposal and insisted that production begin with 50 percent domestic content and reach 95 percent by January 1, 1961.[90]

In February 1959, the Executive Committee approved a revised proposal to manufacture the same vehicle. This time, Ford proposed to start manufacturing with 50 percent domestic content in 1960 and to indicate its "intention to reach 95 percent local content in 1961 under certain conditions only and with no obligation to do so or penalty for failure to accomplish this phase of the program."[91] The project in-

[90] It is interesting to note that at this point, VW and other competitors assumed that Ford, and possibly GM, would enter the car market. In December 1958, VW's Schultz-Wenk reported to Wolfsburg that Mercedes-Benz had given up on passenger cars for the moment, and that he thought it was because Mercedes feared competition from Ford and Chevrolet. He also wrote about the opening of Ford's factory and how Ford planned to use its V-8 engines for passenger cars as well as trucks. November Report on VW do Brasil from Schultz-Wenk to Nordhoff, December 3, 1958, Volkswagen Archives.

[91] According to the proposal, reaching domestic-content levels of 50% by March 1960 would be feasible without major new investments because the car used many of the same components as Ford's small truck produced in Brazil. Reaching 95% domestic content by 1961 would be more complicated because of the inability to use existing sheet metal dies. The additional investment for 1959 would amount to the equivalent of US$542,000, of which US$375,000 would be in dollars and would become an equity investment by Ford, and US$167,000 in cruzeiros. The proposal specified that the following four conditions were necessary for the Ford automobile to reach 95% domestic content by 1961: the availability of sheet metal dies from Ford–United States; favorable market conditions in Brazil; reasonable cost and availability of foreign exchange for imported components; and the ability of local vendors to supply components. Executive communication from Tom Lilley to Members of the Exec-

volved an expenditure of US$375,000 in dollars and the equivalent of US$167,000 in cruzeiros for facilities and tooling. Ford doubted that the Brazilian government would approve its terms but considered it "essential to set forth the conditions clearly both for policy reasons and because of possible legal liability." The proposed program would "[p]rovide Ford of Brazil with a further opportunity to try to persuade the Government to permit them to produce at less than 95 percent local content," and "permit Ford of Brazil to keep 'foot-in-door' with respect to recognition as a car manufacturer and might facilitate our entry as a full scale small car manufacturer later on."[92]

According to Monteiro's communications from Brazil, he felt confident that GEIA would support Ford's proposal but warned that the timing could not be worse in terms of the country's foreign-exchange position.[93] As had occurred with VW's loan guarantee request, the macroeconomic environment was influencing auto sector policies. At the time of Ford's proposal, Brazil's economic team, headed by Finance Minister Lucas Lopes, was in the midst of difficult negotiations with the IMF and facing growing domestic opposition to its economic stabilization program.[94] Meira advised that it would be impossible to obtain approval after April 8 and suggested that Ford's position with Lopes would be strengthened if it included a five-year swap to cover dollar requirements for sheet steel. Ford agreed to include a swap arrangement in its proposal, and GEIA accepted Ford's conditions in principle. Meira remained pessimistic about Lopes but agreed to "use all his influence to push [the] matter."[95]

Once again, Brazilian policymakers relied on the standard trump card to strengthen their bargaining position: the foreign-exchange

---

utive Committee, Brazil–Proposed Manufacturing Program of 1959 Model Ford Car, February 18, 1959, Acc AR-75-63-430, Box 29, Ford Industrial Archives.

[92] Ibid.

[93] Confidential telex from Monteiro to McKee, March 26, 1959, Acc. AR-75-63-430, Box 29, Ford Industrial Archives.

[94] The economic stabilization program had been drafted by Finance Minister Lopes (who had served as Kubitschek's first director of the BNDE) and Roberto Campos, then director of the BNDE, in consultation with the IMF. Kubitschek broke off negotiations with the IMF in June 1959 and both Lopes and Campos were replaced soon after. For more on Brazil's break with the Fund, see Thomas E. Skidmore, *Politics in Brazil 1930–1964* (Oxford: Oxford University Press, 1967), pp. 174–82; and Economic Commission on Latin America (Carlos Lessa), "Fifteen Years of Economic Policy in Brazil," *Economic Bulletin for Latin America* 9, no. 2 (1964).

[95] LT Interford Memo from Monteiro to McKee, April 1, 1959, Acc. AR-75-63-430, Box 29, Ford Industrial Archives.

constraint. In fact, they were upping the ante by raising the entry requirements for any acceptable Ford auto project. The recently approved Mercedes-Benz passenger-car proposal also strengthened Brazil's hand.[96] Ford responded to these pressures and included mechanisms to cover its foreign-exchange requirements in its next proposal.

The next car proposal, presented to the Executive Committee in April 1959, committed Ford to produce the Ford Custom 300 with 95 percent domestic content by 1961. This required significantly greater investments than previous proposals. Initial investments were estimated at US$4 million in dollars and $2.5 million in cruzeiros.[97] In addition, Ford agreed to purchase US$7.8 million worth of Brazilian iron ore from 1959 to 1964;[98] to extend the terms on an open exchange account for truck and car components; and/or to extend a swap loan of US$5 million for five years. Ford officials were evidently becoming increasingly worried that GEIA would soon close the market to new projects.[99]

Lopes's first reaction to the new proposal was again negative. "He insisted, that rather than accept new car programs, GEIA should reduce the present ones." Lopes also insisted that Ford purchase iron ore and asked if it could buy even more than originally planned.[100] In the face of this resistance and, most important, of Brazil's ongoing

---

[96] The project was never implemented; Mercedes produced only trucks and buses in Brazil.

[97] The proposal noted that 50% of the dollar investment could be utilized in production of a car other than the proposed model. After March 1960, Ford expected that imported equipment would become subject to import duties. Ford estimated that by using its US$4 million import license, it would save at least US$2 million on a future car program. On the initial production of 10,000 units, it was expected that Ford–United States would earn economic profits of US$1 million; profits to Ford of Brazil could be as high as US$10 million if the car had a retail price of US$8,500. Executive communication from Tom Lilley to members of the Executive Committee, Brazil – Proposed Manufacturing Program of 1959 Model Ford Car, April 1, 1959, Acc. AR-65-71, Box 27, Ford Industrial Archives.

[98] Ford would only use about 60% and sell 40% to other ore users.

[99] "Conversations with Government officials have . . . indicated their intention to protect companies with approved programs and, since such programs if carried out will provide for capacity of up to 175,000 cars per year, the Government has hinted strongly that it will be very difficult for other manufacturers to enter the market later on." Executive communication from Tom Lilley to members of the Executive Committee, Brazil – Proposed Manufacturing Program of 1959 Model Ford Car, April 1, 1959, Acc. AR-65-71, Box 27, Ford Industrial Archives.

[100] Memorandum from Walter McKee to J. S. Bugas et al., May 1, 1959, Acc. AR-65-71, Box 27, PR archives, Accession no. 742, Ford Industrial Archives.

negotiations with the IMF, Ford's Executive Committee withdrew its car proposal.[101]

Ford continued to float car proposals until at least 1961.[102] For a variety of reasons, they continued to be for mid-sized, rather than small-sized, models. In part, this had to do with economies of scale and scope. The firm had investigated the feasibility of introducing smaller, European-designed models into the Brazilian market.[103] By September 1959, however, Ford had rejected the idea, and all its subsequent proposals were for mid-sized cars. As explained to Walter McKee by Andrew Masset of Ford-Brazil, "We have discarded the possibility of manufacturing the Falcon or any European car simply because the burden of the additional investment required would be too onerous to bear, and would most probably result in a vehicle cost greater than that of the larger Custom 300 passenger car." The high degree of complementarity between Ford's locally produced trucks and the Custom 300 significantly reduced initial investment costs. Most important, a new engine plant would have to be built to supply the Ford Falcon, whereas the Custom 300 used the engine Ford was already producing in Brazil. The estimated investment for the Custom 300 was US$10.5 million, of which US$5.5 million was in dollars. The Falcon program would have required a dollar investment of US$31 million and cruzeiro expenditures of US$25 million. Masset doubted that GEIA would approve a program that required such large investments "to produce a vehicle which would compete directly with vehicles already approved for production in Brazil."[104]

Ford also concluded that large cars, which were not yet being made

---

[101] Telex from McKee to Monteiro, May 7, 1959, Acc. AR-75-63-430, Box 29, Ford Industrial Archives.

[102] No record of later Ford projects was found among Brazilian archives and sources. Ford denied clearance to all Ford Industrial Archive materials pertaining to any aspect of its Brazilian operations after 1961. According to the archives until 1961, the Custom 300 was still being proposed in September 1959, but had been replaced with the 1959 Ford Galaxie by August 1960. According to Brazilian records, the last proposal to be considered, and the most publicized and contentious, was for the 1959 Ford Fairlane.

[103] Possible alternatives included German class D cars, such as the 17M and its successor, the H or N XPD, with 1.5 liter engines, and the Ford Falcon, a Class E car with a 2.5 liter engine. Although both were smaller than the Ford Custom 300, neither would have competed directly with the smaller Class C cars produced by Volkswagen. Letter from Walter McKee to Humberto Monteiro, July 15, 1959, Acc. AR-75-63-430, Box 29, Ford Industrial Archives.

[104] Letter from Andrew Masset, Ford Motor do Brasil, to Walter McKee, Ford International, September 11, 1959, Acc. AR-75-63-430, Box 29, Ford Industrial Archives.

in Brazil, had a better chance of approval because GEIA would protect the market niche of existing producers. As Masset wrote, "Finally, as long as there is GEIA or some governmental control, we would have a very slim chance of getting a Falcon program approved on top of the similar package programs (Vedette and Aero-Willys) under way."[105]

Ford's initial unwillingness to commit additional investments in Brazil and its subsequent late entry into the Brazilian car market precluded its entrance into the small-car market segment, even if it believed that "a smaller car will ultimately be needed to penetrate the developing mass market in Brazil."[106] The sequential nature of the investment process made each decision contingent on previous moves. Ford's strategy to start with light trucks, in combination with GEIA's high domestic-content requirements for cars, determined the type of car Ford would try to get approved, regardless of market requirements. By the time Ford was prepared to make larger investments, small cars remained problematic; the start-up time was longer because of the lack of complementarity with trucks, and GEIA was much less inclined to approve.

Timing was becoming a critical issue. Ford grew increasingly anxious about further delaying entry as its competitors' cars were about to roll off production lines.[107] Ford also wanted to use its duty-free import credits by 1960, when they were expected to expire. Ford assumed that it would become harder to win GEIA's approval as time passed and existing projects came on stream. In 1960, Ford also began to hear worrisome rumors that its U.S. competitors were considering car production. GM was studying some sort of car program that used GM truck engines, and American Motors, after its Rambler proposal was refused, was discussing partnership with existing manufacturers. Ford feared that its negotiating position would be weakened if GEIA had already approved a car project from either of the other firms before considering another Ford proposal.[108]

---

[105] Ibid.

[106] Executive communication from J. S. Bugas to Board of Directors, Brazil – Proposed Passenger Car Manufacturing and Facility Expansion Program, December 14, 1960, Acc. AR-67-14, Box 2, Ford Industrial Archives.

[107] "There is no doubt that we will be facing a new crisis in our already difficult dealer situation as soon as competitors' cars appear in a volume on the market." Letter from Andrew Masset to W. L. McKee (regional director, Latin American Operations), Ford International, September 11, 1959, Acc. AR-75-63-430, Box 29, Ford Industrial Archives.

[108] Memorandum on Brazil Car Manufacturing and Capacity Expansion Programs,

The fact that Kubitschek's administration was going to be replaced in 1961 put an additional premium on time. As a Ford official noted, "Certain members of GEIA who might be helpful in obtaining import licenses for car tooling and components may not be in office after the end of 1960 or January 1961 which would favor a date of approval here on or before December 1, 1960."[109] Ford was particularly concerned about getting government approval to import car tooling as an equity investment without exchange cover, since this had a significant effect on any project's financial feasibility. If such approval were not forthcoming, alternative methods of importing the equipment would be required or the project would have to be resubmitted to the next government.[110]

With these proposals, which met the domestic-content requirements, Ford put GEIA in a difficult position. The pioneers of the auto program clearly had Ford in mind. Ford had set up the first assembly line in Brazil, its name was well known, and mechanics and machine shops had long been familiar with its vehicles. Ford's participation in the automobile program would have brought GEIA credibility and support. The Volkswagen Beetle was still a suspicious novelty, and the program was lacking quality mid-size cars. Again, GEIA was caught in a contradictory position: Ford would have been an asset to the plan, but extending the subsidies would have broken GEIA's pledge of consistency. If Ford were given special consideration one day, others would be on GEIA's doorstep the next.

October 26, 1960, Acc. AR-67-14, Box 2; and executive communication from J. S. Bugas to Board of Directors, Brazil–Proposed Passenger Car Manufacturing and Facility Expansion Program, December 14, 1960, AR-67-14, Box 2, Ford Industrial Archives.

[109] Memorandum on Discussion of Factors, Problems, etc., in Connection with Brazil Car Manufacturing and Capacity Expansion Programs, October 26, 1960, Acc. AR-67-14, Box 2, Ford Industrial Archives.

[110] Letter from J. C. Goulden, finance manager, Ford Motor do Brasil, to W. L. McKee, regional director, Latin American Operations, Ford International, August 17, 1960, discussing the 1959 Ford Galaxie proposal to be submitted to the Executive Committee. Ford assumed that it would be allowed to import US$3 million of equipment duty free and without exchange cover, so that the value of imported equipment would be carried on the books as capital investment. Ford predicted that the return on total added assets employed for car production would be 35% per year after taxes and that the additional fixed investment would be paid for within three years. In his December 14, 1960, executive communication to the Board of Directors on Brazil – Proposed Passenger Car Manufacturing and Facility Expansion Program, J. S. Bugas provided somewhat higher investment figures for the Galaxie but also assumed that all equipment would be imported duty free and without exchange cover. Acc. AR-67-14, Box 2, Ford Industrial Archives.

A debate ensued within GEIA over Ford's proposal to produce the 1959 Fairlane, which was submitted in December 1960, right before Kubitschek was to leave office. Ford requested permission to import US$3.6 million in equipment without exchange cover. In accordance with both the February 26, 1957, decree that established the guidelines for passenger-car production and the tariff reform of 1957, all car proposals had to be submitted for consideration by December 31, 1957. Those against Ford's proposal argued that it would be unfair to firms that had come in under these guidelines to grant latecomers like Ford the same import benefits. They also argued that allowing Ford to import equipment without foreign-exchange cover, as Ford intended, discriminated against national capital. Ford planned to import used equipment, which normally was not permitted if similar products could be domestically produced. These imports, allowed only under Instruction 113, would hurt the development of the domestic metal-working industry. A national firm that did not want to associate with foreign capital could not import this type of equipment. Those opposed to Ford argued that granting foreign firms these foreign-exchange benefits made sense when the industry was in its infancy and when GEIA imposed performance criteria (i.e., domestic-content requirements) on firms. Because the industry was past the installation phase and was now consolidating, new norms were required, and foreign firms' equipment imports should be subject to exchange cover.

Meanwhile, Ford campaigned for its project on several fronts. It argued that Brazil was denying entry, which technically was not the case. Ford insisted that it could not invest without financial incentives. It applied external pressure through officials at multilateral agencies.[111] Inside Brazil, its campaign strategy was to blame GEIA for forcing Brazilians to drive second-rate cars like the VW Beetle when they could be driving Fords. It also solicited and won the support of the Union for the Automotive Parts and Similars Industry (Sindicato da Indústria de Peças para Veículos e Similares [SINDIPEÇAS], which lobbied on Ford's behalf.

Kubitschek's successor, Jânio Quadros, asked GEIA personnel for a summary of their negotiations with Ford, which Lúcio Meira supplied in July 1961. Meira presented the preceding arguments for and against the project and said that GEIA itself was divided. In his opinion, the Fairlane should have been approved if Ford had incorporated itself as an independent subsidiary, rather than remaining a branch plant, and had proved that the imported equipment could not be

---

[111] Interview with Lucas Lopes, May 1985, Rio de Janeiro.

locally procured. He would not have allowed Ford to import equipment without exchange cover, and he would have forced the firm to increase the level of Brazilian equity participation by the same amount as the new investment.[112]

Inexplicably, in August 1961, Quadros had Meira's report reprinted in the *Diário Oficial,* the daily record of government proceedings. Subsequent intragovernmental correspondence indicates that the company continued to apply pressure. Meira held firm, however, saying that GM would certainly follow, which would lead to the "entire denationalization of the sector."[113] Ford finally succeeded with the military regime that took over in 1964, which had a more accommodating position toward foreign capital. Ford presented a new proposal to produce the 1966 Galaxie, which was accepted.

Ford gambled that it would eventually be allowed into the Brazilian market on its own terms. It correctly bet that the Brazilians would be forced to accept a company with Ford's international stature and clout. It is likely, however, that the firm underestimated both how long approval would take and the costs of the delay.

Rather than "stealing a march" on its competitors and getting whatever monopoly profits might accrue to being first, Ford initially would not comply with GEIA demands and let VW test the Brazilian market. In so doing, Ford may have made a strategic error. Its absence from the Brazilian market in these years allowed VW to redefine and capture the Brazilian car market. In pre-GEIA Brazil, Ford had been synonymous with automobiles. At first, Brazilians were forced to drive Beetles and other compact-sized European cars by the lack of alternatives, but they came to do so by preference. In 1968, VW's share of car sales was almost 80 percent; in 1975 (by which time new models had been introduced) it was still high at 62 percent, and in 1980 held at 50 percent.[114]

Subsequent interviews with Ford managers at the time indicate that

[112] Parecer do GEIA, July 28, 1961, published in its entirety in the *Diário Oficial,* August 7, 1961.

[113] Letter from Lúcio Meira to the minister of industry and commerce, January 31, 1963, GEIA archives.

[114] Ford and GM did not benefit from VW's loss of market share. Their respective shares of production in 1975 were 16% and 19%, and in 1980, 13% and 20%. Fiat entered the Brazilian car market in 1976 and by 1980 had 16% of total production, although a larger relative share went to export. It could be argued that VW gained and maintained such a high market share because it had a more appropriate vehicle for Brazil. In countries such as Argentina and Mexico, however, no one firm dominated the domestic car market to the extent that VW did in Brazil.

some view Ford's late entry as a mistake. In retrospect, they offer various explanations for Ford's absence from this market segment.[115] Some attribute it to Dearborn's lack of knowledge or interest in international affairs. Ford International, located in New York until 1956, was still somewhat of a stepchild in the organization. Ford was not manufacturing in any less-developed country at that time and had recently sold its interests in Spain and liquidated in India, rather than comply with the local capital requirements of those countries' automotive programs.[116] Ford-Brazil, though profitable, had been relatively marginal to Ford's total operation. Ford had brought virtually no new capital into the country since it had begun assembling there thirty-seven years before.

Others blame Ford's late entry on the firm's short time horizon. Whereas VW had to buy into the market and was willing to earn a low return per car, Ford was worried about a quick return on investment. The company questioned the overall financial viability of any project in Brazil. Ford's early entry into Argentina and Mexico indicates a possible awareness of this miscalculation.[117]

Consolidation and Concentration

Had all the accepted projects been implemented, planned vehicle production for 1960 would have reached 232,250. Seven firms ultimately withdrew their proposals, leaving eleven firms and a 1960 production target of 170,000. Actual production came to 133,041.

---

[115] Guimarães suggests that a possible explanation for the late entry of Ford and GM was the shortage of managerial capacity in the 1950s, when the two companies were busy expanding in Europe. He also points out that the early and mid-1960s were profitable years for Ford and GM, and that the growth rate of the European market was slowing down ("Industry, Market Structure and the Growth of the Firm in the Brazilian Economy," p. 190).

[116] According to Wilkins and Hill, an important reason for abandoning these markets was that local capital had to have a controlling interest in any project (Wilkins and Hill, *American Business Abroad: Ford on Six Continents*, p. 402).

[117] Bennett and Sharpe also note that Ford was the first to indicate a willingness to begin domestic production in Argentina and Mexico. However, referring to the dynamics of defensive investment, which require that one firm take the lead while the others follow, they claim that Ford has traditionally made the first move in Latin America. In the case of Brazil, Ford was one of the most intransigent before the creation of GEIA; discussions had gone further with both GM and VW toward setting up domestic manufacture. Furthermore, as noted, one must also consider the type of investment firms made. With respect to cars in Brazil, Ford was not a leader but a follower. See Bennett and Sharpe, "The World Automobile Industry and Its Implications," p. 214.

The shortfall was partly due to alterations in some of the original plans and to limited availability of foreign exchange for imported parts. By 1962, 191,194 vehicles were rolling off Brazilian assembly lines. Between 1955 and 1962, the volume of vehicle production had increased by an annual average of 39 percent, compared with 10 percent for manufacturing as a whole.

As described previously, one of GEIA's rationales for allowing so many firms to enter the market was the expectation that some would not survive and the industry would consolidate. There was in fact a competitive shakeout in the industry in the mid-1960s, but it did not occur in the way GEIA had predicted.

The smaller firms were able to survive until the early 1960s because of protection, repressed demand, and rationed market shares. The market was not the price-competitive one GEIA had in mind; even when the industry took a downturn in 1962 and 1963, prices did not respond. Moreover, the Brazilian market was still in formation and therefore did not possess the characteristics of a mature one. Initially, firms faced pent-up demand after years of import controls. Once this pre-existing demand was met, future sales depended on replacement demand and new demand based on income growth and on the incorporation of lower-income groups into the market through price reductions or credit facilities. As estimated by Alfredo Luiz Baumgarten, Jr., demand for automobiles was not elastic with respect to price but with respect to income.[118]

The industry went through a difficult period in the early and mid-1960s. Even before the severe recession partially induced by the military government in 1964, the auto sector was plagued with overcapacity. Firms had built ahead of demand. This can be attributed in part to the technical discontinuities of auto production; investment came in discrete steps, such as engine or stamping plants, each with high scale economies. It can also be traced in part to the "bunched" nature of investment patterns under import substitution, as Albert Fishlow has pointed out.[119] The investment that was initiated under GEIA was coming on-stream. Building extra capacity may also have been an oligopolistic strategy to block entry by competitors and to

---

[118] Alfredo Luiz Baumgarten, Jr., "Demanda de automóveis no Brasil," *Revista Brasileira de Economia* 26 (1972):203–97.

[119] Albert Fishlow, "Some Reflections on Post-1964 Brazilian Economic Policy," in Alfred Stepan, ed., *Authoritarian Brazil* (New Haven: Yale University Press, 1973), pp. 104–5.

strengthen a firm's position in the market.[120] Demand for trucks fell even more than that for cars, as economic activity began to decline in 1963 and 1964. (Truck demand is tied to general economic performance; cars, especially during rapid inflation, may be viewed as investment goods.) Inflation in those years nevertheless made it possible for firms to pass along higher costs to consumers.

The expected growth in demand did not materialize in the short run, however. Rather, the market disintegrated when the military implemented an austerity program after the coup in 1964. Only after two to three years of enormous drops in demand did prices begin to soften. The industry finally demonstrated price-responsiveness, but only in the face of plummeting demand and, more important, of government-imposed price controls, which started in 1965. The trade-off between idle capacity and price reduction was significant. Not until 1967 did the industry really rebound.[121]

The weaker firms did not survive these difficult years. By 1968, the original eleven firms had shrunk to eight. As Meira had feared, only those controlled by transnational capital remained. Already a minority shareholder, in 1966 Chrysler bought 92 percent of Simca in France, gaining control of Simca in Brazil, which had originally been 50 percent Brazilian-owned; Chrysler also purchased International Harvester's truck facility. Volkswagen took over Vemag, which had also been controlled by Brazilian capital, first through its acquisition of the German firm Auto Union, a minority holder, and then through purchase of the remaining shares.[122] In 1967, Ford gained control over Willys, another firm that had been predominantly Brazilian-owned, through its purchase of a controlling interest in Kaiser, and Alfa Romeo took over the previously state-owned FNM. It was at this time of consolidation that Ford and General Motors entered the pas-

---

[120] See Guimarães, "Industry, Market Structure and the Growth of the Firm in the Brazilian Economy," p. 195.

[121] Price rigidity in the face of falling demand is not unique to the Brazilian auto industry but has been demonstrated in other national auto industries and oligopolized industries in general. Within Brazil, this pricing behavior was also characteristic of many other sectors, supporting the structuralists' arguments about the prevalence of market power and markup pricing. Data on production and prices are presented in Chapter 4.

[122] Vemag's president cited the firm's difficulty in raising capital as the primary reason for selling out. Vemag had tried selling stock but could not compete with other financial assets being offered. Another reason given was "that the authorities were not just stimulating but even pressuring the companies to accomplish mergers" (Ventura Dias, "The Motor Vehicle Industry in Brazil," p. 45).

senger-car market through investing in new production facilities and bsorbing existing firms. Replacing Willys and Vemag, they became the second and third largest automobile producers after Volkswagen.[123] (For statistics on the share of the total Brazilian motor vehicle industry of these four producers, see Appendix A.)

Thus, by 1968, the industry resembled that anticipated in GEIA's original blueprint. But the process of consolidation was not exactly as GEIA had imagined. The firms that survived were those with access to resources with which to survive the crisis and not necessarily the most efficient. The American giants of the industry, by delaying entry into passenger-car production, let other firms test the market and the sustainability of market closure. Once Brazilian growth potential was assured, they committed themselves to car production.

The newly structured industry led the so-called economic miracle from 1968 to 1973, growing at rates of 20 percent a year (for basic economic indicators, see Table 3.3). Demand boomed in response to income concentration and new consumer credit instruments; wage compression and the repression of trade unions reduced labor costs. To ensure some price discipline over the increasingly concentrated oligopoly, the military could resort to the instrument that GEIA had lacked – price controls.

Determinants of Firm Entry

Explanations for the specific evolution of the Brazilian automotive industry echo the more general debate on the relative importance of underlying economic variables and structures as compared with state policy and institutional innovation in shaping economic development. A large literature on foreign direct investment explains the entrance of transnational firms into countries like Brazil and the ultimate struc-

---

[123]   This process of concentration appeared to have the government's blessing. Secretary of Planning Roberto Campos encouraged mergers. According to a *Visão* interview, he viewed concentration as "an inevitable international tendency" that would reduce industrial costs and propagate competitive pricing. The denationalization of the motor vehicle industry occurred in other Latin American countries as well. Bennett and Sharpe claim that the speed of the Mexican program unintentionally may have been responsible. The TNCs were in a position to establish themselves more quickly because they had better access to resources and know-how. Moreover, they had ready suppliers for parts in the United States. This was particularly important in Mexico, which instituted only a 60% domestic-content requirement. This was less critical under the 90% domestic-content regime in Brazil, although foreign firms typically forced their major suppliers to accompany them (Bennett and Sharpe, *Transnational Corporations versus the State*, p. 128).

Table 3.3. *Basic Economic Indicators*

	GDP mil. current Cr$	GDP mil. 1949 Cr$	% Growth real GDP	% Growth per capita income	% Change GDP deflator	Exchange rate Cr$ per US$[a]
1947	164.9	200.7				.018
1948	194.6	215.6	7.4	4.7	9.9	.018
1949	229.9	229.9	6.6	4.3	10.7	.018
1950	272.1	244.8	6.5	4.0	11.2	.018
1951	322.7	259.3	6.0	2.8	12.0	.018
1952	397.3	281.9	8.7	5.6	13.2	.018
1953	469.5	289.0	2.5	-0.5	15.3	.043
1954	627.4	318.2	10.1	7.0	21.4	.062
1955	783.4	340.0	6.9	3.7	16.8	.098
1956	995.9	350.8	3.2	0.2	23.2	.112
1957	1,218.0	379.1	8.1	4.9	13.2	.087
1958	1,457.5	408.3	7.7	4.6	11.1	.166
1959	1,989.6	431.1	5.6	2.4	29.2	.221
1960	2,755.7	472.9	9.7	6.6	26.3	.229
1961	4,052.1	521.6	10.3	7.2	33.3	.279
1962	6,601.4	549.0	5.3	2.3	54.8	.387
1963	11,928.6	557.5	1.5	-1.3	78.0	.617
1964	23,055.0	573.8	2.9	0.0	87.8	1.234
1965	36,817.6	589.5	2.7	-0.1	55.4	1.893
1966	53,724.1	619.6	5.1	2.2	38.8	2.220
1967	71,486.3	649.2	4.8	1.8	27.1	2.663
1968	99,879.8	709.7	9.3	6.3	27.8	3.409
1969	133,116.9	773.6	9.0	5.9	22.3	4.076
1970[b]	174,624.1	847.2	9.5	6.4	19.8	4.595
1971[b]	223,966.3	942.8	11.3	8.2	20.4	5.287
1972[b]	302,323.2	1,040.8	10.4	7.3	17.0	5.934
1973[b]	392,358.1[c]	1,159.5	11.4	8.3	16.5[d]	6.126

[a] 1947 - January 1953: official rate.
February 1953 - September 1953: free market rate, Rio de Janeiro.
October 1953 - August 1957: weighted average of five auction rates.
September 1957 - January 1961: general category rate.
March 1961 - July 1968: average of daily quotations of commercial banks.
August 1968 - February 1970: buying rate of Bank of Brazil.
March 1970: buying rate of Central Bank.
[b] New series, published October 1974:
1970 206,564.7
1971 274,267.4
1972 359,132.7
1973 477,163.1
[c] Estimated from real growth and increase in wholesale price index.
[d] Change in wholesale price index.
Source: Albert Fishlow, "Foreign Exchange Regimes and Economic Development: Brazil" (unpublished manuscript, 1976).

ture of industries such as auto by the behavioral characteristics of international industries. Essentially, this literature looks at foreign investment as part of the growth and competitive process of a firm in an oligopolized industry characterized by economies of scale, barriers to entry, and so on. As the industry becomes more concentrated in the home market through technological change and mass production, which drives out weaker firms, the move to external markets becomes critical to a firm's growth strategy. Firms go abroad in order to garner relatively larger rents on the advantages derived from imperfectly competitive market positions.[124]

The number of entrants is also explained by the nature of oligopolistic interdependence. As posited by Knickerbocker, if firms are knowingly interdependent but cannot collude, one firm's option to invest in a particular market will induce a "bandwagon effect."[125] It is this form of competition, rather than expected rates of return, that explains the observed phenomenon of bunched entry in relatively concentrated industries. Therefore, the competitive logic of international capital determines foreign investment and industrial structure in less-developed countries.

These works on the multinational firm have deepened our understanding of international capital flows and the global strategies of oligopolistic industries. In their emphasis on industrial organization, however, they ignore or discount the importance of state policy in determining investment behavior.[126] In contrast, some analysts of the Brazilian auto industry have adopted a more state-centric approach. These authors emphasize the relative autonomy of Kubitschek's executive branch as a critical ingredient to the auto program's success.[127]

---

[124] See Richard E. Caves, *Multinational Enterprise and Economic Analysis* (Cambridge: Cambridge University Press, 1982), for a general discussion; and Stephen Hymer, *The International Operation of National Firms: A Study of Direct Foreign Investment* (Cambridge, Mass.: MIT Press, 1976), on the impetus behind direct foreign investment.

[125] Knickerbocker, citing Yair Aharoni in "Oligopolistic Reaction and Multinational Enterprise," p. 31.

[126] The state is relatively absent in the work of Hymer, and completely absent from Knickerbocker. Knickerbocker is less concerned with the reasons behind a first mover's entry than with why so many follow. However, in the Brazilian case, market closure and a brief window of investment opportunity affected all firms simultaneously.

[127] Indeed, in subsequent interviews and publications, the participants in GEIA refer to its success in grandiose terms. Their language is that of a crusade against the skeptics, the anti-industrialists, and intransigent multinationals. They see themselves as having directed an automotive revolution in five years. GEIA is pointed to as Brazil's first successful planning experiment in which nondiscriminatory treatment

They argue that the creation of executive groups like GEIA allowed technical rationality to dominate key development decisions. It is implied that had it not been for this administrative reform, either the investment climate in Brazil would not have been stable enough to attract foreign capital or penalties would not have been severe enough to force that investment. The Brazilian automobile industry is thus characterized as an example of effective state intervention.[128]

Although apparently presenting a contrary view, those who characterize the Brazilian automotive industry as a planning failure reveal similar underlying assumptions about the scope of state intervention. Bergsman, for example, is highly critical of the industry, pointing to the large number of firms and high domestic-content levels that maintain diseconomies of scale. He suggests that, had Brazil limited production to two firms and fewer models and relaxed domestic-content levels, costs of production would not have exceeded the CIF cost of imports.[129] Similarly, Orosco calls the GEIA experience "an opportunity once again lost for the country." He claims that GEIA accepted more projects than its own market estimates warranted and that it caved in to congressional pressures.[130] Therefore, despite their negative evaluation, Bergsman and Orosco still imply that it was within state power to determine the industry's outcome.

In its focus on institutions, this approach downplays the degree to which structural economic conditions impose boundary conditions on state intervention. Not only changes in the nature of international oligopolistic competition, but also domestic market conditions played a role in determining the shape of the Brazilian industry. On the one hand, the potential market size in a country of over sixty million, whose GNP was growing at average annual rates of 6 to 7 percent, made the high domestic content more feasible than in smaller markets and the loss of market access more costly than in smaller economies.[131]

---

was assured for all participants. Meira claims that in retrospect, he would not have done anything differently (interview with Lúcio Meira, April 1985, Rio de Janeiro).

[128] See Barbara Geddes, "Building State Autonomy in Brazil, 1930–1964," *Comparative Politics* 22, no. 2 (January 1990):217–34; Celso Lafer, "The Planning Process and the Political System in Brazil: A Study of Kubitschek's Target Plan 1956–1961" (Ph.D. diss., Cornell University, 1970), and "O planejamento no Brasil: observações sobre o Plano de Metas (1956–1961)," in Betty Mindlin Lafer, ed., *Planejamento no Brasil* (São Paulo: Editora Perspectiva, 1970), pp. 29–50, on executive groups in general; and Moreira Franco, "Nacionalização de veículos no Brasil," on GEIA in particular.

[129] Bergsman, *Brazil: Industrialization and Trade Policies*, p. 130.

[130] Orosco, *A indústria automobilística brasileira*, p. 14.

[131] Mexico's underlying economic conditions made it more difficult to require such

On the other hand, structural constraints made a gradual approach unrealistic, and political factors made it difficult to restrict market entry.

Recognizing that the independent dynamics of foreign capital are critical but not completely determinant in shaping the pattern of foreign investment, recent bargaining literature has investigated how states can influence the structure, conduct, and performance of transnational industries. It has expanded on work by economists such as Charles Kindleberger, who modeled the relationship between the state and the transnational firm as a bilateral monopoly in which each party bargains over the distribution of monopoly rents, though he did not incorporate any explicit theory of the nature of the peripheral state. This literature has opened up the state itself for analysis, much as industrial organization opened up the black box of the firm, in order to understand the determinants of its bargaining strength.[132] Like the firm in an oligopolized industry, the state is portrayed as having unique behavioral rules. The state is no longer simply defined as representing the "national interest" or even a clearly identifiable group of interests. An attempt is made to clarify the domestic political and economic bases of the state and their implications for policy formation and implementation.

Those who have applied such a bargaining framework to explain the implantation of domestic automotive industries in Latin America have successfully moved beyond the standard state–market dichotomy.[133] They acknowledge that in countries like Brazil, where the

high domestic-content levels. With a smaller population and per capita income level, Mexico did not possess the market potential of Brazil. The country's long border with the United States presented the country with different constraints. Unlike Brazil, its import-substitution process took place in the context of macroeconomic stability and a fixed and unified exchange rate regime. Its auto program required that only 60% of a car's value (based on direct cost and including the engine) be manufactured in Mexico. By setting domestic-content levels at 90–95% of a vehicle's weight, Brazil had ensured that body stamping would be done in the country. In general, the Mexicans were more concerned about relative costs and inflation, and there were large economies of scale in the stamping process. Also, with so much contact with the United States, Mexican consumers were exposed to the trends set by Detroit. A domestic-content level of 60% allowed for body stampings to be imported and also facilitated frequent model changes.

[132] See Peter Evans, Dietrich Rueschmeyer, and Theda Skocpol, eds., *Bringing the State Back In* (Cambridge: Cambridge University Press, 1985). For case studies on various industries in Latin America, see Richard Newfarmer, ed., *Profits, Progress and Poverty: Case Studies of International Industries in Latin America* (Notre Dame: University of Notre Dame Press, 1985).

[133] See Bennett and Sharpe, *Transnational Corporations versus the State;* Guimarães, "In-

state unilaterally mandated local automobile production, the literature that explains firm entry by the behavioral characteristics of the international auto industry must be modified to incorporate the state and its institutions. But they also rightly emphasize how the coincidence of state policies with increased competition between U.S. and European firms in both home and third markets helped attract foreign investment. Clearly, if Brazil's efforts had not coincided with the industry's foray into new forms of global competition, they could not have precipitated the same outcome; ten years earlier, they might not have evoked a similar response. The GEIA plan fortuitously coincided with the return of private capital flows to Latin America in general and with the internationalization of motor vehicle production in particular.

In the absence of change in the international industry, there is little doubt that market closure, financial incentives, and administrative reform would have been insufficient to attract investment into the Brazilian auto industry. Indeed, the emergence of European competitors in the 1950s loosened the relatively tight oligopoly of the U.S. firms that prevailed before World War II, and a new international configuration was not yet consolidated. Other countries were also closing their markets to car imports. Brazil's room for maneuver increased as a result.

Nevertheless, this study suggests that the bargaining literature's approach to the Brazilian auto industry is incomplete in several respects. First, it exaggerates the coincidence of interests between the state and the firms, as well as the degree to which oligopolistic competition explains the pattern of investment. Second, and more important, the objective function of the state must be expanded to include the installation of auto manufacturing capacity not only as an end in itself but as a means to rapid industrialization and the maintenance of political support. The firms, in contrast, aimed to limit their initial commitment to make it easier to recoup their investment and to reduce potential exit costs. Therefore, the timing and form of investment must be included as key elements in the bargaining process.

Douglas Bennett and Kenneth Sharpe argue, for example, "that no

dustry, Market Structure and the Growth of the Firm in the Brazilian Economy," and *Acumulação e crescimento da firma*; Jenkins, *Transnational Corporations and the Latin American Automobile Industry*; and Kenneth S. Mericle, "The Political Economy of the Brazilian Motor Vehicle Industry," in Rich Kronish and Kenneth S. Mericle, eds., *The Political Economy of the Latin American Motor Vehicle Industry* (Cambridge, Mass.: MIT Press, 1984), pp. 1–40.

matter how contentious or conflictive the actual bargaining may become, it rests upon a foundation of shared or convergent interests."[134] Given firms faced with saturating markets in Europe and the United States, and the challenge of realizing full scale economies while producing a wider and changing array of models, one such convergence became "transnational automobile firms looking to promote sales and secure toeholds in LDC markets and LDC governments looking to promote domestic industrialization."[135] Kenneth Mericle characterizes the relationship between the Brazilian state and the transnational firms as supportive and says that there is no evidence to suggest that firms were hostile to the principle of establishing domestic manufacture, although they would have preferred lower domestic-content levels.[136]

If by convergent interests it is meant that firms would have proceeded in the same way in the absence of state action, the evidence suggests otherwise. Only when faced with market closure did firms respond to GEIA's call. Eduardo Augusto de Almeida Guimarães and Rhys Jenkins concluded that market closure was the single policy variable that attracted and set the timing of foreign investment. Subsequent interviews and testimony in which the automotive companies in Brazil credit market closure as the most important incentive support this contention.[137] Without this compulsion, the firms were not inclined to invest. As Ford's J. Sundelson put it, the Brazilians put "a pistol to our head."[138]

Although it is true that the auto companies were not hostile to the principle of domestic manufacturing, but at lower domestic-content levels, it was precisely the level of domestic content, which in fact defines the degree of manufacturing capacity, that was the main issue of contention. High domestic-content levels meant that firms were forced to produce the technological heart of their vehicles in Brazil, which they did not want to do. Having to build engine and stamping

---

[134] Bennett and Sharpe, "The World Automobile Industry and Its Implications," p. 222.

[135] Ibid., p. 208.

[136] Mericle, "The Political Economy of the Brazilian Motor Vehicle Industry," pp. 2, 6.

[137] See Lincoln Gordon and Engelbert L. Grommers, *U.S. Manufacturing Investment in Brazil: The Impact of Brazilian Government Policies 1946–1960* (Cambridge, Mass.: Harvard University Press, 1962); and John C. Goulden, general director of Ford do Brasil, Testimony before the Parliamentary Inquest Commission for the Verification of the Cost of the National Vehicle, October 10, 1967, GEIA Archives.

[138] Mira Wilkins interview with J. Sundelson, May 11, 1960, Wilkins Personal File.

plants, and even foundries, in a short period of time also made it impossible to invest incrementally.

This is not to imply that state policy was sufficient to attract foreign investment; Ford had shown that it was prepared to pull out of other markets when investment conditions were unfavorable. It also followed closely the strategy of its primary rival, GM. Moreover, it is important to distinguish between the initial decision to invest and subsequent decisions, and to understand the relationship between the state and firms once the industry was established. Once the industry was installed, government policies were supportive in that they created conditions under which vehicle demand grew and labor costs were compressed. Negotiations between the firms and the state revolved around price controls, which were set on a cost-plus basis and, starting in the 1970s, around exports. Despite the increased concentration of the industry, the relatively small market was still too fragmented to allow any one firm to reach optimum levels of production in the short to medium run. By influencing factor costs, maintaining protection, and limiting new entry, the government ensured that high costs did not necessarily translate into low profits.[139]

Once Brazil decided to close its markets to imports, the logic of international capital movements takes precedence in most bargaining accounts. A degree of automaticity is implied regarding the number of firms that entered; market fragmentation was the result of oligopolistic competition. Unless Brazil's small-political–economic profile had been radically altered, the argument goes, GEIA could not have prevented market fragmentation, nor was it responsible for it. Also, because expected profits are not the determinant attraction, the incentive structure was insignificant. Finally, even without the government's program, the industry would eventually have located in Brazil. As stated by Guimarães:

> In this context [of internationalization], the first implication which
> foreign producers could derive from the announced Brazilian gov-
> ernment policy was that being absent from the emerging industry
> meant being excluded from the Brazilian market entirely, since ef-

---

[139] Many of the cited authors who have emphasized convergent interests were implicitly or explicitly responding to simpler bargaining models that assumed completely distinct interests and agendas on the part of states and foreign firms. These less sophisticated frameworks assumed that the state represented a vaguely defined national interest. To their credit, these scholars have identified competing interests in the peripheral state and society, some of which may not be distinct from those of transnational firms. I would like to thank an anonymous reviewer for reminding me of this point.

fective protection for new national production should be expected. From this point of view, Brazilian government policy was a decisive inducement in engaging foreign firms to take up manufacturing activities in the country. On the other hand, it can be argued that, due to the very growth dynamics of the international industry, a foreign producer would be induced, sooner or later, to steal a march on [his] competitors by starting to manufacture in Brazil, independent of any prior government incentive, counting only upon future restriction on CBU [completely built-up] and CKD imports. This government policy would have only realized, or at most anticipated an existing trend.[140]

The history of the Brazilian industry shows that this approach, with its emphasis on market closure alone, is insufficient. Such an approach both disregards and cannot account for the form and timing of investment, which, along with firm risk, were highly related and significant factors. For strategic reasons, Brazil wanted fast and large investment projects. Firms could have invested incrementally, reducing their degree of exposure and commitment, but the state would not have met its larger developmental objectives.

The incentive structure must therefore be included in the analysis of firm entry, and the role of these incentives must be understood within the larger context of the international industry and the Brazilian market. The market was potentially large and protected from import competition; years of foreign-exchange rationing had created a situation of repressed demand. This market, in combination with the relative price inelasticity of vehicles, made investment more attractive. However, this was only market potential and not a given. By substantially reducing the cost of investment, the financial incentives offered to the industry reduced the risk. With the exception of BNDE financing, total subsidies on US\$421.4 million of imported investment goods and complementary parts came to US\$202.9 million, or 48 percent (see Chapter 4 for calculations). Even if the market had not fully materialized, subsidies significantly reduced the probability of financial losses.

The incentives also changed the time frame of the industry's birth, for which closing the market alone would have been insufficient. Lowering the costs of investment by a significant amount for a prescribed

[140] Guimarães, "Industry, Market Structure and the Growth of the Firm in the Brazilian Economy," pp. 169–70. He cautions that an individual producer would have had difficulty getting an adequate supply of parts in the absence of a government policy for the sector as a whole.

time period put late entrants at a competitive disadvantage. (Ford was unwilling to invest in passenger-car production without the benefits of Instruction 113.) The firms were all forced to invest within a short time period. A more protracted investment schedule would have had different ramifications for Brazilian industrialization. GEIA had the authority to deny subsidies to firms that entered after a certain date, as evidenced by Ford's attempts to win project approval. Very little new investment was made in the industry after 1960. Only in 1967–8, when a new growth cycle was beginning and subsidies were re-instated, did a second investment phase begin. The incentives, there-fore, increased the barriers to entry for firms that did not invest under the GEIA program and, by compelling large investments in a short period, increased the exit costs as well.

Furthermore, the incentives may have induced a certain degree of excess investment in the auto sector, both for individual firms and for the industry as a whole. By reducing investment costs, they en-couraged firms' tendency to build ahead of demand; firms tried to use import licenses and credits before they expired. These subsidies, in combination with fixed market shares, also made survival possible for marginal firms. Theoretically, closing the market could have been sufficient to attract the financially secure transnationals; they could have covered short-run losses through their international operations and counted on the long-term market potential of Brazil. But re-source-poor firms had to rely on current profits for a greater pro-portion of investment funds. Even companies like Ford, however, were not sufficiently convinced of Brazil's market potential to incur losses and were concerned about earning returns on their investment. For example, the incentives and market quotas (based on foreign-exchange allocations), which guaranteed a niche in the market, pro-vided the minimum threshold that made investment feasible. In fact, the industry as a whole was characterized by relatively high profits in the early years, when firms faced a buoyant sellers' market and before they reached 100 percent domestic content. According to Orosco, the industry, like Ford, was largely self-financed after the initial foreign investments were made.[141] Furthermore, it was precisely these weaker firms that did not survive the crisis of the mid-1960s when this cushion disappeared. Therefore, although the nature of oligopolistic com-petition explains why more firms entered than would be expected in an industry with a less concentrated, more competitive market struc-ture, characteristics of the Brazilian market in combination with in-

---

[141] Orosco, *A indústria automobilística brasileira*, p. 111.

centives meant that more firms may have entered than would otherwise have been the case.

In addition, the threats of market closure and subsidy deadlines would have fallen on deaf ears had they not been *credible*, particularly since Brazil was setting a precedent in the region. In this respect, those who focus on the Brazilian state's administrative capacity have a strong point. To expand on the metaphor of Ford's Sundelson, Brazil had to prove that the pistol was indeed loaded. As evidenced by Ford's intransigence and VW's manipulations, the transnational firms themselves did not take the government's pronouncements at face value. They continually tested the government's resolve.

GEIA's performance was not as stellar as is generally portrayed. It was not immune to pressure from Kubitschek, as shown in the cases of Simca and VW, and its representative agencies did not always coordinate their efforts, as shown by the BNDE's investigation of VW. GEIA did not always have the political mandate or the administrative flexibility to respond to unforeseen events, such as foreign-exchange crises or the 1964 coup, which affected the plan. Stochastic elements introduced by the general political and economic context affected the sector in ways that neither GEIA nor the firms could have predicted.

The transnational firms were more adept than GEIA at manipulating public opinion and Congress. In interviews, several GEIA personnel voiced the suspicion that TNCs supported Bilac Pinto in his attempt to circumvent GEIA's auto plan. The auto firms were attuned to divisions in the state apparatus and to Kubitschek's political need for cars. Whether or not they initiated Article 59, they were poised to take full advantage of it.

Moreover, the fact that GEIA was not able to entice Ford and GM, the two largest car producers with the most international experience, into the market raises questions about the sufficiency of state policy *or* market closure (and the "bandwagon effect") to guarantee firm entry. Within the overall pattern of international competition, firm response varied. GEIA could not persuade the most powerful TNCs to invest in cars when it wanted them to, nor was it empowered to keep them out indefinitely.

Nevertheless, GEIA was able to initiate automobile production on its own time schedule. Overall, it successfully resisted attempts to sabotage the plan. There was no rumor or evidence of corruption.[142] It enforced domestic-content requirements by withholding foreign-

---

[142] According to José Mindlin, Lúcio Meira did not even own a car when he was president of GEIA. Interview with José Mindlin, August 16, 1988, São Paulo.

exchange allocations from those firms that were not in compliance.[143] It prevented Ford from entering the car market on Ford's terms. In effect, it proved that the pistol was "loaded enough" and that the plan would proceed with or without the full participation from Ford and GM, whose executives probably underestimated GEIA's commitment. The two U.S. giants also underestimated the challenge posed by VW. As known entities in the Brazilian market, Ford and GM may have presumed that they could afford to delay car production; a newcomer like VW had to carve out a new market. Even though these firms ultimately were allowed to invest in passenger cars, they had to confront an existing industry and reclaim market share.

Finally, a primary objective of the plan was to kickstart industrial development. From that standpoint, the debate on whether firms would have invested later in the absence of incentives is irrelevant. Kubitschek's automotive program may well have "anticipated an existing trend." But the extent to which Brazil was successful in accelerating the process had vastly different consequences for the country's industrialization. The industry's performance is evaluated in Chapter 4.

---

[143] For example, GEIA withheld Simca's foreign-exchange allotment when the firm failed to meet domestic-content requirements, halting production for six months. Ford also saw its import quotas slashed. Letter from Aranha to Volkswagen explaining the potential consequences of delaying or abandoning local engine production, February 3, 1959, Volkswagen Archives.

4
RENT REDISTRIBUTION AND
LINKAGE EFFECTS

Due to the variety of objectives the auto industry was supposed to achieve, the criteria for evaluating the outcome are not self-evident. The previous chapter documented how government policies successfully met the objectives of attracting foreign capital into Brazil and installing a domestic automotive industry. This chapter further develops the argument that the industrial strategy was a success by assessing several performance indicators. The criteria considered here include the distribution of rents between the transnational auto firms and the Brazilian government, production costs and prices, and linkage effects.

The chapter first considers the special subsidies provided to the auto firms and then studies tax rates, prices, and profit margins. A comparison of subsidies and tax revenues shows that, even in the industry's first five years, the amount of taxes paid by the vehicle assemblers on federal, state, and local levels more than compensated for the indirect subsidies they received. By the mid-1960s, production costs and prices were declining, as were profit margins. Therefore, the indirect incentives provided to the industry did not represent a pure subsidy because the state ultimately recovered all of its forfeited revenues. Also, as production levels increased and firms consolidated, the industry became more efficient and production costs fell.

The chapter then looks at the sector's linkage effects. Brazilian planners explicitly used the U.S. economy as the model they hoped to duplicate. They observed that the job of one in eight U.S. workers was connected to auto production, and they expected the industry similarly to transform the Brazilian economy. A variety of indicators shows that the sector did have an important impact on the economy as a whole.

These performance indicators are clearly only partial. It is beyond this study's purview to undertake a full social cost–benefit analysis of Brazil's attempt to substitute domestically produced vehicles for imports.[1] It is important to acknowledge, however, that following a development strategy centered around the automotive industry had broad ramifications, many of which are difficult to quantify. Some relate to the more general implications of a development effort based on a capital-intensive consumer durable industry. Alternative development models that focus on labor-intensive goods have been proposed for Brazil because of the presumed employment-generating effects, lower investment and import costs relative to output and employment, and different demand profiles. Questions have also been raised about the wisdom of building a transportation system around private motor vehicles in a country with a highly skewed distribution of income, dense urban environments, and a dependence on imported fuel.[2]

As discussed in Chapter 2, the decision to build a domestic auto industry emerged from a particular political, economic, and historical context. The industry fulfilled a variety of objectives for President Juscelino Kubitschek and fit the developmental assumptions of the era. Brazil was not alone in its fascination with the automobile: India, South Africa, and Australia were beginning their own motor vehicle programs at the time, soon to be followed by Argentina, Mexico, and South Korea. Following an alternative development path would presume a different political–economic profile for the country.

Subsidies

The financial incentives offered to the automobile companies included various foreign-exchange subsidies and import duty exemptions.

Instruction 113

One of the most important investment incentives for the Brazilian automotive industry was the foreign-exchange benefit derived from Instruction 113, which was issued by the Monetary Authority (Superintendência da Moeda e do Crédito [SUMOC]) in 1955 – before

---

[1] For example, it is beyond the range of this study to assess whether the Mill-Bastable criterion – that the discounted present value of social gains exceeds that of social costs – was satisfied. The value of subsidized inputs provided by the public sector, such as steel and electricity (which were not unique to the auto industry or to foreign capital), were also not estimated.

[2] See Richard Darbera and Remy Prud'homme, *Transports urbains et développement économique du brésil* (Paris: Ed. Economica, 1983).

President Juscelino Kubitschek took office in 1956. This policy instrument allowed all equipment entering the country as direct foreign investment to be imported without exchange cover. Firms could thereby bypass the auction system through which foreign exchange was allocated between 1953 and 1957 and avoid the implicit tax involved in exchange transactions. The subsidy was the difference between the higher, third-category cruzeiro/dollar exchange rate at which capital goods would otherwise be imported, and the free rate, at which the investment was valued and on which profit remittances were calculated (see Table 4.1). After the exchange reform of 1957, the subsidy was the difference between the general import rate and the free rate.

As shown in Table 4.2, the automotive industry as a whole (including the parts sector) was responsible for almost half of all investment entering Brazil under Instruction 113 during the Kubitschek administration: US$200.7 million of the US$419 million total. US$114.7 million of that amount was invested in the terminal sector, while the rest went into the parts industry.[3] This represented almost three-fourths of total foreign investment in the terminal sector. The implicit exchange subsidy on this investment was worth US$28.7 million, 25 percent of the value of the investment (see Tables 4.3 and 4.4).

Financing at the "Cost of Exchange"

For foreign equipment not imported as direct investment but requiring foreign financing, the exchange rate at which amortization and interest payments were remitted was also subsidized. Smaller firms that were either controlled or had substantial participation by Brazilian capital relied on this type of financing (see Table 4.5). The larger transnational firms relied exclusively on Instruction 113; Bra-

---

[3] Superintendência da Moeda e do Crédito (SUMOC), *Boletim* and *Relatório do Exercício* (Rio de Janeiro, various months and years). Other studies of the industry have provided different investment figures. Data originating from GEIA usually represent investment approved by that agency. For example, ANFAVEA and Summa each cite GEIA as the source for approved investment totals under Instruction 113 of US$133,959,000 in the terminal sector and US$99,306,000 in parts until August 1960 (ANFAVEA, *Indústria automobilística brasileira* [São Paulo: ANFAVEA, various years]; and Aimone Summa, *A indústria automobilística brasileira* [São Paulo: CEPAL, 1963]). SUMOC provides data on investment it has authorized, rather than on actual equipment imports. The figures provided here were arrived at by totaling each firm's monthly importation of equipment during this period as registered by SUMOC. For investment figures provided by Almeida, see Appendix B.

Table 4.1. Exchange Rates (cruzeiro/U.S. dollar)

Category	1956	1957 Jan.- Aug.	1957 Sept. - Dec.	1958	1959	1960	1961
I	73.76	58.29					
II	81.29	74.51					
III	103.15	100.60					
IV	115.46	138.03					
V	222.36	299.07					
General import rate	--	--	80.29	148.45	199.45	233.00	--
Cost of exchange (custo de câmbio)	43.82	43.82	43.82	54.84	78.49	100.00	200
Free rate	73.60	75.67	75.67	130.06	156.60	189.73	255
Bergsman's "free trade rate"	71.00	81.00	81.0	95.00	160.00	210.00	350

Note: Rates equal to official rate (1956-8: 18.82; 1959-61: 18.82) plus agio.

Source: All from Superintendência da Moeda e do Crédito (SUMOC), Relatório do Exercício (Rio de Janeiro, various years), except cost of exchange: 1957 from Albert Fishlow, "Foreign Trade Regimes and Economic Development: Brazil" (unpublished manuscript, 1976); 1958-61 from José Almeida, "A indústria automobilística brasileira" (unpublished manuscript; Rio de Janeiro: Fundação Getúlio Vargas, Instituto de Economia Centro de Estudos Industriais, 1969); and from Joel Bergsman, Brasil: Industrialization and Trade Policies (London: Oxford University Press, 1970).

Table 4.2. *Foreign Financing Authorized By SUMOC - Direct Investment Licensed by CACEX According to the Target Plan (US$ millions)*

	1955				1956				1957			
	Financing		Investment	Total	Financing		Investment	Total	Financing		Investment	Total
	With exchange priority	Without exchange priority			With exchange priority	Without exchange priority			With exchange priority	Without exchange priority		
I. General total	79.4	--	31.3	110.7	253.7	57.5	55.7	366.6	234.7	217.1	108.2	560.0
II. Targets total	78.1	--	15.2	93.3	241.1	57.5	16.4	315.0	204.8	217.1	47.7	469.6[a]
A. Energy	40.4	--	2.5	42.9	23.9	--	--	23.9	67.2	--	0.7	67.9
B. Transport	31.4	--	0	31.4	82.7	--	--	82.7	105.2	--	0.8	106.0
C. Food	--	--	1.4	1.4	8.1	--	0.4	8.5	7.3	28.9	3.3	39.5
D. Basic industries	6.3	--	11.3	17.6	126.4	57.5	16.0	199.9	25.1	188.2	42.9	256.2
1. Steel	6.3	--	0.5	6.8	51.6	--	3.5	55.1	10.5	--	--	10.5
2. Automotive	--	--	--	--	45.6	57.5	6.2	109.3	2.3	188.2	32.3	222.8
E. Education	--	--	--	--	--	--	--	--	--	--	--	--
III. Other	1.3	--	16.1	17.4	12.3	--	39.3	51.6	29.9	--	60.5	90.4

	1958				1959			
	Financing		Investment	Total	Financing		Investment	Total
	With exchange priority	Without exchange priority			With exchange priority	Without exchange priority		
I. General total	392.4	115.0	82.5	589.9	325.8	42.6	65.8	435.2
II. Targets total	372.5	114.9	72.1	559.5	316.2	41.1	53.7	411.0
A. Energy	133.7	--	--	133.7	117.7	--	--	117.7
B. Transport	185.4	--	1.1	186.5	28.9	1.5	--	30.4
C. Food	4.5	11.3	0.7	16.5	1.2	8.2	--	9.4
D. Basic industries	48.9	103.6	70.3	222.8	168.4	31.4	53.7	253.5
1. Steel	18.6	--	--	18.6	124.6	1.1	--	125.7
2. Automotive	25.0	98.7	59.1	182.8	16.1	28.1	46.8	91.0
E. Education	--	--	--	--	--	--	--	--
III. Other	19.9	0.1	10.4	30.4	4.6	1.5	12.1	18.2
Later reductions	--	--	--	--	6.0	--	--	6.0

Table 4.2 (*continued*)

	1960				1961			
	Financing		Investment	Total	Financing		Investment	Total
	With exchange priority	Without exchange priority			With exchange priority	Without exchange priority		
I. General total	242.1	62.8	106.8	411.7	115.8	14.4	39.2	169.4
II. Targets total	226.1	53.6	84.8	364.5	103.1	14.0	27.5	144.6
A. Energy	64.2	--	--	64.2	19.1	--	--	19.1
B. Transport	41.0	--	--	41.0	46.4	--	--	46.4
C. Food	3.0	39.2	12.2	54.4	0.3	--	4.0	4.3
D. Basic industries	113.4	14.4	72.6	200.4	37.3	14.0	23.5	74.8
1. Steel	89.6	10.0	5.5	105.1	31.4	--	2.8	34.2
2. Automotive	11.0	--	56.3	67.3	2.7	14.0	3.5	20.2
E. Education	4.5	--	--	4.5	--	--	--	--
III. Other	13.9	9.2	22.0	45.1	11.0	--	11.7	22.7
Later reductions	2.1	--	--	2.1	1.7	0.4	--	2.1

140

	1956-60					1956-61				
	Financing		Total	Investment	Grand total	Financing		Total	Investment	Grand total
	With exchange priority	Without exchange priority				With exchange priority	Without exchange priority			
I. General total	1,449.7	495.0	1,944.7	419.0	2,363.7	1,565.5	509.4	2,074.9	458.2	2,533.1
Automotive industry	100	372.5	472.5	200.7	673.5	102.7	386.5	489.2	204.2	693.4
% of total	7	75	24	48	28	7	76	24	45	27

[a] Error in original.

Sources: SUMOC, *Relatório do Exercício* (Rio de Janeiro, various years), Financed Investment Data for 1959 was revised in the 1961 volume. Financing with exchange priority is that which could be repaid at the "cost of exchange" (*custo de câmbio*). Financing without exchange priority in 1956 included only complementary parts and components for the auto industry; in 1957, it also included agricultural machinery; in 1958 and 1959, other categories were included.

Table 4.3. *Instruction 113 Investments by Firm (US$ millions)*

	1955	1956	1957	1958	1959	1960	Total 1956-60
FNM	--	--	--	--	3.224	--	3.224
Ford	--	--	16.420	--	--	6.000	22.420
General Motors	--	--	10.100	10.300	.041	1.718	22.159
International Harvester	--	--	--	4.547	.029	--	4.576
Mercedes-Benz	3.630	--	--	2.291	.719	5.877	8.888
Scania Vabis		--	--	.538	.071	.171	.780
Simca	--	--	--	--	1.904	4.550	6.454
Toyota	--	--	--	--	--	1.548	1.548
Volkswagen	--	.969	2.498	--	.087	7.619	11.173
Vemag	--	.516	.180	.240	1.659	.119	2.714
Willys Overland	--	3.255	3.708	10.172	11.485	2.198	30.819
Total 1956-60	3.630	4.740	32.906	28.088	19.219	29.800	114.755

Source: SUMOC, *Boletim* (Rio de Janeiro, various years).

zilian firms without foreign participation were essentially barred from importing under Instruction 113.

As shown in Table 4.2, the amount of equipment financed under these terms for the automotive sector as a whole came to US$100 million between 1956 and 1960. This represented only 7 percent of the total amount of investment thus financed. The terminal sector was responsible for US$41.6 million of that amount. More than 60 percent of foreign-financed equipment came into Brazil under this exchange category; the auto sector was atypical in this respect. Because of foreign firms' predominance, most auto-related investment entered under Instruction 113.

The subsidy on this financing scheme was the difference between the third category rate, which is what firms would have had to pay for the foreign financing, and the *custo de câmbio* ("cost-of-exchange") rate, which is what they did pay. As shown in Table 4.1, the difference between these two rates was even greater than the subsidy offered for Instruction 113 imports, since the cost-of-exchange rate was substantially lower than the free rate. This has generally been considered the biggest exchange subsidy provided to the industry. José Almeida, who does not calculate an implicit subsidy for Instruction 113, found this to be the case. Eugênio Gudin, the author of Instruction 113, considered the cost-of-exchange rate oversubsidized and different from 113, which, in his view, compensated foreign investors for an

Table 4.4. *Instruction 113 Subsidy*

	1956	1957	1958	1959	1960	1956-60
I. Subsidy						
Category III rate minus Free rate (1956-7); General rate minus Free rate (1958-60)	29.55	24.93[a]	18.39	42.85	43.27	--
II. 113 investment (US$ millions)	4.7	32.9	28.1	19.2	29.8	114.7
III. Total subsidy (Cr$ millions) (I x II)	138.9	820.2	516.8	822.7	1,289.4	
IV. Total subsidy (US$ millions)	1.89	10.84	3.97	5.25	6.79	28.74
(Cruzeiro subsidy divided by free market rate)						
V. Subsidy as a percentage of investment	40	33	14	27	23	25

[a] The Category III rate minus Free rate was used for the entire year of 1957. This exaggerates the subsidy for the year as the difference between the general rate and the year's average free rate was 4.62.

overvalued cruzeiro.[4] Both of their measurements of this subsidy left out an important factor.

These and other measurements of this subsidy fail to evaluate the impact of the exchange reform of 1961.[5] With that reform, the *custo de câmbio* rate of exchange was abolished. According to SUMOC, "The measure [the reform] functions like a brake on external expenditures and frees the Government from the internal subsidy based on exchange benefits as well as from the subsidies it was obliged to concede ... to national producers."[6]

Whereas the foreign financing entered the country between 1956 and 1960, when the cost-of-exchange rate was still in force, the subsidy – that is, the exchange differential – was derived only at the time of payment. Moreover, the rates used for this calculation were those existing not when the loan was contracted but at the time of payment. Decree No. 39.412, which established the norms for the industry, clearly states that foreign-financed equipment that met the necessary criteria would be "subject to liquidation at the cost of exchange, *in accordance with legislation in force at the time of contractual payments*" (emphasis added).[7]

According to SUMOC *Relatórios*, most of this type of financing for the auto industry was granted with at least a three-year grace period. Therefore, a loan contracted in 1958, for example, did not require payment until 1961, by which time the cost-of-exchange rate had been abolished. In essence, this effectively eliminated the implicit subsidy for foreign financing. No alternative or exceptional rate appears to have been set for those firms that had borrowed under those assumptions, and, according to the statement in the SUMOC *Relatório* cited previously, an explicit goal of the reform was to spare the government the onus of the subsidy.[8]

[4] Eugênio Gudin, "The Chief Characteristics of the Postwar Economic Development of Brazil," in Howard S. Ellis, ed., *The Economy of Brazil* (Berkeley: University of California Press, 1969), pp. 3–25.
[5] Orosco and Latini briefly mention how the reform eliminated much of the subsidy, but neither measured its impact; see Eros Orosco, *A indústria automobilística brasileira* (Rio de Janeiro: Consultec, 1961), p. 79, and Sydney Latini, Testimony before the Parliamentary Inquest Commission for the Verification of the Cost of the National Vehicle (Comissão Parlamentar de Inquérito Destinado a Verificar o Custo de Veículo Nacional), October 26, 1967, GEIA Archives, Conselho do Desenvolvimento, Ministério de Indústria e Comércio, Rio de Janeiro.
[6] SUMOC, *Relatório do Exercício*, 1961.
[7] Decree No. 39.412, *Diário Oficial*, June 16, 1956.
[8] Gudin calculated the total subsidy by measuring the difference between the market rate and the cost-of-exchange rate times the total financing in the year the loans were

Table 4.5. *Financed Equipment Imports by Firm (US$ thousands)*

	1956	1957	1958	1959	1960	Total
FNM[a]	1,145 (1956-7)	--	6,697 (1958-63 & 1959-64)[b]	4,500 (1961-6)	4,500	16,842
Simca[a]	--	--	--	6,183 (1962-7)	--	6,183
Scania Vabis	--	--	232 (1964-73)	35 (1964-73)	85	352
Vemag	--	250 (?)	160 (1958-63)	--	2,250	2,660
Volkswagen	--	--	--	2,400 (1959-67)	1,905	4,305
Willys	1,600 (1956-63)	--	4,018[c] (1958-63 & 1963-6)	--	5,618	11,236
Total	2,745	250	11,107	13,118	14,358	41,578

Note: Years in parentheses indicate payback period.
[a] Simca and FNM (1958, 1959: US$ 3,400,000 of 1960) loans guaranteed by BNDE.
[b] Separate loans: US$ 4,348,487 in 1958-63; remainder in 1959-64.
[c] Separate loans: US$ 518,350 in 1958-63; US$ 3,500,000 in 1963-6.
Source: SUMOC, *Relatório* and *Boletim* (Rio de Janeiro, various years).

Although not insignificant, the total subsidy was substantially reduced by the exchange reform. Based on the term structure of these loans as reported by SUMOC, an amortization schedule for 1956–60 is presented in Table 4.5. Interest payments are not calculated because interest rates were not available. Of the US$41.6 million in financed equipment, only US$7.5 million was repaid at a subsidized rate. The subsidy came to US$3.6 million, or 48 percent of the value of payments. Had this subsidy continued throughout the payment period, it would have been quite substantial. As a percentage of total financed imports, however, the subsidy amounted to only 9 percent (see Tables 4.6 and 4.7).

Exchange Quotas

During the period 1956–60, when firms were not yet producing at 100 percent domestic-content levels, each firm was allocated a foreign-exchange quota for importing parts and components based on

contracted (see Gudin, "The Chief Characteristics of the Postwar Economic Development of Brazil"). Almeida also measures the subsidy using the cost-of-exchange rate at the time the loan was contracted (see Appendix B).

Table 4.6. *Subsidized Loans (at Cost of Exchange) and Amortization Schedule (US$)*

		1956	1957	1958	1959	1960[a]
FNM	Loans	1,145,000 (1956-7)		4,348,000 (1958-63) 2,349,000 (1959-64)		
	Amortization	572,500	572,500	869,600	869,600 469,800	869,600 469,800
Vemag	Loans		250,000 (1957-62)[b]	160,000 (1958-63)		
	Amortization		50,000	50,000 32,000	50,000 32,000	50,000 32,000
VW	Loans				2,400,000 (1959-67)	
	Amortization				300,000	300,000
Willys	Loans	1,600,000 (1957-63)		518,000 (1958-63)		
	Amortization	320,000	320,000	320,000 103,600	320,000 103,600	320,000 103,600
Total Amortization		892,500	942,500	1,375,200	2,145,000	2,145,000

Note: Numbers below loans indicate terms of loan (years due).

a The term structure for finance authorized in 1960 was not available; it was assumed that amortizations came due only after 1961.

b Assumed.

Source: See Table 4.5.

Table 4.7. *Subsidy in Financing*

	1956	1957	1958	1959	1960	1956-60
I. Subsidy						
Free rate minus cost of exchange	29.8	31.9	75.2	78.1	89.7	--
II. Payments (US$ thousands)	892.5	942.5	1,375.2	2,145.0	2,145.0	7,500.2
III. Total subsidy (Cr$ millions) (I x II)	26.597	30.066	103.415	167.525	192.407	--
IV. Total subsidy (at free rate) (US$ thousands)	361.4	397.3	795.1	1,069.8	1,014.1	3,637.7
V. Subsidy as a % of:						
Payments	40	41	58	50	47	48
Total finance	--	--	--	--	--	9

planned production targets. In this way, production and market shares were rationed. Foreign exchange was the binding constraint on production during these years; production could not exceed the level of required parts available through imports.

As described in Chapter 2, foreign exchange was made available at beneficial rates, a policy rationalized on the grounds that consumer prices would be lower as a result of cheaper inputs. High-priority vehicles such as trucks and jeeps received better rates than passenger cars, and rates improved once a high domestic-content level was attained in engines. The subsidy became particularly significant after the 1957 exchange reform; the average import rate for the first six months of 1957 was maintained until June 30, 1959. Afterward, it was set arbitrarily. According to SUMOC, the exchange subsidy was eliminated in 1960.

Available data on parts imports are sketchy and contradictory. Complementary parts imports appear in the SUMOC-authorized finance tables under financing without exchange priority. These figures were not used to calculate subsidies, as they represent authorized, rather than actual, imports and are significantly different from all other sources. Other data sources indicate that these were not equal. Data from the vehicle producers' association (ANFAVEA) were used for 1957, 1958, and 1960; specific SUMOC data for imported parts and exchange-rate subsidies were used for 1959.

As shown in Table 4.8, US$265.1 in complementary parts were imported from 1957 to 1960. The foreign-exchange subsidy was significant, especially in 1959 (see Table 4.9) when it came to 59 percent of the value of the imports. For the four-year period, the subsidy represented 33 percent of total imports.

National Bank for Economic Development Financing and Loan Guarantees

During the Kubitschek administration, the National Bank for Economic Development (Banco Nacional do Desenvolvimento Econômico [BNDE]) shifted its almost exclusive emphasis away from railroad transportation and electrical energy to basic industries. Between 1957 and 1961, basic industries absorbed 39 percent of domestic currency operations.[9]

---

[9] BNDE, *Relatório do BNDE* (Rio de Janeiro, various years). The auto industry as a whole accounted for 4.8% of total loans. Metallurgy, steel, and electrical energy dominated, representing 47%, 46%, and 24% of the total, respectively.

Table 4.8. *Complementary Parts Imports and Subsidies, 1957-1960*

	1957[a]	1958[a]	1959[b]	1960	1957-60
1) Total imported parts, US$ millions	10.9	54.8	100.5	98.9	265.1
2) Imported parts for trucks, jeeps & buses, US$ millions	9.9	40.6	93.2		
3) Subsidy — trucks,[c] Cr$	26.09	66.51	[b]	0	
4) Total subsidy (trucks, etc.), Cr$ millions (2x3)	258.29	2,700.31	9,304.86		
5) Imported parts for cars, US$ millions	1.0	14.2	7.3		
6) Subsidy — cars,[c] Cr$	37.43	22.15	[b]	0	
7) Total subsidy (cars), Cr$ millions (5x6)	37.43	314.53	-25.93		
8) Total subsidy (all vehicles), Cr$ millions	295.72	3,014.84	9,278.9	0	
9) Total subsidy US$ millions at free rate	3.91	23.18	59.25	0	86.34

[a] For 1957-8 assumed percentage of total parts imports for trucks and cars proportional to production shares.
[b] See Table 4.9.
[c] 1957: Subsidy on trucks: category III rate-category II rate; on cars: category IV-III.
1958: General rate--average conceded import rate for January-June 1957.
1959: SUMOC--See Table 4.9.

Although categorized as a basic industry, the auto industry accounted for a small share of BNDE funding, and, in turn, the BNDE was responsible for only a small share of the sector's total finance. As seen in Table 4.10, the industry (including the parts sector) received Cr$1,872.1 million (nominal) from 1956 to 1960, which was 3.7 percent of total BNDE-authorized finance; Cr$1,448 million of this total was granted to the terminal sector. The National Motor Factory (FNM), Volkswagen (VW), Willys, and Simca, all firms either dominated or with significant participation by Brazilian capital, were the only vehicle manufacturers to receive these cruzeiro loans (see Table 4.11).[10] It is important to note that of these firms, the FNM was by far the biggest beneficiary of BNDE assistance; the bank ultimately became a stockholder in the firm.

The value of the BNDE subsidy is difficult to quantify. Usury laws

[10] Vemag had a credit of Cr$60 million approved in January 1958, but apparently never used it.

Table 4.9. *Complementary Parts Imports and Subsidies, 1959 and First Semester 1960*

Vehicles (1)	Imported parts US$ (2)	Premiums				Tariff		Total Cr$/US$ (5)+(8)	Estimate of incentives (9)x(2)
		Average general category (3)	Conceded (4)	Difference[a] (5)	Estimation (6)	Conceded (7)	Difference (8)		
First semester, 1959									
Trucks (medium & heavy), buses, & jeeps	31,632,568.10	180.53	63.12	117.41	34.4	--	34.4	151.81	4,802,140,163.00
Utilities & light trucks	14,274,954.10	180.53	107.48	73.05	34.4	--	34.4	107.45	1,533,843,818.00
Passenger cars	2,735,131.80	180.53	186.87	-6.34	34.4	--	34.4	28.06	76,747,798.00
Total	48,642,654.00								6,412,731,779.00
Second semester, 1959									
Trucks (medium & heavy), buses, & jeeps	39,937,848.50	180.53	76.00	104.53	34.8	5.2	29.6	134.13	4,954,473,619.00
Utilities & light trucks	7,387,556.50	180.53	130.00	50.53	34.8	5.2	29.6	80.13	519,964,902.00
Passenger cars	4,567,815.10	180.53	182.41	-1.88	34.8	5.2	29.6	27.72	126,619,834.00
Total	51,893,220.10								5,673,058,355.00
First semester, 1960									
Trucks, buses, utilities, jeeps, & passenger cars	41,747,529.90	204.30	204.30	--	34.8	5.2	29.6	29.60	1,235,726,864.00
Total									1,235,726,864.00

[a] This column used to estimate exchange-rate subsidy in Table 4.8.
Source: SUMOC, *Relatório do Exercício* (Rio de Janeiro, various years).

Table 4.10. *BNDE Authorized Finance (Cr$ millions)*

	1952-5	1956	1957	1958	1959	1960	1961	1952-61[a]	1956-60	1956-61
Total	8,265.8	7,122.6	8,414.7	12,241.8	9,932.4	13,555.0	23,872.5	83,404.8	51,266.5	75,139
Transport	5,364.9	4,882.8	1,629.6	530.0	1,952.6	646.7	222.0	--	--	--
Electric energy	2,121.9	928.8	4,668.1	5,548.9	3,483.8	1,366.6	15,703.8	--	--	--
Basic industries	658.9	939.6	1,838.9	5,679.7	4,339.0	11,482.6	7,175.7	--	--	--
Auto industry[b] (which is part of basic industries)	194.3	--	187.7	421.8	1,106.6	156.0	--	2,066.4	1,872.1	1,872.1
Other	120.1	371.4	278.1	483.2	157.0	59.1	771.0	--	--	--
Autos % of total	2.3	--	2.2	3.4	11.1	1.1	--	2.5	3.7	2.5

[a] Cr$ 200,000,000 of the 1952-61 total in the form of "participação societária" and Cr$ 118,800,000 as direct investment. The rest are repayable loans.
[b] Includes the parts sector.
Source: BNDE, *Relatórios do BNDE* (Rio de Janeiro, various years).

Table 4.11. *BNDE Cruzeiro Loans until 1961*

	Cr$ thousands	Date authorized	Date contracted
FNM	115,315	March 15, 1954	March 29, 1954
	237,708	August 20, 1957	June 24, 1958
	710,400	July 3, 1959	July 12, 1961
VW	150,000	April 30, 1957	March 24, 1958
Willys	350,000	July 7, 1959	February 3, 1961
Vemag	60,000	January 1958	Never

Source: See Table 4.10.

forbade banks from charging more than 12 percent interest on loans, which made the real interest rate highly negative during this period of rising inflation. Parallel credit markets emerged, and banks added fees and other costs in order to raise the effective interest rate charged. Nevertheless, real interest rates on commercial loans remained negative and funds were scarce, so that simply getting credit in this rationed market represented a subsidy. The supply of real financial resources declined between 1957 and 1964, despite the fast growth in domestic product.[11]

For basic industries, the BNDE charged an average annual interest rate of 11 percent usually with a grace period of at least six months and an amortization period of at least five years.[12] As shown in Table 4.12, the subsidy was calculated as the difference between that rate and the rate charged by commercial banks, a close alternative. The effect of inflation on real interest rates was not considered, because the impact on these rates was the same. (As inflation heated up in these years, the relative difference in interest rates became less important, as each rate became significantly negative in real terms.) It was assumed that the loans were paid in five installments beginning with

[11] The Bank of Brazil's share in the supply of credit to the private sector decreased after 1953 when it devoted increasing amounts of its finance to the government to cover its Treasury deficits. The real value of its loans to the private sector was 5% lower in 1961 than in 1952. In 1958, BNDE credit was only 7% of the total amount extended by the private commercial banking system to the private sector. Its resources also were reduced from 1958 to 1960; after Brazil broke with the IMF, all credit lines with international agencies were cut. An important caveat, however, is that a significant portion of the Bank of Brazil's public loans was recycled to the private sector via government contracts. See A. C. Sochaczewski, "Financial and Economic Development of Brazil, 1952–1968" (Ph.D. diss., University of London, 1980).

[12] BNDE, *Relatório do BNDE*, 1959.

Table 4.12. *Subsidy on BNDE Loans*

	(1)	(2)	(3)	(4)	(5)[a]	(6)	(7)	(8)
		Nominal interest rates (%)						
	Bank of Brasil	Commercial banks	Comm. banks "effective"	BNDE	Inflation	Subsidy (3-4)	BNDE loans Cr$ thousands	Total subsidy Cr$ thousands (6x7)
1956	6.9	15.1	18.9	11	23.2	7.9		
1957	8.6	16.0	20.0	11	13.2	9.0		
1958	8.4	16.1	20.1	11	11.1	9.1	387,708.0	35,281.4
1959	9.0	17.8	22.3	11	29.2	11.3	310,166.4	35,048.8
1960	9.3	19.1	23.9	11	26.3	12.9	232,624.8	30,008.6
1961	14.7	18.5	23.1	11	33.3	12.1	1,215,483.2	147,073.5

[a] Inflation figures provided to indicate real interest rates. They have not been used to calculate subsidy because commercial bank loans, considered the alternative, also were subsidized in this way.

Sources: (1)(2) and (3) from A.C. Sochaczewski, "Financial and Economic Development of Brazil, 1952-1968" (Ph.D. diss., University of London, 1980). Effective rate defined as 25% greater than nominal rate (includes fees, etc.).
(4) BNDE, *Relatório do BNDE* (Rio de Janeiro, 1959) — rate charged to basic industry with minimum of six months' grace period and at least five-year amortization.
(5) Albert Fishlow, "Foreign Trade Regimes and Economic Development: Brazil" (unpublished manuscript, 1976).
(6) BNDE, *Relatório do BNDE*, various years. It is assumed that the loans are paid in five installments so that interest is charged on the full amount in year 1, on 4/5 in year 2, etc.

Table 4.13. *Deferred Fiscal Income*

A. *Deferred import tax revenue*
I. Investment under Instruction 113

	(1) Investment US$ millions	(2)[a] Tariff Cr$/US$	(3) Total Cr$ millions (1x2)	(4)[a] Customs tax Cr$/US$	(5) Total Cr$ millions (1x4)	(6) Total Cr$ millions (3+5)	(7)[b] Total US$ millions	(8) % (7÷1)
1957	32.9	30.57	1,005.8	3.82	125.7	1,131.5	14.95	45.0
1958	28.1	52.04	1,462.3	6.51	182.9	1,645.2	12.65	45.0
1959	19.2	73.64	1,413.9	9.21	176.8	1,590.7	10.16	52.9
1960	29.8	78.00	2,324.4	9.75	290.6	2,615.0	13.78	46.2

II. Financed equipment imports

	(1) Financed imports US$ thousands	(2)[a] Tariff	(3) Total Cr$ thousands (1x2)	(4)[a] Custom tax Cr$/US$	(5) Total Cr$ thousands (1x4)	(6) Total Cr$ thousands (3+5)	(7)[b] Total US$ thousands	(8) % (7÷1)
1957	250	30.57	7,642.5	3.82	955.0	8,597.5	113.6	45.0
1958	11,107	52.04	578,008.3	6.51	72,306.6	650,314.9	5,000.1	45.0
1959	13,118	73.64	966,009.5	9.21	120,816.8	1,086,826.3	6,940.1	52.9
1960	14,358	78.00	1,119,924.0	9.75	139,990.5	1,259,914.5	6,640.6	46.3

III. Total Cr$ millions

1957	1,140.1
1958	2,295.5
1959	2,677.5
1960	3,874.9

B. *Consumption tax deferred*
I. Investment under Instruction 113

	(1) Investment US$ millions	(2)[a] Conversion rate to fiscal dollar	(3) Cr$ millions (1x2)	(4)[a] Consumption tax (%)	(5) Total Cr$ millions (3x4)	(6)[b] Total US$ millions	(7) %
1957	32.9	114.58	3,769.7	5	188.5	2.49	7.6
1958	28.1	206.66	5,807.1	5	290.4	2.23	7.9
1959	19.2	282.09	5,416.1	8	433.3	2.77	14.7
1960	29.8	310.50	9,252.9	8	740.2	3.90	13.1
II. On financed equipment							
1957	.250	79.67	19.9	5	.995	.013	5.2
1958	11.107	113.39	1,259.4	5	62.97	.484	4.4
1959	13.118	161.34	2,116.5	8	169.32	1.081	8.2
1960	14.358	165.90	2,382.0	8	190.56	1.004	7.0

C. *Totals (A and B)*

	Cr$ millions	US$ millions[b]
1957	1,329.6	17.57
1958	2,648.9	20.37
1959	3,280.1	20.95
1960	4,805.7	25.32
1957-60		84.21

[a] Taken from José Almeida, "A indústria automobilística brasileira" (unpublished manuscript; Rio de Janeiro: Fundação Getúlio Vargas, Instituto Brasileiro de Economia, Centro de Estudos Industriais, 1969).
[b] Converted at the free exchange rate.

the year in which they were contracted. Converted into dollars at the free market rate, the total subsidy from 1956 to 1961 amounted to about US$1.23 million.

The industry was also eligible for BNDE foreign loan guarantees, but it is difficult to ascribe an implicit subsidy to them. The guarantees were not very important to the terminal producers, as only two firms – Simca and the FNM – benefited from them.

Fiscal Benefits

Equipment imports were exempt from custom duties and consumption taxes. Historically, importers of capital goods had been exempt from import taxes. By the mid-1950s, their value was virtually nil: They had been fixed taxes, eroded by inflation. With the 1957 exchange reform, they were replaced by an ad valorem tax. Table 4.13 shows that they were between 45 and 52 percent of the value of the imports. Consumption taxes were not as high, ranging from 4 to 15 percent.

Total Subsidies

Omitting BNDE financing, total subsidies on US$421.4 million of imported investment goods and complementary parts came to US$202.9 million, or 48 percent (see Table 4.14). Proportionally, the biggest subsidies were custom-duty exemptions and the cost-of-exchange import rate. Had the latter continued to apply to all financed imports, the rate of subsidization would have been significantly higher. The elimination of the exchange subsidy on imported parts – a smaller percentage but applied to a larger value – in 1960 also reduced the overall subsidy. Although this figure represents 48 cents per dollar of investment in the terminal sector, it is lower than José Almeida's previous estimate of 89 cents for the entire industry (including the parts sector).[13]

Taxes

The Brazilian tax system underwent a variety of changes during this period. Indirect taxes on production and sales, as compared with income taxes, represented a significant and growing portion of total

[13] José Almeida, *A implantação da indústria automobilística no Brasil* (Rio de Janeiro: Fundação Getúlio Vargas, 1972), p. 41.

Table 4.14. *Total Subsidy*

	1956	1957	1958	1959	1960	1961	1956-60
Investment (US$ millions)							
I. Instruction 113	4.7	32.9	28.1	19.2	29.8		114.7
II. Financing	2.7	.3	11.1	13.1	14.4		41.6
III. Parts		10.9	54.8	100.5	98.9		265.1
Total	7.4	44.1	94.0	132.8	143.1		421.4
BNDE (Cr$ millions)						1,060.4	
Subsidies (Cr$ millions)							
A. Exchange subsidies							
I. Instruction 113	138.9	820.2	516.8	822.7	1,289.4		
II. Financing	26.6	30.1	103.4	167.5	192.4		
III. Parts		295.7	3,014.8	9,278.9	--		
B. Fiscal subsidies							
IV. Import taxes		1,140.1	2,295.5	2,677.5	3,874.9		
V. Consumption taxes		189.5	353.4	602.6	930.8		
VI. BNDE Interest subsidy			35.3	35.0	30.0	147.1	
Total subsidy							
VII. Excluding BNDE							
(Cr$ millions)	165.5	2,475.6	6,283.9	13,549.2	6,287.5		
(US$ millions) at free rate	2.25	32.7	48.3	86.5	33.1		202.9
As % of total investment	30.4	74.2	51.4	65.1	23.1		48
VIII. Excluding BNDE and parts (Cr$ millions)	165.5	2,179.9	3,269.1	4,270.3	6,287.5		
US$ millions at free rate	2.25	28.8	25.1	27.3	33.1		115.2
As % of Instruction 113 and financing	30.5	87	64	84.5	74.8		73.7

tax revenues.[14] The annual taxes paid by the assemblers alone (not including the parts sector) are listed in Table 4.15. These figures, which do not include exchange agios or income taxes paid to the federal government, indicate that tax revenues covered the costs of all subsidies by 1960. It is fair to assume that most subsidies on investment and on imported components ended by 1961. Little new investment was made from that time until the industry entered its second growth cycle in 1967. Moreover, because of reforms in the foreign-exchange regime, the differentials in import rates all but disappeared. Therefore, all tax revenues received after 1960 were net gains to the public sector.

Furthermore, until the tax reform of 1967, which replaced the cascading value-added state tax on sales and consignments (*imposto sobre vendas e consignações*) with a sales tax (*imposto de circulação de mercadorias*), the total tax earnings originating in the industry were much greater than those paid by the assemblers, because the sector was taxed at each stage of production and distribution. Total taxes, including those paid by suppliers and dealers, were 26.9 percent of a vehicle's final sales price in 1962 (30.71 percent for cars, 23.44 percent for trucks).[15] According to Almeida, taxes were approximately 20 percent of GNP in the early 1960s and 24 percent in 1966.[16] The auto sector, therefore, apparently was taxed at a higher than average rate.

Tax revenues generated by the industry increased with expanded sales volumes, and tax rates also went up, so taxes represented a significant and rising share of vehicle sales during this period. As shown in Table 4.16, cars were taxed at higher rates than trucks. In 1962, taxes represented 17.05 percent of factory costs for automobiles and only 9.87 percent for trucks. In 1964, the numbers were 23.2 and 11.0 percent, respectively.[17] Taxes were then reduced in 1965 as part of an anti-inflation package.[18] The tax reform of 1967 ended the

---

[14] Between 1956 and 1960, the share of direct taxes in total tax revenues fell relative to indirect taxes. The latter's share rose from 66% in 1956 to 72% in 1960. Demosthenes Pinho, "The Brazilian Economic Policy in the Late 1950s: A Tentative Outline of the Period" (unpublished manuscript; University of California, Berkeley, 1987).

[15] ANFAVEA, *Indústria automobilística brasileira*, 1963.

[16] José Almeida, "*A indústria automobilística brasileira*" (unpublished manuscript; Rio de Janeiro: Fundação Getúlio Vargas, Instituto de Economia, Centro de Estudos Industriais, 1969).

[17] ANFAVEA, *Indústria automobilística brasileira*, 1963 and 1964.

[18] The comparison with Mexico is noteworthy in this regard. Brazil was generally less concerned with the inflationary impact of policy and therefore with the implications

Table 4.15. *Taxes Paid by Motor Vehicle Producers*

	Taxes	Subsidy
1957	Cr$ .984 billions	Cr$ 2.5 billions
1958	3.3	6.3
1959	6.8	13.5
1960	12.1	6.3
1961	18.9	
1962	32.6	
1963	80.9	
1964	*a*	
1965	NCr$ 226,425,000	
1966	407,362,828	
1967	625,601,522	
1968	854,168,519	
1969	1,058,901,014	
1970	1,538,541,867	
1971	2,064,012,224	

Notes: Taxes only on motor vehicle production not including tractors. Excludes exchange agios and income taxes.
Includes the following:
1) Imposto de vendas e consignações: 4.8% (São Paulo) of sales price to dealer
2) Consumption tax: 3-30%
3) Industry and professions tax
4) Import tax: rate depends on vehicle type and value of components not yet nationalized
5) Customs tax
6) Port improvement tax
7) Tax for the renovation of the merchant marine
8) Additional custom taxes
9) Federal stamp tax
10) Union tax
11) Patent registry
12) Rural land tax
13) License tax
14) Urban land and building tax
15) Road conservation tax
a Unknown.
Sources: 1957: estimated from 1958, Conselho do Desenvolvimento-GEIA, *Relatório*.
1958-62: ANFAVEA, *Indústria automobilística brasileira* (São Paulo: ANFAVEA, 1963).
1963 : ANFAVEA, *Indústria automobilística brasileira* (São Paulo: ANFAVEA, 1964).
1965: Congresso Nacional, Câmara dos Deputados, "Relatório da Comissão Parlamentar de Inqúerito Destinado a Verificar o Custo de Veículo Nacional," *Diário do Congresso Nacional*, Suplemento (A) ao no. 152, September 5, 1968.
1966-71: ANFAVEA, *Indústria automobilística brasileira* (São Paulo: ANFAVEA, 1971).

Table 4.16. *Tax Rates: Taxes as a Percentage of Consumer Sales Price*

	1962	1963	1964	1965	1966	1967	1968
I. All vehicles							
Taxes	29.5	31.8	33.1	32.4	36.0	29.9	31.8
Parafiscal contributions and compulsory loans	3.0	3.4	3.3	2.9	3.7	4.4	4.3
Total	32.5	35.2	36.4	35.3	39.7	34.3	36.1
II. Cars and utility vehicles							
Taxes	30.4	33.8	35.6	34.3	38.3	32.0	34.0
Parafiscal contributions and compulsory loans	3.0	3.3	3.2	2.9	3.7	4.5	4.4
Total	33.4	37.1	38.8	37.2	42.0	36.5	38.4
III. Trucks and buses							
Taxes	28.4	28.3	29.1	29.3	32.7	27.3	29.1
Parafiscal contributions and compulsory loans	3.1	3.5	3.4	3.0	3.8	4.3	4.2
Total	31.5	31.8	32.5	32.3	36.5	31.6	33.3

Note: There is some discrepancy between these tax rates and those provided by ANFAVEA. Almeida covers the entire sector.

Source: José Almeida, "A indústria automobilística brasileira" (unpublished manuscript; Rio de Janeiro: Fundação Getúlio Vargas, Instituto Brasileiro de Economia, Centro de Economia, Centro de Estudos Industriais, 1969).

intermediate value-added taxes. Over time, the bulk of taxes came to fall on final production as the intermediate value-added taxes were removed.

Manufacturers complained about Brazil's relatively high tax bite.[19] They pointed to it as a major reason for high sales prices and claimed that it reduced the size of the market.[20] In blaming tax policy for shrinking demand, they implicitly assumed that Brazilian demand for motor vehicles was sensitive to price. However, demand elasticity with respect to price was relatively low, particularly in the industry's early days of inadequate supply. As Alfredo Luiz Baumgarten, Jr., has shown, in these years the Brazilian market differed from that in developed countries, because its growth was based on new demand rather than on reposition; he estimated price elasticity to be -1.9, as compared to income elasticity of 6.3.[21] The nature of the product and the market is precisely what permitted the government to increase both the tax rate and total revenues over time. Until the mid-1960s, passenger cars were luxury goods facing relatively inelastic demand with respect to price. Even as the tax rate was increased, firms were able to pass these additional costs along to consumers without reducing demand or tax revenues.

The emphasis here is on whether the industry was self-financing from the government's point of view rather than on its intrinsic revenue-generating capacity. By that criterion, it was a successful high-taxed sector. Furthermore, given that automobile consumption was restricted to the upper classes at this time, the tax was a progressive one – an unusual feature in Brazil.

of high tax rates on the price level. It could continue to generate tax revenues in this way and ultimately pay for the costs of establishing the industry. Mexico, in contrast, was more constrained with respect to inflation. According to Baranson, Mexico controlled prices and profit margins of the end producers (Jack Baranson, *Automotive Industries in Developing Countries*, World Bank Occasional Staff Paper no. 8 [Washington, D.C.: World Bank, 1969], p. 37, n. 8).

[19] According to Baranson, indirect taxes (corporate, excise, and social security) were 11.4% of U.S. factory costs for light trucks and cars in 1967. His comparable figures for Argentina, Brazil, and Mexico were 31.9%, 33.8%, and 10.8%, respectively (Baranson, *Automotive Industries in Developing Countries*, p. 34).

[20] See John C. Goulden, general director of Ford do Brasil, and Damon Martin, Jr., president of General Motors do Brasil, Testimonies before the Parliamentary Inquest Commission for the Verification of the Cost of the National Vehicle, October 10, 1967, and October 11, 1967, GEIA Archives, Conselho do Desenvolvimento, Ministério de Indústria e Comércio, Rio de Janeiro.

[21] Alfredo Luiz Baumgarten, Jr., "Demanda de automóveis no Brasil," *Revista Brasileira Econômica* 26 (1972): 290.

Table 4.17. *Tax Revenues Net of Potential Imports*

	(1) Vehicles produced	(2) Taxes Cr$ billions	(3) Taxes per vehicle Cr$	(4) Vehicles produced minus 40,000	(5) Tax revenue on (4) Cr$ billions
1957	30,542	.98	32,218	--	--
1958	60,983	3.30	54,113	20,983	1.14
1959	96,114	6.80	70,749	56,114	3.97
1960	133,041	12.10	90,949	93,041	8.46
1961	145,584	18.90	129,822	105,584	13.71
1962	191,194	32.60	170,507	151,194	25.80

Nevertheless, it must be noted that the government would also have earned tax revenues had Brazil continued to import vehicles. To avoid double-counting, revenues from import taxes foregone would have to be netted out of revenues gained from domestic production. How many vehicles Brazil would have imported in the absence of domestic production is not clear or imputable from the postwar data. If one assumes a continual foreign exchange constraint, a high import volume would not have been sustainable. It is arguable, therefore, that the number of imported vehicles would have been lower than the amount produced domestically.

To get a rough estimate of the net tax revenues generated by domestically produced vehicles, it was assumed that an average of 40,000 vehicles would have been imported annually.[22] Total tax revenues were divided by the number of vehicles produced to arrive at average taxes per vehicle. Tax payments for 40,000 vehicles were then subtracted from each year's actual total. The net tax revenues listed in Table 4.17 indicate that tax revenue still would have outstripped the value of subsidies by 1960, although by a smaller margin.

From these data, therefore, a circular, self-financing program can be observed: Firms were given indirect subsidies, and consumers reimbursed the government through production and sales taxes. As will be discussed, firms were forced to absorb an increasing portion of this tax incidence from the mid-1960s.

Given this circularity, the question arises of why the subsidies were

[22] Average annual vehicle imports from 1946 to 1956 were about 48,000 units. In 1951 and 1952, years of import liberalization, vehicle imports climbed to over 109,000 and 85,000, respectively (see Table 2.3). Kubitschek's Working Group on Motor Vehicles (GEIA's predecessor) estimated that the total demand for vehicles would be 115,000 by 1962.

necessary to begin with. It seems to support foreign firms' skepticism about subsidies as described in Chapter 3, which was based on their presumption "that what the government gives with one hand it may well take away with the other."[23] As previously mentioned, this perception overlooks the state's absorption of all the risk involved in establishing the industry. As a result of subsidies, the firms were protected whether or not the market materialized. Had it failed to do so, the state would have been left with the losses.

Prices, Costs, and Profits

While taxes increased as a percentage of total costs, profits' share declined. The data also show that vehicle production costs and prices fell over time. Rents paid by the consumer were not simply redistributed from the transnational firms to the state through the increased tax rate, however. Rather, significant idle capacity, intensified competition, increased demand sensitivity to price, and, ultimately, price controls forced firms to pass along some of the production savings to the consumer and to absorb part of the tax bite themselves.

Ex-Factory Prices

Data on wholesale prices are available for 1962–8 and for some earlier years. Almeida provides the most complete data set on an aggregate level. These data were culled from questionnaires completed by eight terminal producers that accounted for 90 percent of vehicle production, 88 percent of the total value of production, and 81.5 percent of registered capital in the industry in 1967.[24] The Conselho do Desenvolvimento–GEIA price study of 1958 and the 1968 report of the Parliamentary Commission on Vehicle Cost provide firm data for 1957 and 1963–7, respectively.[25] Data on consumer prices are more difficult to come by. Wholesale prices probably are an adequate proxy because the firms tried to maintain a constant percentage markup for their

---

[23] Richard E. Caves, *Multinational Enterprise and Economic Analysis* (Cambridge: Cambridge University Press, 1982), p. 258.

[24] Almeida, "A indústria automobilística brasileira," p. 13.

[25] Presidência da República, Conselho do Desenvolvimento-GEIA, "Relatório dos Trabalhos do Subgrupo de Estudo de Formação dos Preços na Indústria Automobilística Brasileira" (Rio de Janeiro, January 1958); and Congresso Nacional, Camara dos Deputados, "Relatório da Comissão Parlamentar de Inquérito Destinada a Verificar o Custo de Veículo Nacional," *Diário do Congresso Nacional,* suplemento (A) ao no. 152, September 5, 1968.

Table 4.18. *Passenger Car Relative Price Index, According to*
Alternative Deflators, 1961-1978 (1968=100)

Year	I	II	III	IV	General price index
1961	133	140	140	143	5.72
1962	122	127	130	131	8.68
1963	140	131	152	152	15.2
1964	134	134	145	148	29.0
1965	125	115	128	125	45.5
1966	105	103	105	106	62.8
1967	98.6	104	97.1	98.1	80.5
1968	100	100	100	100	100
1969	96.5	95.0	95.7	95.0	121
1970	90.0	84.2	87.0	88.8	145
1971	84.7	83.2	81.8	82.8	174
1972	81.2	82.8	79.2	78.9	204
1973	78.1	78.5	77.8	75.9	235
1974	72.3	67.2	72.5	72.0	302
1975	77.0	71.3	76.4	75.5	386
1976	68.5	67.5	67.7	69.8	545
1977	67.9	72.5	66.6	70.2	777
1978	68.0	78.1	66.7	70.6	1,078

Notes: Values correspond to a Laspeyres chain price index deflated by:
I: General price index – goods and services for domestic use (column 2 of *Conjuntura Econômica*).
II: Metal and metal products price index (column 21 of *Conjuntura Econômica*).
III: Rio de Janeiro cost-of-living index *(Conjuntura Econômica).*
IV: São Paulo cost-of-living index *(Conjuntura Econômica).*
Source: Computed from ANFAVEA production data and producers' price lists published in *Quatro Rodas* by Eduardo Augusto de Almeida Guimarães, "Industry, Market Structure and the Growth of the Firm in the Brazilian Economy" (Ph.D. diss., University of London, 1980).

dealers.[26] Eduardo Augusto de Almeida Guimarães's data on retail price trends for passenger cars are in fact similar to those found with respect to wholesale prices (see Tables 4.18 and 4.19).

As seen in Table 4.20 and Figure 4.1, wholesale prices for all vehicles remained essentially unchanged in real terms from 1960 to 1968. However, prices had risen dramatically by 1963 and then proceeded to fall to their 1960 levels. The pattern is clearly countercyclical, with the largest price increases occurring in years when production fell most sharply. High inflation, particularly in 1963, also facilitated real

---

[26] The 1968 "Relatório da Comissão Parlamentar" comes to a similar conclusion and also relies on wholesale costs.

Table 4.19. *Average Price of Passenger Cars by Size Class, 1961-1978*
(1978 Cr$ thousands)

Year	Small cars	Medium cars	Medium-large cars	Large cars
1961	126	168	220	--
1962	113	164	195	--
1963	133	191	230	--
1964	126	188	226	--
1965	116	144	235	--
1966	102	139	200	259
1967	98.8	140	193	266
1968	101	139	189	255
1969	97.7	138	174	269
1970	94.8	126	158	254
1971	88.1	120	144	215
1972	82.8	114	134	215
1973	85.9	109	136	201
1974	81.4	104	132	192
1975	88.3	110	132	218
1976	80.9	101	121	185
1977	79.1	110	130	224
1978	80.7	103	127	241

Notes: Annual average prices weighted by annual output. Values inflated by the general price index (column 2 of *Conjuntura Econômica*).
Source: See Table 4.18.

price increases. Pricing policies did change when price controls were implemented in 1965. These controls essentially were cost-plus, however, which still allowed prices to accommodate rising costs as production levels fell.

Production and pricing trends differed between automobiles and utility vehicles on the one hand and trucks and buses on the other. Automobile production, with the exception of a slight dip in 1965, continuously increased from 1960 to 1968. Real prices also fell, with the exception of 1963, a high-inflation year. There was also much less idle capacity in car facilities. A spurt of new investment came on-line in 1961 and helped push idle capacity up to 48.5 percent; but thereafter production levels increased annually so that idle capacity fell to 33 percent by 1967, before the next wave of investment in 1968. Furthermore, as shown in Tables 4.21 and 4.22, aggregate data obscure the great disparity among firms' individual performances. Volkswagen, responsible for more than 50 percent of car production, had no idle capacity from 1963 to 1967 and essentially determined

Table 4.20. *Real Price Changes Relative to Production*

	I. Nominal price increase		II. GDP deflator		III. Real price changes		IV. Production	
	Change (%)	Index	Change (%)	Index	Change (%)	Index	Change (%)	Index
A. All vehicles								
1960		100		100		100		100
1961	38.5	138.5	33.3	133.3	5.2	105.2	4.7	104.7
1962	43.4	198.6	54.8	206.3	-11.4	93.2	25.4	131.3
1963	117.6	432.2	78.0	367.2	39.6	130.1	-11.8	115.8
1964	83.9	794.8	87.8	689.6	-3.9	125.0	8.3	125.4
1965	48.7	1,181.9	55.4	1,071.6	-6.7	116.6	-2.2	122.6
1966	21.4	1,434.8	38.8	1,487.4	-17.4	96.3	28.7	157.8
1967	35.6	1,945.6	27.1	1,890.5	8.5	104.5	4.2	164.4
1968	24.2	2,416.4	27.8	2,416.1	-3.6	100.7	29.3	212.6
B. Cars and utility vehicles								
1960						100.0		100.0
1961	23.4				-9.9	90.1	28.3	128.3
1962	43.7				-11.1	80.1	20.8	155.0
1963	114.6				36.6	109.4	6.3	164.8
1964	80.0				-7.8	100.9	8.2	178.3
1965	46.7				-8.7	92.1	-3.5	172.1
1966	23.1				-15.7	77.6	19.9	206.3
1967	35.4				8.3	84.0	10.6	228.2
1968	24.9				-2.9	81.6	18.2	269.7

C. Trucks and buses

1960		100		100
1961	26.4	126.4	-28.5	71.5
1962	-11.8	111.5	34.3	96.0
1963	45.1	161.7	-36.3	61.2
1964	1.7	164.4	9.3	66.9
1965	-2.8	159.8	.4	67.2
1966	-21.4	125.6	45.7	97.9
1967	8.8	136.7	-7.8	90.3
1968	-4.8	130.1	50.0	135.5

Source: José Almeida, "A indústria automobilística brasileira" (unpublished manuscript; Rio de Janeiro: Fundação Getúlio Vargas, Instituto Brasileiro de Economia, Centro de Estudos Industriais, 1969), for raw data.

167

Perct. Chng./Production & Real Prices

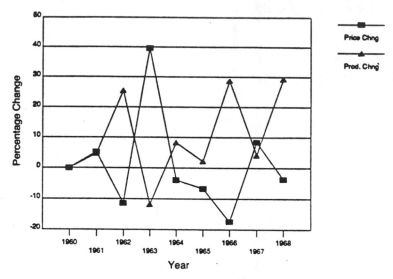

Indices of Production and Real Prices

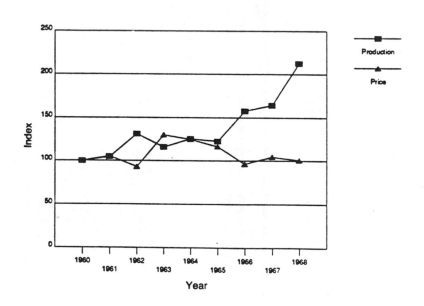

Figure 4.1. Real Price Changes Relative to Production; (A) *All vehicles.*

168

Perct. Chng./Production & Real Prices

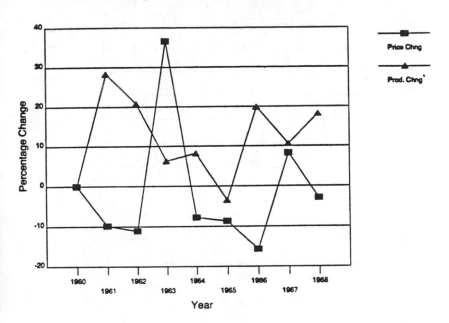

Indices of Production and Real Prices

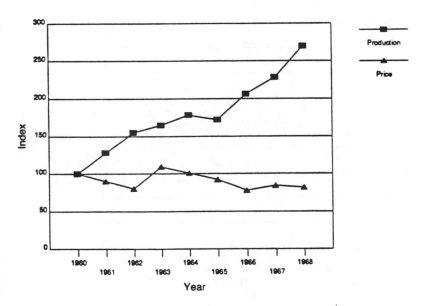

Figure 4.1. (B) *Cars and utility vehicles.*

169

Perct. Chng./Production & Real Prices

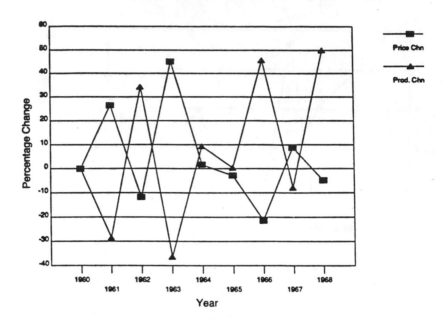

Indices of Production and Real Prices

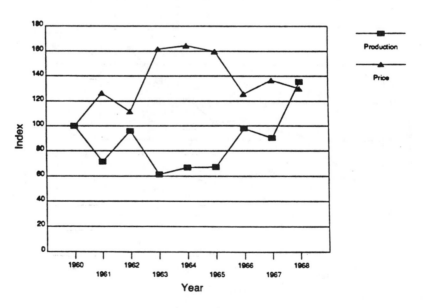

Figure 4.1. (C) *Trucks and buses.*

170

Table 4.21. *Idle Capacity, 1957-1968*

Year	Installed capacity			Effective production			Idle capacity (%)		
	All vehicles	Autos	Trucks	All vehicles	Autos	Trucks	All vehicles	Autos	Trucks
1957	30,700	11,853	18,847	30,700	10,845	19,855	0.0	8.5	0.0
1958	84,030	50,200	33,830	61,129	25,521	35,608	27.3	49.2	0.0
1959	138,630	81,040	57,590	96,243	48,679	47,564	30.6	39.9	17.4
1960	199,180	116,520	82,660	133,078	81,753	51,325	33.2	29.8	37.9
1961	335,500	208,000	127,500	145,674	107,218	38,456	56.6	48.5	69.8
1962	345,700	218,200	127,500	191,194	138,542	52,652	44.7	36.5	58.7
1963	354,700	227,200	127,500	174,126	140,500	33,626	50.9	38.2	73.6
1964	361,700	234,200	127,500	183,735	148,835	34,900	49.2	36.4	72.6
1965	369,700	242,200	127,500	185,173	152,581	32,592	49.9	37.0	74.4
1966	380,700	262,200	118,500	224,575	180,581	43,994	41.0	31.1	62.9
1967	374,700	274,200	100,500	225,389	183,634	41,755	39.8	33.0	58.5
1968	482,200	380,200	102,000	279,715	219,920	59,795	42.0	42.2	41.4

Source: See Table 4.20.

Table 4.22. *Idle Capacity by Firm (%)*

	1963	1964	1965	1966	1967[a]
Chrysler	20	74	15	43	26
Ford	64	64	67	61	45
GM	39	30	45	20	24
Mercedes-Benz	57	53	49	21	17
Scania Vabis[b]	60	32	24	--	48
Toyota	50	25	68	70	34
Vemag	35	50	49	45	42
Volkswagen	0	0	0	0	0
Willys Jeep	46	46	49	39	35

[a] For production until August 1967.
[b] Obtained from declared idle capacity in August 1967.
Source: Congresso Nacional, Camara dos Deputados, "Relatório da Comissão Parlamentar de Inquérito Destinada a Verificar o Custo de Veículo Nacional," *Diário do Congresso Nacional,* Suplemento (A) ao no. 152, September 5, 1968.

the performance of the automobile sector. As will be discussed, its real costs and prices fell over this period.

Trucks, on the other hand, suffered a severe drop in demand and did not recover 1962 levels of production until 1968. The truck sector was operating with almost twice the idle capacity of the passenger-car sector for many of these years. Truck pricing exhibits a clearer countercyclical pricing trend, and real prices in 1968 were higher than in 1960. As a result, and despite the quickly increasing share of automobiles in total production, the average price for all motor vehicles was virtually the same in 1968 as it had been in 1960.

Cost Structure

Although total ex-factory prices rose slightly from 1962 to 1968 and fell from 1963, not all costs rose at the same rate, so that the cost structure at the end of the period had changed substantially. As shown in Table 4.23, indirect costs rose relative to direct costs. This increase was almost completely due to a rise in taxes from 16.7 percent in 1962 to 26.2 percent in 1968. Components' share of total costs fell from 44.1 to 33.7 percent (including components purchased from third parties and those made in-house), and profits per vehicle fell from 5.5 to 3.1 percent.

Looking from another angle, Almeida also breaks up total costs into intermediate consumption and value added, the latter including taxes and remuneration of labor and capital (see Table 4.24). Value added

Table 4.23. *Automotive Industry Cost Structure, 1962-1968 (%)*

	1962	1963	1964	1965	1966	1967	1968
Direct costs	56.5	46.7	46.4	50.6	51.6	48.8	47.4
Raw materials	8.8	6.5	6.9	8.3	9.2	8.2	8.7
Components	44.1	36.7	35.7	37.7	37.2	35.2	33.7
Combustibles and lubricants	.4	.4	.5	.5	.5	.5	.4
Electric energy	.2	.2	.3	.6	.6	.6	.5
Labor	3.0	2.9	3.0	3.5	4.1	4.3	4.1
Indirect costs	38.0	46.8	48.9	44.2	45.5	50.7	49.5
Administrative expenses	4.8	5.6	5.2	4.7	5.0	5.4	5.4
Sales expenses	11.3	16.6	12.3	11.6	12.0	12.9	11.8
Financial expenses	2.0	1.5	2.1	2.1	1.3	1.6	1.2
Taxes	16.7	20.9	22.2	18.6	21.2	24.9	26.2
Depreciation	3.2	2.2	7.1	7.2	6.0	5.9	4.9
Total costs	94.5	93.5	95.3	94.8	97.1	99.5	96.9
Profit	5.5	6.5	4.7	5.2	2.9	.5	3.1
Value of production	100	100	100	100	100	100	100

Source: See Table 4.20.

Table 4.24. *Automotive Industry Value Added (%)*

	1962	1963	1964	1965	1966	1967	1968
1. Value of production	100	100	100	100	100	100	100
2. Material used in production	79.3	79.5	75.8	72.8	76.6	77.3	78.8
3. Gross value-added	20.7	20.5	24.2	27.2	23.4	22.7	21.2
Depreciation	3.2	2.2	7.1	7.3	6.0	5.8	4.9
4. Net value-added	17.5	18.3	17.1	19.9	17.4	16.9	16.3
Salaries	8.4	8.3	8.6	10.7	11.4	11.4	10.9
Return on capital	9.1	10.0	8.5	9.2	6.0	5.5	5.4
Profits	5.5	6.5	4.7	5.2	2.9	2.3	2.9
Interest	2.0	1.5	2.1	2.1	1.3	1.7	1.2
Royalties and technical assistance	1.6	2.0	1.7	1.9	1.8	1.5	1.3

Source: See Table 4.20.

as a percentage of total costs remained fairly constant over this period, but its composition changed. Profits as a percentage of the value of production fell from 5.5 to 2.9 percent; their share of value added net of depreciation fell from 31 to 18 percent. Almeida concludes from these and pricing data that the full tax increase was not passed on to consumers but was partly absorbed by the producers.

Individual firm data support Almeida's conclusions. As shown in Tables 4.25 and 4.26, cars were taxed at a higher rate than trucks, and taxes as a percentage of vehicle price were increasing over this period for all vehicles. Real costs net of taxes fell from 1963 to 1967 for most firms, although these decreases become less substantial or disappear if 1964 is taken as the base year. Factory prices fell faster than costs, so the profit share per vehicle declined. The fall in factory price is more notable from 1963. In that year, high inflation allowed real price increases that more than compensated for the high costs incurred (from inflation and low volumes of production).

Performance did vary by firm to some degree. General Motors, Volkswagen, and Mercedes-Benz all had reductions in production costs, whereas the costs of Toyota and Vemag increased. They all suffered absolute reductions in profits. However, GM and Volkswagen (with the exception of the Kombi van in 1966) were the only two firms that managed to avoid losses. Ford began to show losses on all its vehicles in 1967, and Toyota, Mercedes, and some of the Willys lines showed losses for most of these years.

The reasons for these trends are various. First, the nature of the market was changing. By 1961 the industry began to experience its first difficulties; planned investment was mostly on-stream, and total capacity now greatly surpassed market capacity. The repressed demand from the 1950s had been largely satisfied.[27] Future growth would now depend on replacement demand and on new demand from increased incomes, population growth, and so on. GNP growth rates fell in 1962 and plummeted in 1963, which especially affected the demand for trucks. Minimum wages plunged 20 percent from 1964 to 1967. High inflation rates in 1963 and 1964 facilitated the transfer of cost increases (including taxes) to the consumer, which became more difficult when inflation ebbed. Price controls further complicated matters. Firms began to compete more intensely for market share, and new forms of competition emerged. Also, as would be

---

[27] Eduardo Augusto de Almeida Guimarães, "Industry, Market Structure and the Growth of the Firm in the Brazilian Economy" (Ph.D. diss., University of London, 1980), pp. 180–4.

Table 4.25. *1957 Cost Structure by Firm (Cr$)*

	DKW Vemag	GM Chevrolet	Ford	Mercedes	Willys Jeep
Industrial costs	197,628.00	264,736.00	289,333.30	349,725.00	159,941.62
Indirect costs	28,206.50	25,045.00	17,432.40	51,429.23	32,960.86
Taxes	13,985.20[a]	48,152.00	49,188.10	42,025.36	23,506.15
Subtotal	239,819.70	337,933.00	355,953.80	443,179.59	216,408.63
Net profit	7,054.00	31,367.00	37,046.20	53,470.41	23,591.37
Factory price	246,873.70	369,300.00	393,000.00	496,650.00	240,000.00
Expenses and profits of dealers	100,426.30	98,700.00	131,000.00	148,350.00	55,000.00
Price to public	347,300.00	468,000.00	524,000.00	645,000.00	295,000.00
Taxes					
% of total costs	5.83	14.25	13.82	9.49	10.86
% of factory price	5.66	13.03	12.52	8.46	9.79
Profits					
% of total costs	2.94	9.28	10.41	12.07	10.90
% of factory price	2.86	8.49	9.43	10.77	9.83

[a] Not including income tax on profits.

Source: Presidência da República, Conselho do Desenvolvimento-GEIA, "Relatório dos Trabalhos do Subgrupo de Estudos da Formação dos Preços na Indústria Automobilística Brasileira" (Rio de Janeiro, January 1958).

expected as replacement demand became a larger part of the market, some price elasticity was becoming evident. Volkswagen claimed in its 1967 annual report,

> The past year demonstrated that market difficulties can only be overcome by rationalization measures which result in cost reductions and productivity increases. The conquest of the client was no longer limited to arguments about quality. Much more than that and already without the influence of violent inflation, the decisive argument was price. A consolidation of the process of monetary stabilization is transferring the center of decision-making, from a seller's market insensitive to criticisms to a demanding buyer's market that is better informed about conditions of competition.[28]

Second, as shown earlier, the tax rate on motor vehicles increased. Thus, tax-rate increases, together with price controls and a weak market, resulted in lower profits per vehicle.

Profits on Capital

Attempts to measure profits on capital encounter many problems. Generating a consistent series is very difficult because of high inflation rates. Fixed assets were maintained at their historic rates, whereas profits were calculated in current cruzeiros. Consequently, profits on fixed capital were artificially increased. Moreover, firms were forced to revalue their assets in 1965, so the performance of those firms that had not yet revalued appeared worse than in previous years. Also, in 1967 companies were allowed to depreciate their revalued assets, so the rate of depreciation increased. Finally, profits can be hidden within other accounts such as technical assistance and depreciation.

From survey data on the industry, Almeida calculated profits on fixed assets, on total assets, and on firms' own capital. The results, listed in Table 4.27, indicate that profit rates fell significantly from 1962 to 1968. In particular, profits on fixed assets fell from 18.4 percent in 1962 and a high of 24.1 percent in 1963 to 6.7 percent in 1968. Because of the revaluation, it is difficult to make strong inferences from this declining ratio. From profits on sales, it is fair to say that prices were not increasing as fast as costs and that greater volumes did not compensate for reduced profits per vehicle; the end result was a declining return on capital. Nevertheless, firms were able to

---

[28] Almeida, citing the *Relatório Anual do Exercício de 1967, Volkswagen do Brasil*, in "A indústria automobilística brasileira," p. 199.

Table 4.26 a. Cost Structure by Firm: Ford, General Motors, and Mercedes-Benz, 1963-1967

		Ford			General Motors		Mercedes-Benz
		F-350	F-600	F-100A	Mixed use truck	Medium truck	Cargo truck	Medium truck
I. Costs (pretax and preprofit)								
1963=100	1963	100.0	100.0	100.0				100.0
	1964	103.3	98.8	97.6				102.7
	1965	98.4	95.4	92.1				119.6
	1966	92.6	89.8	92.5				90.5
	1967	96.0	90.9	97.7				85.1
1964=100	1964	100.0	100.0	100.0	100.0	100.0	100.0	100.0
	1965	95.0	97.0	94.0	73.7	93.6	92.8	116.0
	1966	90.0	91.0	95.0	61.6	79.3	79.3	88.0
	1967	93.0	92.0	100.0	62.4	77.0	79.2	83.0
II. Costs (including taxes)								
1963=100	1963	100.0	100.0	100.0				100.0
	1964	103.1	99.7	98.9				105.0
	1965	99.7	97.6	95.0				121.0
	1966	94.8	93.0	96.7				94.2
	1967	98.6	93.6	101.3				91.0
1964=100	1964	100.0	100.0	100.0	100.0	100.0	100.0	100.0
	1965	96.0	98.0	96.0	73.1	93.2	92.3	115.0
	1966	92.0	93.0	98.0	61.6	79.7	79.6	90.0
	1967	96.0	94.0	102.0	63.1	77.2	79.8	87.0
III. Factory price								
1963=100	1963	100.0	100.0	100.0				100.0
	1964	91.1	95.0	96.1				117.9
	1965	87.5	96.5	92.9				102.6
	1966	82.2	88.2	91.2				96.7
	1967	77.0	81.4	86.2				94.0

				1964=100			
1964	100.0	100.0	100.0	100.0	100.0	100.0	100.0
1965	96.0	102.0	97.0	66.0	88.0	86.7	87.0
1966	90.0	93.0	95.0	58.0	80.8	80.1	82.0
1967	84.0	86.0	90.0	53.6	75.4	74.3	80.0
IV. Taxes as % of factory price							
1963	9.7	9.7	12.0	--	--	--	9.4
1964	10.9	10.9	13.0	6.0	6.0	6.1	10.3
1965	11.7	11.7	14.8	6.0	6.0	6.0	12.5
1966	13.2	13.3	16.0	6.4	6.4	6.3	13.0
1967	14.8	14.0	17.5	8.0	6.4	7.3	15.0
V. Profits as % of factory price							
1963	19.8	5.2	9.5	--	--	--	-5.6
1964	8.8	1.0	6.5	16.0	7.0	11.7	6.0
1965	9.0	4.1	7.4	7.0	1.5	6.0	-24.6
1966	7.2	--	4.0	12.1	8.3	12.2	-2.9
1967	-2.8	-9.0	-6.3	1.1	4.9	5.1	-2.3
VI. Production							
1963	1,513	6,909	4,541	763	7,004	4,298	4,613
1964	1,850	6,470	3,704	501	7,176	6,123	4,119
1965	2,016	6,435	3,303	1,253	6,624	3,077	4,752
1966	2,734	8,684	2,603	1,416	9,567	4,974	8,062
1967	2,715	6,242	1,816	2,136	9,031	5,967	8,795

Source: Raw data from Congresso Nacional, Camara dos Deputados, "Relatório da Comissão Parlamentar de Inquérito Destinado a Verificar o Custo de Veículo Nacional," *Diário do Congresso Nacional*, Suplemento (A) ao no. 152, September 5, 1968; production data from ANFAVEA, *Indústria automobilística brasileira* (São Paulo: ANFAVEA, various years).

Table 4.26 b. *Cost Structure by Firm: Toyota, Vemag, and Volkswagen, 1963-1967*

	Toyota		Vemag		Volkswagen		
	Truck	Jeep	Belcar	Vemaguet	Sedan	Van	Karmann Ghia
I. Costs (pretax and preprofit)							
1963 = 100							
1963	100.0	100.0	100.0	100.0	100.0	100.0	100.0
1964	102.6	109.1	77.2	90.6	98.8	103.0	95.3
1965	123.0	126.5	75.8	72.6	96.5	98.7	92.7
1966	111.2	112.6	95.6	99.2	85.0	91.5	81.6
1967	114.4	126.0	93.4	91.3	84.2	93.2	83.6
1964 = 100							
1964	100.0	100.0	100.0	100.0	100.0	100.0	100.0
1965	120.0	116.0	98.0	80.0	98.0	96.0	97.0
1966	108.0	103.0	124.0	109.0	86.0	89.0	86.0
1967	112.0	115.0	121.0	101.0	85.0	90.0	88.0
II. Costs (including taxes)							
1963 = 100							
1963	100.0	100.0	100.0	100.0	100.0	100.0	100.0
1964	102.4	110.5	80.4	92.6	101.3	105.2	97.7
1965	117.8	110.8	77.6	74.6	93.4	102.3	89.6
1966	112.5	113.6	94.9	105.5	87.4	100.2	83.5
1967	113.5	122.6	95.4	98.9	88.4	96.1	85.7
1964 = 100							
1964	100.0	100.0	100.0	100.0	100.0	100.0	100.0
1965	115.0	100.0	97.0	81.0	92.0	97.0	92.0
1966	110.0	103.0	118.0	114.0	86.0	95.0	85.0
1967	110.0	100.0	119.0	107.0	87.0	91.0	88.0
III. Factory price							
1963 = 100							
1963	100.0	100.0	100.0	100.0	100.0	100.0	100.0
1964	89.6	110.8	87.6	95.4	96.5	98.8	93.0
1965	80.4	100.9	77.7	74.1	86.8	91.9	82.7
1966	86.2	90.0	70.5	86.9	80.2	85.4	77.1
1967	79.4	86.4	86.7	90.8	81.8	88.6	78.5

1964 = 100							
1964	100.0	100.0	100.0	100.0	100.0	100.0	100.0
1965	90.0	91.0	89.0	78.0	90.0	93.0	90.0
1966	96.0	81.0	80.0	91.0	83.0	86.0	83.0
1967	89.0	78.0	99.0	95.0	85.0	90.0	84.0

IV. Taxes as % of factory price

1963	11.9	9.3	17.2	11.4	17.2	11.3	17.2
1964	13.4	10.5	18.6	12.7	19.9	13.7	20.0
1965	12.7	10.2	18.9	13.6	16.0	15.5	16.0
1966	16.6	12.9	22.5	19.8	20.8	20.8	24.3
1967	15.8	10.0	20.8	19.3	22.2	14.6	20.7

V. Profits as % of factory price

1963	15.5	-6.9	5.4	6.2	11.7	12.9	11.9
1964	3.5	-6.5	13.2	8.9	7.3	7.9	7.4
1965	-23.8	-32.4	5.5	5.6	5.0	3.6	4.5
1966	-10.2	-35.0	-12.8	-13.9	3.8	-1.4	4.6
1967	-20.4	-51.4	-4.1	-2.3	4.7	0.1	3.8

VI. Production

1963	291	1,001	7,541	6,267	42,362	14,428	1,868
1964	642	1,014	6,291	4,975	51,755	12,378	2,285
1965	423	367	5,519	3,847	59,966	13,114	1,951
1966	438	167	6,980	5,392	77,624	15,098	2,400
1967	367	88	6,007	5,009	91,821	20,221	3,009

Source: See Table 4.26 a.

Table 4.26 c. *Cost Structure by Firm: Willys, 1963-1967*

	Year	Aerowillys	Rural 4x2 and 4x4	Jeep	Gordini	Pick-up
I. Costs (pretax and preprofits)						
1963 = 100	1963	100.0	100.0	100.0	100.0	100.0
	1964	102.3	97.2	104.8	104.9	104.9
	1965	94.5	94.8	96.5	90.4	114.9
	1966	81.9	87.8	89.0	87.1	100.2
	1967	91.8	95.8	98.0	105.1	115.2
1964 = 100	1964	100.0	100.0	100.0	100.0	100.0
	1965	92.0	98.0	92.0	86.0	110.0
	1966	80.0	90.0	85.0	83.0	96.0
	1967	90.0	99.0	94.0	100.0	110.0
II. Costs (including taxes)						
1963 = 100	1963	100.0	100.0	100.0	100.0	100.0
	1964	105.9	98.8	106.6	106.8	107.7
	1965	92.1	98.3	97.8	89.0	101.0
	1966	92.2	96.3	92.0	89.6	99.0
	1967	99.6	101.0	100.3	106.2	106.0
1964 = 100	1964	100.0	100.0	100.0	100.0	100.0
	1965	87.0	99.0	92.0	83.0	94.0
	1966	87.0	97.0	86.0	84.0	92.0
	1967	94.0	102.0	94.0	99.0	98.0
III. Factory price						
1963 = 100	1963	100.0	100.0	100.0	100.0	100.0
	1964	104.3	93.8	106.2	70.9	104.9
	1965	95.0	88.9	91.8	54.7	93.2
	1966	90.4	83.1	82.7	51.4	86.2
	1967	90.0	83.1	85.7	52.0	88.0
1964 = 100	1964	100.0	100.0	100.0	100.0	100.0
	1965	91.0	95.0	86.0	77.0	89.0
	1966	87.0	89.0	78.0	72.0	82.0
	1967	86.0	89.0	81.0	73.0	84.0
IV. Taxes as % of factory price						
	1963	21.1	12.3	9.8	11.2	12.1
	1964	24.0	14.3	11.4	18.2	14.6
	1965	18.7	16.6	11.6	16.9	13.7
	1966	26.0	22.3	14.1	22.1	17.7
	1967	25.0	20.0	13.7	24.0	17.7
V. Profits as % of factory price						
	1963	4.7	9.2	5.0	-.7	11.3
	1964	3.2	4.4	4.6	-4.7	8.9
	1965	7.6	-.3	-1.1	-3.0	3.9
	1966	2.8	-5.1	-5.7	-10.4	-1.9
	1967	-5.5	-10.4	-11.7	-29.3	-6.9
VI. Production						
	1963	14,541	13,252	12,408	7,908	4,937
	1964	15,056	15,141	10,714	10,185	4,156
	1965	14,095	11,643	9,096	6,591	5,262
	1966	11,109	14,031	14,039	7,417	9,052
	1967	8,603	10,922	7,971	3,553	5,927

Source: See Table 4.26 a.

Table 4.27. *Profits (%)*

	Profit Own capital	Profit Fixed assets	Profit Total assets	Profits[a] Sales
1962	11.7	18.4	6.7	5.2
1963	13.8	24.1	8.6	6.5
1964	7.0	11.4	4.8	4.9
1965	7.5	10.4	5.3	5.2
1966	4.9	6.5	3.3	3.0
1967	0.8	1.0	0.6	0.6
1968	5.3	6.7	3.8	3.2

[a] Different ratios are offered by other sources. According to ANFAVEA, profits as a percentage of sales were 2.93% in 1962 and 4.0% in 1963. According to the "Relatório da Comissão Parlamentar," the percentage was 3.2% in 1965.
Source: See Table 4.20.

finance their investments through retained earnings and depreciation during each of these years except 1967.[29]

Production Costs

Individual firm data show that production costs net of taxes and profits fell from 1963 (see Table 4.26). Using 1963 as a base year is somewhat deceptive because production had fallen and the industry was operating with high rates of idle capacity. The drop in production costs is less significant if 1964 is used as a base. Total costs fell more substantially and, for most firms, profit reduction was responsible. Almeida found taxes to be responsible for the biggest percentage of ex-factory price increases.

The data are not available to explain fully the performance of those firms whose direct production costs did fall. In order to distinguish learning-by-doing from scale effects, it would be necessary to cover a particular plant over time, holding production volume constant. The Brazilian case is particularly complicated, as domestic content was increasing over time and the nature of the product was changing due to diversification. Some firms were reaping the benefits of scale economies as their production levels markedly increased. As shown in Chapter 3, although the industry was fragmented among many firms, by 1968 production was concentrated in just a few. Again, Volkswagen was largely responsible for the falling cost curve of the overall in-

[29] Almeida, "A indústria automobilística brasileira," p. 95.

dustry. Its production costs net of profits and taxes fell by about 15 percent from 1963 to 1968 as well as from 1964 to 1968. Its share of total production rose from 34 to 55 percent over this period; by 1968, it was producing over 150,000 vehicles.

In light truck production, Jack Baranson found that ex-factory costs in Brazil were 1.7 times those of the United States in 1967 (see Table 4.28).[30] Jack Behrman found that for Latin America in general, the low scale of production accounted for over 50 percent of the cost differential with U.S. production.[31] In Brazil, taxes were responsible for the largest part of that differential. Baranson found that, net of indirect taxes, Brazil's costs were only 1.28 times those of the United States.[32] As shown earlier, productivity varied considerably among firms, and many were no doubt producing at many more times the cost of similar U.S. vehicles. Nevertheless, given the industry's youth and the low volume of production, the differential is surprisingly small.

The data in this section show how profits fell from relatively high levels while tax rates increased, indicating a redistribution of the sector's rents. Production costs fell slightly but remained high as a result of idle capacity, fragmentation, and high-cost parts and raw materials. Costs would fall further during the years of the economic "miracle" as production volumes soared.

The extent to which this outcome was intentional is unclear. Most of the policies were macro-oriented and consequently only affected the auto industry. Those involved in the industry were aware of the impetus that cascading taxes had on vertical integration, but the individual states' needs for revenue took precedence. Economywide price controls were imposed to fight inflation rather than to broaden the market. GEIA assumed a degree of price elasticity and thought lower prices would have a positive impact on demand. More by luck than by design, they came across a winning combination: high tax rates and high revenues. The nature of the market and the product was responsible for this fortuitous combination. If the policy had been reproduced in a smaller market, it probably would have necessitated an ongoing and pure subsidy that the state would have been unable to recoup. In the mid-1960s, the military government did assume a role in reactivating demand by providing mechanisms for consumer credit. It also supported the move toward consolidation and concen-

---

[30] Baranson, *Automotive Industries in Developing Countries*, p. 34.
[31] Jack N. Behrman, *The Role of International Companies in Latin American Integration: Autos and Petrochemicals* (Lexington, Mass.: Lexington Books, 1972), p. 57.
[32] Baranson, *Automotive Industries in Developing Countries*, p. 34.

Table 4.28. *Comparison of Internal Costs, Cars and Light Trucks, Argentina, Brazil, Mexico, and the United States, January 1967 (US$ equivalents)*

	Latin American costs[a]					U.S. costs				Ratios		
	Domestic value added at market prices (1)	C.i.f. value of imported content[b] (2)	Ex-factory (3) (1)+(2)	Taxes[c] (4)	Cost net of taxes (5) (3)-(4)	Ex-factory[d] (6)	Net of taxes[e] (7)	C.i.f. Latin America[f] (8)	Foreign exchange savings (9) (8)-(2)	Ex-factory Latin America U.S.A. (10) (3)÷(6)	Cost of domestic value added[g] (11) (1)÷(9)	Resource cost net of taxes Latin America U.S.A. (12) (5)÷(7)
Argentina												
Car	$4,244	$371	$4,615	$1,463	$3,152	$1,775	$1,573	$2,475	$2,104	2.60	2.02	2.00
Light truck	3,476	593	4,069	1,290	2,779	1,634	1,448	2,469	1,876	2.50	1.85	1.92
Brazil												
Light truck	2,841	155	2,996	1,013	1,983	1,752	1,552	2,587	2,432	1.71	1.17	1.28
Mexico												
Car (small)	1,902	978	2,880	311	2,569	1,756	1,556	1,956	978	1.64	1.95	1.65
Car (large)	2,564	1,203	3,767	407	3,360	2,297	2,035	2,497	1,294	1.64	1.98	1.65
Light truck	1,728	902	2,630	284	2,346	1,604	1,421	1,804	902	1.64	1.92	1.65

[a] Cost in local currency converted to dollars at official exchange rate at time of procurement. (In the case of Argentina, this was prior to devaluation in March 1967, or 250 pesos = US$1.00.) Figures for annual production runs of 20,000 to 30,000 vehicles, which is 5% to 10% the size of production for comparable vehicles in the United States.

[b] These figures, calculated from base figures given in column 8, include allowances for import content of domestically supplied parts (estimated at 15% for Argentina, 30% for Mexico, and 10% for Brazil).

[c] Roughly 31.9% of manufacturing price in Argentina, 33.8% in Brazil, and 10.8% in Mexico.

[d] Cost estimate for a "reconstituted" vehicle equivalent to the overseas model.

[e] Based on estimated average of 11.4%. This includes all federal, state, and local taxes (corporate income, excise, and social security). A comparable concept is used in estimating tax component for the Latin American countries.

[f] Difference between "C.i.f. Latin America" (column 8) and "U.S. ex-factory" (column 6) costs represents ocean freight, insurance, and port handling fees; it does not include import duties.

[g] This is akin to the "Bruno ratio."

Source: Jack Baranson, *Automotive Industries in Developing Countries,* World Bank Occasional Staff Papers, no. 8 (Washington, D.C.: The World Bank, 1969), calculated from data furnished by an American vehicle manufacturer.

tration in order to attain economies of scale in the industry, even at the cost of losing nationally owned firms.

Linkages

As a result of its rapid growth rate, the automotive sector came to represent a larger share of GDP and industrial production. From a negligible percentage, its share in GDP was 2.9 by 1960 and 3.3 by 1967. It accounted for 4.1 percent of industrial employment in 1960 and 8 percent by 1968.[33]

An industry's growth rate alone does not provide a full picture of its relative contribution, because it does not incorporate its impact beyond a given sector or on overall development. Import substitution is a process by which the composition of the output of a less developed country shifts to resemble that of a developed economy. The goal is to produce domestically previously imported commodities that, through their input demands, will fill in the rows and columns found in the input–output tables of industrialized countries but are lacking in less-developed countries. Although import-dependent sectors like motor vehicles may generate an import leakage in the short run, they expand the domestic market for those inputs. Once produced domestically, the inputs will consequently reduce the import demands of other sectors that use them as well.[34] Indeed, the automobile industry's potential impact on the growth of other industrial sectors was one of the planners' arguments in its favor. They anticipated Albert Hirschman's idea of inducement mechanisms by arguing that the industry's demand for significant amounts of intermediate inputs would induce their domestic production.[35]

The standard input–output matrix indicates the structure of a sector's intermediate inputs and can be manipulated to show how a sector's own growth rate affects that of other sectors. Based on the Brazilian input–output table of 1970, the automotive industry had

[33] Almeida, *A implantação da indústria automobilística no Brasil*, p. 64.

[34] Using this argument to support domestic production of industries with high forward linkage effects is more problematic. Theoretically, forward linkage effects could be induced by imports. In fact, a replacement parts industry had sprung up in Brazil to supply the fleet of imported vehicles. Nevertheless, one could argue that until an adequate demand was created, a domestic industry would not be forthcoming. More relevant for Brazil than the size of this market was its variance, given the instability of foreign exchange supply.

[35] See Albert O. Hirschman, *The Strategy of Economic Development* (New York: W. W. Norton, 1978).

relatively high linkage effects compared with other sectors. Out of eighty-seven sectors, trucks ranked sixth in total linkage effects, and cars ranked seventeenth.[36]

Although input–output tables do provide useful information, the limitations of this type of static input–output analysis are well known.[37] Such analysis indicates that, in Brazil and elsewhere, food processing, textiles, apparel, and basic metals show the highest total linkage effects. By and large, these are low value-added sectors whose primary input is food or raw materials. Their growth impulse is not dispersed beyond their own general category or primary basic input. Moreover, they rely on existing sectors rather than on inducing the creation of new ones. In contrast, motor vehicles served as an industrial platform, because their effects were dispersed among various sectors and generated new ones. The parts sector, the most direct beneficiary, represented only 36.3 percent of intermediate inputs for automobiles and 48.9 percent for trucks. In comparison, leather, skins, and rubber

---

[36] The first Brazilian input–output table was calculated for 1959, but was quite sketchy (see Willy van Rijckegham, "An Intersectoral Consistency Model for Economic Planning in Brazil," in Ellis, ed., *The Economy of Brazil*). The first detailed input–output table for Brazil was done for 1970, by which time the industry was firmly established IBGE, *Matriz de relações intersectoriais: Brasil 1970* [Rio de Janeiro: IBGE, 1978]. In 1970, the backward linkage effects as measured by the ratio of purchased inputs to the value of total production was .5995 for automobiles and .7701 for trucks and buses. Their combined ratio was .6262. Forward linkages were relatively small: .0015 for cars and .0093 for trucks; these are likely to be understated because sales to other industries are considered as part of capital formation and therefore appear as final demand rather than intermediate inputs. The total linkage effect, which includes the indirect effects from the direct backward and forward linkages, was 1.9598 for automobiles and 2.2032 for trucks and buses. The "power of dispersion" indicator was 1.1648 for automobiles and 1.3095 for trucks and buses (S. Schultz, "Approaches to Identifying Key Sectors Empirically by Means of Input–Output Analysis," *Journal of Development Studies* 14 [1977]:91; Werner Baer and Isaac Kerstenetsky in "Import Substitution and Industrialization in Brazil," *American Economic Review* 54 [1964]:411–25, came up with similar measurements for Brazil using the 1947 U.S. input–output table).

[37] For instance, the presumed fixed coefficient technology implies constant returns to scale, which does not characterize motor vehicle production. Also, the relative inefficiency of the parts and metallurgical sectors exaggerates the extent of backward linkages. The industry's relatively high degree of vertical integration (see Chapter 5), especially in passenger cars, will cause it to register lower dispersion effects. (This may partly explain why the sector overall and why cars in particular register higher linkage effects in the United States than in Brazil.) Moreover, the assumption of fixed relative prices is especially tenuous with respect to Brazil where inflation is high and prices are administered. Due to changes in the exchange rate, this is particularly relevant to the assumption of fixed import coefficients.

were 60 percent of consumed inputs in shoe manufacture, and textiles were 73 percent in the clothing industry.[38]

Moreover, static input–output does not take into account technical change, which is the core of this process. Testimony from those involved indicates that the auto industry imposed higher technological standards on intermediate inputs. The pressure on the parts sector is undeniable. Ongoing complaints about the quality of domestically produced specialty steels brought attention to that area. How effective this pressure was in bringing forth quality improvement in the short run is unclear, but it certainly wrought changes in the medium run. Furthermore, as the bulk of capital equipment came to be purchased in Brazil, the technical specifications provided and rigor demanded by the auto firms had an impact on the capital goods industry. These productivity-improving aspects of the industry have benefited other users of these inputs.

From this evidence, it is safe to conclude that the automotive industry had relatively high linkage effects. Unlike other sectors so ranked, it generated the development of new sectors to produce its intermediate inputs, particularly in the metallurgical industry. It played a key role in the industrial sector and in the economic recovery of the late 1960s. Its role in economic development and growth is hard to quantify, but these larger effects must be considered within any cost–benefit analysis.

Motor vehicles are credited with leading the economic recovery of 1968–73, the so-called miracle years. Production began to recover in 1966 and 1967, and the economywide recovery began in 1968. The industry grew at a compound annual rate of 22 percent from 1968 to 1974, twice the rate of the economy as a whole.[39] This fast growth rate was made possible by the degree of idle capacity in the industry and by expansionary macroeconomic policies. New credit institutions created especially for consumer durables were also responsible for this boost in demand.

---

[38] It is useful to restate Hirschman's words of caution with respect to using power of dispersion measurements as indicators of high-inducement sectors. According to him, they are based "on a mental experiment subject to numerous qualifications." He gives the example of grain mills, which show high linkage effects. Grain mills, however, clearly were not responsible for inducing new sectors; on the contrary, they came after wheat cultivation. The input–output tables provide no evidence of causation or timing (Hirschman, *The Strategy of Economic Development*, p. 108).

[39] Kenneth S. Mericle, "The Political Economy of the Brazilian Motor Vehicle Industry," in Rich Kronish and Kenneth S. Mericle, eds., *The Political Economy of the Latin American Motor Vehicle Industry* (Cambridge, Mass.: MIT Press, 1984), p. 1.

Simulations by Regis Bonelli and Dorothea Werneck using Brazilian input–output tables have shown that if the final demand for consumer durables alone had grown at observed rates while final demand for other sectors remained fixed, so that their growth was due only to linkage effects, the total growth rate of production would have grown at 2.37 percent a year from 1965 to 1973. This is notable given the small weight of durables in the manufacturing sector: In 1970, they comprised 8.9 percent of total manufacturing, as compared with capital goods' 11.9 percent share, intermediate goods' 37.5 percent share, and consumer nondurables' 41.7 percent share. Based on this simulation, Bonelli and Werneck concluded that durables, of which auto and parts comprised 69.1 percent, led the recovery, even though the absolute contribution of nondurables was greater.[40]

In some ways, Brazil's automotive program can be seen as a classic import-substituting strategy. The Kubitschek government targeted a high-linkage "leading sector," which expanded demand for domestic steel and parts. Resources were transferred from abroad and internally among sectors, the industrial structure was altered, and the resource and administrative capacity of the state was enlarged. Initial demand for motor vehicles was guaranteed by protection; domestic production could simply substitute for imports. This aspect, in combination with repressed demand from the postwar years and the relative price inelasticity of vehicle demand, provided the industry with breathing space; future demand would depend on market growth. Also, the fact that auto was an oligopolized and high-rent sector allowed the industry to generate profits in the early years and, later, to be taxed.

The military regime made a clear choice between efficiency and protecting Brazilian capital. It encouraged consolidation and mergers to eliminate excess capacity and to rationalize the industry; Brazilian capital in both the terminal and the parts sectors (discussed in Chapter 5) was sacrificed. The military's capacity to control prices and increase taxes was key, but the regime did not use its authority to protect domestic firms.

One could argue, paradoxically, that the early industry was a success because its forward linkage effects were not more dispersed throughout the industrial sector. Because cars were not productive inputs, their high prices did not then inflate the cost structure of dependent

[40] Regis Bonelli and Dorothea F. F. Werneck, "Desempenho industrial: auge e desaceleração nos anos 70," in Wilson Suzigan, ed., *Indústria: política, instituições e desenvolvimento* (Rio de Janeiro: IPEA/INPES, 1978), pp. 167–226.

industries. Final consumers paid for the initial subsidies and inefficiencies and transferred resources to the state. The state's administrative and fiscal capacities were less strained, as fewer sectors clamored for their own compensatory subsidies.

As production increased, however, firms were able to attain some economies of scale and became more efficient. By the early 1970s, the cost differential with U.S. passenger-car production was estimated at 35 percent. In the early 1980s, the World Bank found that the prices of Brazilian vehicles (excluding taxes) were below those of similar foreign models and characterized the industry as an infant on the verge of maturity.[41]

---

[41] Bernhard Fischer, Peter Nunnenkamp, Juan-Carlos Herken-Krauer, and Matthias Lücke, *Capital-Intensive Industries in Newly Industrializing Countries: The Case of the Brazilian Automobile and Steel Industries* (Tubingen: J. C. B. Mohr, 1988), p. 25; World Bank, *Brazil: Industrial Policies and Manufactured Exports* (Washington D.C.: World Bank, 1983), p. 116.

5

THE AUTOMOTIVE
PARTS SECTOR

The establishment of a Brazilian-owned parts sector was a critical component of the development strategy vis-à-vis the automotive industry. Because of the parts sector's diversity and its lower capital and technological requirements relative to vehicle production, Brazilian planners assumed that local capital could play a significant role in its development. Promoting a nonvertically integrated industry and a Brazilian-controlled parts sector was seen as a means of directing a portion of the rents accruing from protection to domestic capital. The intrasectoral redistribution of resources between transnational corporations (TNCs) and local firms was expected to strengthen the Brazilian industrial sector and to create a basis for further accumulation. A locally controlled parts sector was also used to legitimate foreign dominance of the terminal sector.

This chapter shows, however, that the parts sector effectively came under foreign control, either through vertical integration by the terminal producers or through independent foreign direct investment. With a few notable exceptions, the process generated a bifurcated parts sector: Foreign capital predominated in large, capital- and technology-intensive firms that operated in a relatively concentrated market and sold most of their output to the terminal sector; local capital was centered in the small- and medium-sized firms that produced more standardized parts, faced more competition, and sold a greater portion of their output as replacement parts. The auto program's rapid domestic-content schedule forced terminal firms to work with domestic parts suppliers and initially made them somewhat dependent upon them. But by the mid-1960s, the tendency toward vertical integration, along with the relative bargaining power of the TNCs, appears to have become more pronounced. Based on their stronger bargaining position over the fragmented, locally owned segment, the TNCs were able to restrict profit rates and thereby maintain a greater share of the sector's rents.

The auto program's protectionist policies and domestic-content requirements were not sufficient to preserve the parts sector for domestic capital. The Executive Group for the Automotive Industry (GEIA) had surmised that independent firms producing parts for a variety of vehicle models and companies could attain economies of scale not available to terminal producers, so that the industry's natural structural evolution would benefit Brazilian capital. No special provisions were adopted to prevent the industry's vertical integration or foreign capital's domination of the parts sector. To the extent that GEIA was expected to play the role of *fiador* ("guarantor")[1] of this "horizontally integrated" system, it failed. As in the terminal sector, national capital had more difficulty surviving the crisis of the mid-1960s.

GEIA apparently did not fully appreciate the implications of the sector's diversity and of its dependence on the terminal producers. First, parts are much less homogeneous than finished vehicles. The sector accounts for a diverse range of products, characterized by different technological requirements and economies of scale. Some parts are standardized, whereas others are fabricated to meet a particular vehicle's specifications. Firm type is also heterogeneous, with some firms producing primarily for the replacement market, others for the terminal TNCs. The production of some parts is controlled by only a few large firms, whereas others are produced by hundreds. Firms therefore range from simple repair shops to large-scale factories, so average sectoral data are deceptive. The parts industry at that time was not an international oligopoly of a handful of transnational producers, as was the terminal sector.[2] Large firms existed, but they were still primarily restricted to national markets. The parts sector itself is also interdependent. Most of the ten to fifteen thousand parts[3] in an automobile fit into components and are often assembled before reach-

---

[1] The term was used by Ramiz Gattás, who was himself a parts manufacturer and an ex-president of the Union of Parts Producers, SINDIPEÇAS (Gattás, *A indústria automobilística e a segunda revolução industrial: origens e perspectivas* [São Paulo: Prelo, 1981], p. 207).

[2] Tire manufacturers are an exception, but generally are not included in the parts sector.

[3] James P. Womack, Daniel T. Jones, and Daniel Roos, *The Machine That Changed the World* (New York and Toronto: Rawson Associates and Collier Macmillan Canada, 1990), p. 58, suggest 10,000 parts; Lawrence J. White, *The Automobile Industry since 1945* (Cambridge, Mass.: Harvard University Press, 1971), p. 19, suggests 15,000. The difference between the two estimates may reflect the impact of technological change in the past twenty years.

ing the terminal plant. Bottlenecks often arise due to this interdependence.[4]

Moreover, parts are not final goods but face a derived demand from motor vehicles. Because so much of the sector's production is directed to the terminal sector, it is dependent on it for markets and, often, for technical designs. Licensed distributors also played an important role in the replacement market. In the case of the Brazilian automotive industry, given the nature of the product and the purchasing industry, protection was not enough to preserve the parts sector for local capital or to guarantee it a share in the rents.[5]

In general, the auto industry is characterized by asymmetric bargaining power between terminal and parts producers. With few exceptions, the parts sector is less concentrated. Therefore, an oligopolistic sector faces a predominantly competitive one. Moreover, the terminal producers have monopsonistic power as the primary purchasers of parts. Design and technological changes typically originate in the terminal sector, on which the parts sector usually depends for design instruction. Not only is the terminal sector more concentrated, but its firms also have an absolute size differential: Barriers to entry created by enormous capital costs prevent parts firms from ever moving up into vehicle production.[6] In contrast, vertical integration is a real threat to most parts producers and provides the terminal sector with enormous bargaining power regarding the terms of production.

Independent parts makers can often produce at lower costs, because they supply more than one firm and therefore can attain economies of scale. Terminal firms will integrate backward when lower costs do not compensate for uncertainty of supply and where quality control and coordination are critical. Complete integration is highly unlikely, however. The lower costs attainable by independent suppliers frequently outweigh the reduced risks of in-house production. Also, although integration provides greater control over supply, it turns

---

[4] According to the Delft sample of medium and small parts producers, in 59% of cases a firm's parts were incorporated into components, 27% were applied directly, and 14% were a combination of the two. Programa Delft (Research coordinator: Dorival Teixeira Vieira), *Pequenas e médias indústrias de autopeças* (São Paulo: Programa Delft, 1967), p. 171.

[5] This is not to imply that it is sufficient to protect a consumer item, either, as foreign firms often set up local production facilities to jump tariff walls.

[6] See Rhys Owen Jenkins, *Transnational Corporations and the Latin American Automobile Industry* (Pittsburgh: University of Pittsburgh Press, 1987), p. 121.

variable costs into fixed costs and makes distribution of risk more difficult.[7] Moreover, the parts sector typically pays lower wages and also allows terminal producers to pass along the impact of demand fluctuations.[8]

It bears stressing that consolidation, asymmetric bargaining, and vertical integration are not characteristics particular to the Brazilian automotive industry. They are typical of auto industries everywhere that were based on the mass production model first adopted by vertically integrated U.S. auto companies. Companies such as General Motors perfected the top-down command structure to coordinate the myriad activities of a vertically owned company.[9]

It does appear, however, that the Brazilian auto industry came to be more vertically integrated than the U.S. industry, which requires explanation. Moreover, the issue of ownership is one unique to follower countries. Some of the same types of explanations arise for the parts sector's structure and efficiency as arose for the terminal sector. Some commentators claim that the sector's fragmented structure and inefficiency resulted from government mismanagement, thereby forcing the TNCs to integrate more extensively than they otherwise would have. Others blame the competitive strategy of the TNCs for generating a multiplicity of suppliers.

This chapter shows that the structure and performance of the sector resulted from the nature of the automotive industry and transnational strategy, contradictions in Brazil's sectoral policies, and the impact of the macroeconomic environment. It argues that government policy, particularly with respect to speed of implementation and high do-

---

[7] This discussion on the causes of vertical integration is primarily based on White, *The Automobile Industry since 1945*. He also cites the following motivations: First, when economies of joint production, often with respect to coordination, exist between two activities, in-house production of components with nonstandardized and frequently changing design may be required for effective control; and, second, to receive a larger share of the profits from a good jointly purchased by final consumers, such as spare parts, the ability to manipulate prices for both markets may result in a greater combined profit.

[8] Jenkins, *Transnational Corporations and the Latin American Automobile Industry*, p. 125. "Tapered integration," in-which a firm produces part of its needs in-house and buys the fluctuating remainder is also an option. In this way, a firm can fully utilize its own productive capacity and suppliers absorb the risks of changes in demand. This strategy also strengthens the firm's bargaining position in these areas, because it substantiates the threat of 100% vertical integration. Firms can also diversify their suppliers for individual parts to avoid a monopsonistic relationship.

[9] On GM's success in this regard, see Alfred D. Chandler, Jr., *Giant Enterprise: Ford, General Motors, and the Automobile Industry* (New York: Harcourt Brace and World, 1964).

mestic-content levels, was important for setting up the initial conditions. Nevertheless, it was not the only critical variable. The diversity of the sector, the nature of the technology, and the asymmetric bargaining position between the terminal and the parts producers defied simple solutions.

Early Years

The first five years of the industry were chaotic, as would be expected from such rapidly imposed domestic-content requirements. Suddenly cut off from imports, final assemblers became dependent on domestic parts to meet GEIA's demands. If these domestic-content schedules were not met, the firms were no longer eligible for financial benefits. Most important, they forfeited their foreign-exchange allocations for the importation of components not yet produced in Brazil or falling outside the domestic-content guidelines. While their own facilities were being built, these firms had to rely on Brazilian firms. Some companies such as Ford also turned to domestic suppliers as a means to reduce their investments in fixed assets. The parts producers were therefore presented with a virtual sellers' market. Import restrictions meant an almost guaranteed absorption of supply.

Although production plans had to be submitted to and approved by GEIA to receive special financial incentives, little coordination was involved. As was demonstrated with respect to the terminal producers, GEIA did not have any clear criteria by which to limit the number of firms, even if it questioned the impact of additional capacity on economies of scale.[10] In light of the mad scramble for parts, GEIA focused its attention on increasing supply. In fact, dissatisfied with the initial investment response, in 1958 GEIA increased the level of incentives offered to parts manufacturers.[11]

TNCs complained bitterly about the quality and reliability of Brazilian-made parts. Until that time, more complicated components had not been produced in Brazil. The sector focused primarily on simple, standardized parts. Therefore, new productive capacity had to be installed to manufacture those previously imported, more technologically advanced parts, which were usually the last ones to be incor-

---

[10] This is evidenced in minutes from GEIA meetings, GEIA Archives, Conselho do Desenvolvimento, Ministério de Indústria e Comércio, Rio de Janeiro.

[11] Presidência da República, Conselho do Desenvolvimento-GEIA, "Relatório dos Trabalhos do Subgrupo de Estudo da Formação dos Preços na Indústria Automobilística Brasileira" (Rio de Janeiro, January 1958), p. 56.

porated into domestic content. Even with technical assistance, the TNCs were skeptical about local suppliers' ability to meet their specifications, especially under GEIA's rigid schedule.[12]

One alternative available to the TNCs was to bypass the Brazilian-owned sector completely by fabricating the newly nationalized parts themselves. There is some evidence that, from the beginning, the TNCs' Brazilian plants were more vertically integrated than their operations elsewhere. For example, despite its initial efforts to rely on domestic suppliers, Ford's truck plant was more integrated than its plants in Germany and France at that time, and more integrated than its U.S. plant had been in its starting years. Having its own foundry particularly separated Ford's Brazilian plant from the others.[13] In fact, General Motors, Volkswagen, Willys, and International Harvester all had foundries in place by 1962. Generally, vertical integration was used to compensate for the country's primitive industrial infrastructure.

Another alternative to complete dependence on Brazilian parts firms was to encourage suppliers from the home countries to invest in Brazil. Particularly for custom-made parts, TNCs preferred those suppliers with whom they had long-standing relationships and who were familiar with their technical specifications. There is evidence that some parts firms came to Brazil under threat of losing their primary market at home.[14]

These threats notwithstanding, the investment was potentially attractive to foreign parts firms for many of the same reasons it was to Brazilian capital. Moreover, they could bring in equipment without exchange cover under Instruction 113, which local firms could not. This also provided an opportunity to import reconditioned, second-hand machinery that had become obsolete in home markets.[15]

---

[12] According to Paulo Dias, who worked with suppliers at Ford-Brazil, the company's quality control department and engineers were initially over-cautious from lack of experience. Accustomed to dealing with imported parts from the United States, they followed specifications without exception so as not to risk error, even though certain divergences would not have mattered or might even have made an improvement. In his view, they could not correctly distinguish those specifications that were critical from those that were not. Interview with Paulo Dias, August 4, 1988, São Paulo.

[13] Mira Wilkins and Frank Ernest Hill, *American Business Abroad: Ford on Six Continents* (Detroit: Wayne State University Press, 1964), p. 416.

[14] Lincoln Gordon and Engelbert L. Grommers, *U.S. Manufacturing Investment in Brazil: The Impact of Brazilian Government Policies 1946–1960* (Cambridge, Mass.: Harvard University Press, 1962), p. 58.

[15] Due to the fact that this equipment was used and had been depreciated, there was

Unlike the TNCs in the terminal sector, the foreign firms typically entered the market in association with pre-existing Brazilian firms. As mentioned, parts producers had not yet followed the motor vehicle firms around the world; these firms were still focused on their domestic markets and had little experience with foreign manufacturing. Moreover, in contrast to terminal production, a domestic parts sector, although small, already existed in Brazil. Especially given the speed of the program, cooperation brought potential benefits to the foreign firms unfamiliar with the Brazilian market.[16]

These "marriages"[17] between Brazilian and foreign parts firms, often arranged by the TNCs, involved technical assistance contracts or equity participation via direct investment under Instruction 113. In fact, forming joint ventures with foreign capital was a way for local firms to become eligible for Instruction 113, which they otherwise were not. It also potentially gave foreign firms easier access to BNDE financing.

GEIA encouraged foreign participation in the parts sector as a method to achieve full domestic content and to improve the technological capacity of the sector. Lúcio Meira had made this clear in the pre-GEIA days of Vargas's subcommission. In response to assemblers' complaints about the quality of domestic oil filters, after their importation had been banned by the Law of Similars, he said: "We do not want inferior oil filters, as we also know that they are a problem. And only you [TNCs] can force the national manufacturers to improve the quality. Otherwise, encourage the large filter manufacturers from the U.S. and Europe to come to Brazil."[18] GEIA itself directly recruited foreign parts producers; it particularly solicited project proposals from firms producing "high-tech" parts.[19] Given the high expected growth rates for the sector once the Target Plan was in place, GEIA saw no necessary conflict between national and foreign ownership. The market would be able to accomodate everyone.

continual controversy over what value it should be given as foreign investment in Brazil.

[16] Gordon and Grommers, *U.S. Manufacturing Investment in Brazil: The Impact of Brazilian Government Policies 1946–1960*, pp. 142–3.

[17] The term is from Gordon and Grommers, ibid.

[18] "Um almirante pé na tábua, entrevista com Lúcio Meira," *Quatro Rodas*, January 1966.

[19] Gordon and Grommers, *U.S. Manufacturing Investment in Brazil: The Impact of Brazilian Government Policies 1946–1960*, p. 59; and interview with Lúcio Meira, April 1985, Rio de Janeiro.

Furthermore, technology licensing was expected to transfer know-how to Brazilian suppliers.

The market conditions – the large demand backlog for vehicles coupled with import protection – guaranteed a high-price industry in the short run. The parts sector could pass along its high costs to vehicle producers, who in turn passed them on to consumers in final prices.[20] Profit margins were high in both sectors, and there was little incentive to cut costs or to improve quality. It was a particularly easy time for parts producers, given the vehicle manufacturers' dependence on them. Also, because domestic-content requirements rose each year from 1956 to 1960, the parts sector potentially contributed an increasing percentage of each car produced.

Foreign and domestic capital responded to these profit opportunities, and many new firms entered the market. An estimated thirteen hundred parts firms were operating by 1960.[21] During the GEIA years of 1957–60, new cruzeiro investment into the parts sector totaled over Cr$8 billion. Foreign participation became significant for the first time: US$86 million in equipment was imported under Instruction 113, and about US$58.4 million came in with foreign financing subsidized at the "cost-of-exchange" rate.[22] It was during

[20] However, concern with inflation turned public attention to high-priced vehicles. As discussed in Chapter 3, high prices provided ammunition for the congressional opposition, which pushed for increased imports as an anti-inflationary measure and partly succeeded with the passage of Article 59. GEIA was put on the defensive and, in 1957, commissioned a price study of the industry. This study found that the parts sector presented a bottleneck for the industry but that all price increases could not be attributed to that sector since some firms had already reached 50% domestic content by weight before the GEIA plan went into effect. It acknowledged that the level of technology and skill in the parts sector was low, and that quality control was lacking. But the report underscored GEIA's belief that over time, supply would increase and competition would drive down prices and improve quality. It opposed any form of price control, arguing that high profits were necessary to stimulate investment and production (Presidência da República, Conselho do Desenvolvimento-GEIA, "Relatório dos Trabalhos do Subgrupo de Estudo da Formação dos Preços na Indústria Automobilística Brasileira," p. 63). See Chapter 4 for more details on vehicle cost and price.

[21] ANFAVEA, *Indústria automobílistica brasileira* (São Paulo: ANFAVEA, 1961).

[22] Superintendência da Moeda e do Crédito (SUMOC), *Boletim* and *Relatório* (Rio de Janeiro, various months and years). As noted in Chapter 4's discussion on foreign investment and financial subsidies in the terminal sector, there is some discrepancy among different sources' investment data. ANFAVEA, *Indústria automobilística brasileira*, various years, and Aimone Summa, *A indústria automobilística brasileira* (São Paulo: CEPAL, 1963), each cite GEIA as the source for approved investment under Instruction 113 of US$99.3 million. The same source states that US$44 million of imported equipment was financed at the "cost-of-exchange" rate,

these years that names like Bosch and Bendix appeared on the Brazilian scene.[23]

The abbreviated time schedule forced a certain amount of collaboration between the assemblers and the auto parts sector. Out of necessity, foreign firms had to transfer technology and quality control systems. The industry as a whole had to confront the lack of equipment and the shortage of skilled labor. From this basis, a local parts industry was established.[24]

Crisis

As discussed in the previous chapter, the industry's growth rate slowed from 1962 and did not begin to recover until 1966. The entire automotive sector – parts included – was caught with excess capacity and high fixed costs. Neither industry segment faced a seller's market any longer. The full impact of this crisis will be discussed more fully, but it is important to mention at the outset that the sectors' relative bargaining positions had reversed. On the one hand, the TNCs were less dependent on the parts sector because of slack demand and because their own productive capacity had come on stream (for in-house production of components); domestic-content requirements had been met. On the other hand, the TNCs were in a better position to protect themselves against the market downturn. They could more easily pass along their costs through markup pricing, and they also had more bargaining power to squeeze the parts sector to protect profit rates.

It appears that the TNCs took advantage of the changing supply and demand conditions. José Mindlin, then president of the parts producers association SINDIPEÇAS testified before a 1967 parlia-

US$10 million by other financing arrangements. For Almeida's investment figures, see Appendix B.

[23] Before GEIA, the sector was generally small scale and locally owned, producing relatively simple parts. Foreign participation was virtually nonexistent. Using data from the 1953 Motor Parts Show, in which 112 firms participated, Ventura Dias found that of the 80 firms on which data were available, 77 were Brazilian-owned and only 3 were foreign. Fifty-six of the Brazilian firms each employed fewer than 100 workers; the remaining firms employed more than 100 workers. Vivianne Ventura Dias, "The Motor Vehicle Industry in Brazil: A Case of Sectoral Planning" (Master's thesis, University of California, Berkeley, 1975), pp. 63–5.

[24] Some conclude that as a result of this mutual dependence, the collaborative relationship between the terminal and parts sectors resembled that of the Japanese, as opposed to the U.S., industry. See Caren Addis, "Failed Models and Fortuitous Outcomes: The Brazilian Motor Vehicle Industry" (Ph.D. diss., Massachusetts Institute of Technology, 1993).

mentary commission on vehicle prices that the industry found itself "sandwiched between the big supplier [i.e., nationally owned steel] and the big client."[25] Apparently, the terminal firms were in the habit of diversifying their suppliers as much as possible, which generated uncertainty and made investment planning and attaining economies of scale difficult. For example, GM's representative testified in 1967 that they had a total of thirteen hundred suppliers. "For each item that we buy we try to establish at least two and when possible three suppliers for each part, in the hope that we create competitive conditions to reduce costs."[26] This practice gave the firms more bargaining power, because they could make realistic threats of canceling orders and switching suppliers. In his industry surveys, José Almeida also found that many firms considered three suppliers per part as the minimum required to protect themselves from monopsonistic practices.[27]

Mindlin also testified that, when sales were slack, the firms delayed payment by taking longer with quality inspection procedures.[28] (Dealers paid on delivery; the TNCs did not.) VW reportedly took up to 120 days.[29] This practice exacerbated the cyclic irregularities characteristic of the industry. According to Mindlin, annual demand was more or less uniform, but varied considerably during the year.[30] As a result, inventory costs were high.

These years of weak demand were also characterized by high inflation, making this payment practice particularly burdensome to parts manufacturers. Furthermore, expensive short-term credit made financing inventories extremely costly. Austerity measures, including tight credit policies, were imposed by the military soon after it took power in 1964. The entire automotive industry – terminals included

[25] José Mindlin, Testimony before the Parliamentary Inquest Commission for the Verification of the Cost of the National Vehicle (Comissão Parlamentar de Inquérito Destinada a Verificar o Custo de Veículo Nacional [hereafter referred to as Parliamentary Commission on Vehicle Cost]), October 20, 1967, GEIA Archives.
[26] Damon Martin, Jr., president of General Motors do Brasil, Testimony before the Parliamentary Commission on Vehicle Cost, October 11, 1967, GEIA Archives.
[27] José Almeida, "A indústria automobilística brasileira" (unpublished manuscript; Rio de Janeiro: Fundação Getúlio Vargas, Instituto Brasileiro de Economia, Centro de Estudos Industriais, 1969), p. 110.
[28] José Mindlin, Testimony before the Parliamentary Commission on Vehicle Cost, October 20, 1967, GEIA Archives.
[29] Congresso Nacional, Cămara dos Deputados, "Auto-Peças," addendum to "Relatório da Comissão Parlamentar de Inquérito Destinada a Verificar o Custo de Veículo Nacional," 1968, GEIA Archives.
[30] José Mindlin, Testimony before the Parliamentary Commission on Vehicle Cost, October 20, 1967, GEIA Archives.

– was affected, but the situation was especially difficult for independent Brazilian firms (and, as shown in Chapter 3, for weaker terminal firms) without access to other sources of finance. In effect, the parts sector provided finance to the terminals by accepting their delays in payment.

It is unclear how price controls, established in 1965, affected relative prices between sectors. At first, the controls were voluntary. Those firms that increased prices by only 15 percent a year were eligible for tax rebates. In 1966, the maximum increase was reduced to 10 percent. According to Eduardo Augusto de Almeida Guimarães, all the vehicle producers complied with these restrictions.[31] In November 1966, adherence became compulsory. Those firms that raised prices by less than 30 percent of the general price index received tax rebates. Those that increased prices by 10 percent more than the index received fines. In late 1967, proposed price increases, justified on the basis of costs, had to be submitted to a new price control agency, CONEP, for prior approval. Essentially, the new system institutionalized markup pricing in the terminal sector.[32]

For the parts sector, as Maria Fernanda Gadelha points out, CONEP-approved increases established only the maximum price firms could charge; the actual price was determined through the bargaining process with the terminal firms. Parts producers with some market power were more likely to charge the maximum.[33]

According to a report on the parts sector included in the 1967 parliamentary commission report, parts producers commonly had to defend themselves against TNC complaints about approved price increases: "When, for strongly justifiable reasons (by law and by GEIMEC), we propose an increase in the price of our products, initially we are invaded by legions of auditors from the assemblers who, not being able to negate the facts, . . . still engage in long superfluous debates, unnecessarily delaying payment."[34]

---

[31] Eduardo Augusto de Almeida Guimarães, "Industry, Market Structure and the Growth of the Firm in the Brazilian Economy" (Ph.D. diss., University of London, 1980), p. 238.

[32] CONEP was changed to the Interministerial Price Council (CIP) in 1968. Firms seldom charged prices lower than those approved by CIP. In 1974, the industry was permitted to raise prices before approval was given. See Guimarães, ibid., for fuller discussion.

[33] Maria Fernanda Gadelha, "Estrutura industrial e padrão de competição no setor de autopeças – um estudo de caso" (Master's thesis, State University of Campinas, 1984), p. 55.

[34] According to the report, most of these complaints were directed toward Volkswagen. For example, GEIMEC (the Executive Group for Mechanical Industries, which absorbed GEIA and other related executive groups in 1964) and the Finance Ministry

In his testimony, Mindlin cited a SINDIPEÇAS study showing that parts prices had risen more slowly than vehicle prices since 1964 and, hence, were not responsible for final price increases: "Price control that has been exercised over the auto parts industry has determined, in reality, the absorption of cost increases in such proportion that a majority of firms are becoming gradually decapitalized."[35]

Consolidation

The process of consolidation began in the parts sector even before the crisis of the mid-1960s. Using a survey gathered on 156 firms by Banas in *Brasil Industrial*, an industry directory, Vivianne Ventura Dias shows the extent to which the sector had already consolidated by 1962. As shown in Table 5.1, of 156 firms, 132 were controlled by local and 24 by foreign capital. Unlike most of the domestic firms, which predated GEIA, most of the foreign firms came in after 1955. More important, despite their numerical inferiority, foreign firms controlled 51.67 percent of the sample's total capital and were more typically large in terms of labor and capital.[36]

Ventura Dias also provides examples of how locally owned firms came under foreign capital's control. Albarus, S.A., incorporated in 1947, had sold transmission parts to Ford since 1949. In 1955 it signed a contract for technical assistance with the Dana Corporation, and by 1957 the latter controlled 62.6 percent of the capital. Dana had brought in equipment under Instruction 113 which, in addition to royalties, allowed it to gain control.[37] Filtros Mann, S.A., also began leasing technology for oil and gas filters, but Tilterwerke Mann and

---

approved a 15% price increase for COFAP, a parts firm. In response to the ministry's request, the firm agreed to spread the increase over a three-month period (implementing one-third of the increase each month). After the second month, the finance minister asked the company not to implement the third increase, and the firm agreed. Two months later, the ministry called back COFAP's president and accused him of not keeping his word. COFAP denied the allegation and presented its correspondence with the assemblers that explained that the increase would remain at 10%. The finance minister explained that VW had nevertheless attained a price increase based on a 15% increase in COFAP products. The report states that it knew of no action taken against VW (Congresso Nacional, Camara dos Deputados, "Auto-Peças").

[35] José Mindlin, Testimony before the Parliamentary Commission on Vehicle Cost, October 20, 1967, GEIA Archives.

[36] Ventura Dias, "The Motor Vehicle Industry in Brazil: A Case of Sectoral Planning," p. 65.

[37] Albarus had received Cr$15 million in BNDE financing in 1960 (BNDE, *Relatório do BNDE* [Rio de Janeiro, 1960]).

Table 5.1. *Automotive Parts Industry, 1962*

	Local			Foreign		
	Firms	%	Cumulative	Firms	%	Cumulative
Operations period						
Before 1959	49	37.12	37.12	3	12.50	12.50
1951-4	25	18.94	56.04	6	25.00	37.50
1955-8	40	30.31	86.37	11	45.83	83.33
1959-61	15	11.36	97.73	4	16.67	100.00
After 1961	1	.75	98.48	--	--	--
No information	2	1.52	100.00	--	--	--
Total	132	100.00		24	100.00	
Labor (workers)						
Less than 19	16	12.12	12.12	--	--	--
20-99	58	43.94	56.06	3	12.50	12.50
100-199	25	18.94	75.00	4	16.65	29.15
200-499	16	12.12	87.12	7	29.15	58.30
More than 500	10	7.58	94.70	10	41.70	100.00
No information	7	5.30	100.00	--	--	--
Total	132	100.00		24	100.00	
Capital (Cr$ millions)						
Less than .99	10	7.57	7.57	--	--	--
1.00-9.99	39	29.54	37.11	--	--	--
10-49.99	42	31.81	68.92	4	16.65	16.65
50-99.99	21	15.91	84.83	3	12.50	29.15
100-499.99	14	10.60	95.43	8	33.35	62.50
More than 500	4	3.03	98.46	9	37.50	100.00
No information	2	1.54	100.00	--	--	--
Total	132	100.00		24	100.00	

Note: Proportion of foreign capital in the sample of 156 companies: local companies, 48.33%; foreign companies, 51.67%; total capital 100%.
Source: Vivianne Ventura Dias, "The Motor Industry in Brazil: A Case of Sectoral Planning" (Master's thesis, University of California, Berkeley, 1975), p. 65.

Hummell became the major shareholder after 1961. Amortex, S.A., was obliged to sign technical assistance contracts with Fischtel and Sacks in order to supply shock absorbers to Volkswagen and Merccdes-Benz. It also paid a percentage of sales as royalties. In 1958 and 1959, the German firm underwrote equipment investment, and by December 1960, Sacks GmbH had total control of the enterprise.[38]

The process became more pronounced in the mid-1960s. As mentioned earlier, restrictive macroeconomic policy especially hurt domestic firms without access to outside capital. Domestic credit became restricted and expensive. Inflation also reduced the book value of these firms, and they appeared to be bargains. According to the report on parts provided to the 1967 parliamentary commission: "In the absence of pressure requiring new undertakings, foreign capital followed the shortest path, buying, for a ludicrous price, Brazilian firms debilitated by long crises and the lack of support from official power."[39]

Trends in the industry most likely accelerated this process. For example, the absorption of Brazilian-owned terminal firms by TNCs probably hurt smaller independent suppliers and benefited those parts producers either controlled by or associated with foreign capital. Foreign-owned motor vehicle companies behaved differently toward the parts sector because of their established contacts with home suppliers. According to Vicente Mammana Netto, once president of SINDIPEÇAS, VW bought parts only from firms with technology licenses from its German suppliers. VW's explanation was that because it did not make these parts in Germany, it had no capacity for independent quality evaluations. In general, big firms like Ford, GM, and VW required licensing, whereas the FNM, International Harvester, and Willys did not.[40]

Finally, according to Richard Newfarmer and Willard Mueller, acquiring existing firms, rather than forming new subsidiaries, became the dominant form of entry into the Brazilian manufacturing sector for all U.S. firms during this period.[41] This represented a displacement of Brazilian capital in the manufacturing sector. In the transportation industry, 50 percent of new U.S. affiliates were introduced through acquisition. In this survey, the industry is not disaggregated to allow an independent analysis of the parts sector, but the general trend in manufacturing supports the arguments given here.

---

[38] Ventura Dias, "The Motor Vehicle Industry in Brazil: A Case of Sectoral Planning," pp. 64–6.

[39] Congresso Nacional, Camara dos Deputados, "Auto-Peças."

[40] Vicente Mammana Netto, Testimony before the Parliamentary Commission on Vehicle Cost, November 9, 1967, GEIA Archives.

[41] Richard Newfarmer and Willard F. Mueller, *Multinational Corporations in Brazil and Mexico: Structural Sources of Economic and Noneconomic Power*, Report to the Subcommittee on Multinational Corporations of the Committee on Foreign Relations, United States Senate (Washington D.C.: U.S. Government Printing Office, 1975), p. 122.

In *Brasil Industrial,* Banas does provide data indicating that the participation of foreign capital in large parts firms did increase. National capital's share of fixed capital in these firms fell from 73 percent in 1965 to 62 percent in 1968. Interestingly, Brazilians controlled 60 percent in 1964. The worst years apparently came after 1965.[42] Those firms that were diversified and had access to capital were better able to survive these years of crisis, and they were more likely to be foreign.[43] Smaller firms, dependent on a few parts and facing a more competitive market, were less secure.

By the late 1960s, therefore, the auto parts industry was segmented into three categories: large firms, 80 percent of whose product was geared directly to the terminal sector; small- and medium-sized firms, 50 and 30 percent of whose output, respectively, went to vehicle producers; and a remainder directed to the spare parts market.[44] Local capital dominated the fragmented small- and medium-sized firms. The large firms were both nationally and foreign-owned, but all foreign investment in the sector was located in this segment.

Vertical Integration

Accurate data on vertical integration are almost impossible to come by. Firms are generally reluctant to reveal the extent of in-house production and publish data only on aggregate purchases of all material inputs, which include raw materials and finished components. It is difficult to make inferences from parts data because of that sector's heterogeneity.

Different proxies have been used to measure vertical integration and to ascertain whether it increased over time. José Almeida used purchases of materials and services as a percentage of total costs. By this measure, he found that the Brazilian automotive industry as a whole was more vertically integrated than its major constituent firms in their home countries and was becoming increasingly so. In 1962–3, these purchases represented 62 percent of the total cost for cars

[42] Editôra Banas, *Brasil Industrial* 1968–9, p. 263.
[43] There were some notable exceptions. COFAP, for example, went into joint ventures with foreign firms under Instruction 113. It had developed diversified product lines and buyers. Its survival through the 1960s was based on the fact that it supplied almost all the assemblers, and not only those controlled by national capital that folded. It also invested in the absorption and development of its own technology. For a complete study of this firm, see Gadelha, "Estrutura industrial e padrão de competição no setor de autopeças – um estudo de caso."
[44] Editôra Banas, *Brasil Industrial* 1968–9.

and utility vehicles and 67 percent for trucks and buses. In 1965, these numbers were 56.6 and 58.5 percent, respectively, and by 1967–8, 50 and 57 percent.[45]

In the Brazilian case, this measurement may not be a good proxy for vertical integration because it does not distinguish between raw materials and components.[46] Even if one assumes the same technology, input prices did not rise at a uniform rate over this period. The percentage costs per unit would have fallen from the price freeze alone. Also, reforms in the state tax system in 1967 removed cascading taxes and thereby lowered input costs relative to total costs. On the other hand, some prices from state-owned sectors like steel were "corrected" – that is, increased relative to the general price level -- after the military coup. Disaggregated input data, along with their price indices, would be needed to verify that these percentages signified a greater degree of vertical integration.[47]

There is a fair amount of partial and impressionistic evidence, however, showing that vertical integration did increase in these years. In testimony before the 1967 parliamentary commission investigating vehicle prices, both terminal firms and parts producers noted an increased tendency toward vertical integration. Ford's representative, for example, stated that there had been some movement toward vertical integration in Ford's operations, although it was not pronounced and was strictly tied to costs.[48] General Motors also said that, though it happened infrequently, the company did begin in-house production of a part if it could be produced more cheaply.[49] The tendency was also noted in *Visão* and by Banas at this time.[50]

---

[45] Almeida, "A indústria automobilística brasileira," p. 113.

[46] Even data on the value of parts and components bought from third parties as a percentage of total cost would understate vertical integration. As Gadelha points out, purchases from parts firms owned by terminal TNCs should not be considered as completely independent transactions. Gadelha, "Estrutura industrial e padrão de competição no setor de autopeças – um estudo de caso," p. 33.

[47] Almeida's conclusions would be tenable only if relative prices had remained the same. Capacity utilization increased over these years, so that the ratio of fixed costs per unit should have decreased while material costs increased. Even according to his data, the opposite happened.

[48] John C. Goulden, general manager of Ford do Brasil, Testimony before the Parliamentary Commission on Vehicle Cost, October 10, 1967, GEIA Archives.

[49] Damon Martin Jr., president of General Motors do Brasil, Testimony before the Parliamentary Commission on Vehicle Cost, October 11, 1967, GEIA Archives.

[50] "Quem é Quem na economia brasileira," *Visão*, 1967; and Editôra Banas, *Brasil Industrial*. According to *Brasil Industrial*, "The representative share supplied by the

The change in product mix away from trucks to cars also leads to the conclusion that vertical integration was increasing. According to some sources and substantiated by the firms' original plans submitted to GEIA, the manufacture of automobiles entailed more in-house production than trucks. In testimony before the previously mentioned committee, Mindlin also observed that truck producers, notably GM and Ford, tended to be less vertically integrated. (But he noted that Mercedes-Benz, which did not produce cars, produced a large portion of its own parts, having its own foundries. Purchased parts represented only 30 percent of the vehicle's sale price.)[51] The second growth cycle starting in 1967 was based on the fast growth of automobiles, which came tó dominate production. Therefore, it is likely that a greater percentage of parts was produced in-house and that the independent parts sector shared a smaller percentage of the recovery than it otherwise would have. Furthermore, vertical integration would have facilitated frequent model changes, which became part of firms' competitive strategies.

Along with its own independent move into car production, Ford's purchase of Willys Overland in 1967 also indicated that it would become more integrated and raised concern about the merger's impact on Ford's suppliers. Willys, which began as a virtual assembly line and outsourced almost every part, had become highly integrated with a diversified product mix. When asked whether the purchase would result in increased vertical integration, Ford gave ambiguous testimony. Its representative responded that it would depend on cost comparisons and that the company was under no contractual obligations with its current suppliers.[52] Mindlin was less circumspect: "We have noted the tendency [toward vertical integration] but we often have difficulties with real substantiation. Even so, there exist widely known facts. Ford's acquisition of a firm like Willys, which is quite

autoparts industry . . . oscillates between 12% and 42% of the vehicle's final price, not including taxes and dealers' commissions. There is a tendency for these percentages to decline."

[51] José Mindlin, Testimony before the Parliamentary Commission on Vehicle Cost, October 20, 1967, GEIA Archives. The fact that Ford was not vertically integrated as this time also reflected its initial strategy to minimize investment.

[52] John C. Goulden, general manager of Ford do Brasil, Testimony before the Parliamentary Commission on Vehicle Cost, October 10, 1967, GEIA Archives. With the purchase of Willys, Ford bought a complete line of vehicles, a diversified, skilled labor force, market share, and a distribution network. According to interviews with ex-Ford employees, Ford did in fact become more vertically integrated after absorbing Willys.

vertically integrated, will obviously imply a verticalization of Ford itself."[53]

It does seem clear that the Willys plant allowed Ford to produce the automobile Corcel with a high degree of vertical integration. It produced its own stamped metal body parts, engines, gear boxes, and axle parts. According to Ventura Dias, in its proposal for the Corcel passenger car, which entered the market in 1968, Ford planned to purchase only 32.1 percent of the vehicle's sale price, excluding the dealer's markup, from outside sources.[54] In its 1967 testimony, Ford indicated that the comparative 1966 figures for its F-100 pickup truck and Galaxie automobile were 74 percent (20 percent in-house, 6 percent imported) and 69.9 percent (22 percent in-house, remainder imported), respectively.[55] To the extent that its plans were realized, the difference in outside sourcing is significant.

Examples of terminal producers purchasing parts firms outright provide additional evidence of vertical integration. In the mid-1960s, Mercedes-Benz bought Sofunge, one of the larger foundries in Brazil. In 1955, Sofunge had produced Brazil's first diesel engine block on an industrial scale for Mercedes-Benz trucks. With the purchase, Mercedes joined the ranks of Ford, GM, VW, Willys, and International Harvester, all of whom owned their own foundries and were major producers of engine blocks.[56] In the same period, Willys (and then Ford) got control of Bongotti, a radiator plant, and purchased the metal works, São Francisco.[57] VW bought Forchedo, a foundry.

In effect, consolidation and vertical integration formed part of the same process. Both were responses to the fragmentation and low productivity found particularly at the small-firm end of the parts sector. Combining small firms into medium-sized firms was viewed as a productivity-enhancing measure that would also give the firm better

[53] José Mindlin, Testimony before the Parliamentary Commission on Vehicle Cost, October 20, 1967, GEIA archives.
[54] Ventura Dias, "The Motor Vehicle Industry in Brazil: A Case of Sectoral Planning," p. 49. It is not clear whether this includes imported material as well as local purchases.
[55] John C. Goulden, general manager of Ford do Brasil, Testimony before the Parliamentary Commission on Vehicle Cost, October 10, 1967, GEIA Archives.
[56] Ventura Dias, "The Motor Vehicle Industry in Brazil: A Case of Sectoral Planning," p. 68.
[57] An associate of Mindlin, in José Mindlin, Testimony before the Parliamentary Commission on Vehicle Cost, October 20, 1967, GEIA Archives. São Francisco had brought equipment to Brazil to produce parts but never got to the point of effectively operating. Willys bought the equipment and started a foundry for its own needs. The old supplier, which had based its investment on the Willys original project presented to GEIA, was put in a difficult position and had to revamp its operations.

access to resources. Without such consolidation, in-house manufacture on the part of the vehicle producers would be inevitable.[58] Those parts that did not require a high degree of technical sophistication and that did not exhibit economies of scale in production were prime candidates.

Explanations for This Pattern

The observed process of consolidation and vertical integration is characteristic of the automotive industry, particularly in the start-up stages, and, to some extent, would have occurred anywhere. To the extent that the Brazilian industry was more vertically integrated than that in developed countries, the question remains as to whether policy accentuated this tendency.

Almeida and Jack Baranson both blame government policy for the excessive fragmentation found in the Brazilian parts sector. As a result of this fragmentation, they argue, the sector was highly inefficient and firms had no choice but to integrate. Even if in-house production was costly, it was relatively less so than outside purchasing. The direction of causation, therefore, is policy–structure–high-cost sector.

Almeida targets government incentives as the major culprit: "The fundamental causes of fragmentation and the low technical level of the Brazilian auto parts industry are the excessive favors conceded by the Government for the installation of the automotive industry in Brazil... and the speed with which it reached such a high nationalization coefficient."[59] The high number of firms prevented the attainment of economies of scale, and the speed of the process prevented coordinated development. Therefore, the sector could provide parts neither punctually nor of reasonable technical quality. According to his survey, "Internal production of parts or components always resulted from national suppliers' incapacity to meet the technical requirements, to comply with the terms of delivery, or from high prices."[60] A high degree of vertical integration guaranteed a high-cost sector, but terminal producers found that in-house production, although costly, was still cheaper than outside procurement. Almeida does add that the terminal producers themselves share some of the blame for creating a competitive climate among the parts producers

---

[58] Editôra Banas, *Brasil Industrial* 1968–9, p. 215.
[59] Almeida, "A indústria automobilística brasileira," p. 110.
[60] Ibid., p. 111.

and for creating a high number of small- and medium-sized firms to avoid dependence on a single supplier for any given part.

Baranson, too, tends to blame industrialization policies for the high-cost automotive industries found in Latin America. Protection and import controls raised the cost structure. Rapid movement to high local-content requirements added inflationary pressure, as demand for materials and capital grew faster than supply. In a remark referring to Argentina, but applicable to Brazil, he states: "In the indiscriminate pursuit of autarchy, engineering and managerial skills were spread too thin in too wide a range of components and parts manufactured for too many low volume vehicle models."[61]

He claims that Brazilian firms were forced to integrate in response to inadequately supplied parts of dubious quality. He found that in 1967, outside-plant procurements were 40 percent of total costs, whereas the average in developed countries was 60 percent. This intensified the diseconomies of scale already prevalent in the industry due to low levels of production. He provides the example of Willys, which produced its own transmission and engine components in Brazil but did not do so in the United States.[62]

Brazilian parts producers and other observers blamed the TNCs in the terminal sector for the fragmentation of parts. They also found the government's credit policies and a costly input sector responsible. Oligopolistic practices on the part of the TNCs encouraged excessive fragmentation and high production costs. For example, Mindlin argued that the insecurity caused by the terminal firms' practice of diversifying suppliers made investments risky, as did the threat of vertical integration. Terminal firms complained that the parts sector was ill-prepared to meet the expected growth in demand but, in his view, the TNCs themselves created the conditions of uncertainty under which the parts firms were unwilling to invest.[63]

At the time, parts producers also criticized government policy for weakening the financial position of small parts firms. The 1967 parliamentary commission's report on parts and parts producers' testimony contended that the government encouraged consolidation under the false assumption that it would make the industry more efficient. They claimed that the credit crunch of the mid-1960s se-

---

[61] Jack Baranson, *Automotive Industries in Developing Countries,* World Bank Occasional Staff Papers, no. 8 (Washington, D.C.: World Bank, 1969), p. 52.

[62] Ibid., p. 26.

[63] José Mindlin, Testimony before the Parliamentary Commission on Vehicle Cost, October 20, 1967, GEIA archives.

verely hit the small producer, whereas the large ones, particularly those with access to foreign capital, could expand their market share and offer attractive terms of payment. Small firms were left with no option but to sell out.[64]

The suspicion was voiced that other motives besides cost cutting and guaranteeing supply were at work. Mindlin claimed that economically, vertical integration did not make sense: "We believe that there are internal reasons — taking advantage of equipment brought from the exterior that is no longer being used in the countries of origin."[65] The congressional report also targeted 1967 tariff legislation, which again provided incentives to the terminal producers to import capital goods. It claimed that such incentives encouraged them to integrate vertically.[66]

In these early years, high start-up costs, low levels of capacity utilization, and transition costs inevitably resulted in a high-cost industry. The speed of implementation alone would have accounted for increased costs, as did the high domestic-content requirements. Using firm data for 1967, Baranson has shown how cost differentials between Brazilian and U.S. production rose as domestic-content percentages increased.[67] The low levels of production and the technical requirements of the more complicated – and last to be produced domestically – parts were the cause. As explained in previous chapters, gradualism was not seen as an option.

Moreover, the imposition of the industry at an advanced stage as opposed to the gradual, parallel development of the parts sector alongside the terminal sector that occurred in the United States meant that the terminal sector had more bargaining power. In the United States, some designs originated in the parts sector and created a degree of technological interdependence, whereas in Brazil technological transfer was unidirectional. Thus, the asymmetric bargaining power characteristic of the industry was even more uneven in Brazil.

As occurred in the terminal sector, subsidies may have induced excessive entry into and fragmentation of the parts sector. In particular, the GEIA deadline for investment under Instruction 113 may have contributed to this tendency. According to Lincoln Gordon and Engelbert Grommers, "In a number of cases machinery was 'rushed

[64] Congresso Nacional, Camara dos Deputados, "Auto-Peças"; and Mindlin and Mammana testimonies.
[65] José Mindlin, Testimony before the Parliamentary Commission on Vehicle Cost, October 20, 1967, GEIA archives.
[66] Congresso Nacional, Camara dos Deputados, "Auto-Peças."
[67] Baranson, *Automotive Industries in Developing Countries*, p. 31.

in,' and at least one company feels that the need to meet the [113] deadline led to a larger investment than would have been made on strictly economic grounds."[68] However, it is unlikely that subsidies were the primary cause of excessive fragmentation, as Almeida claims. According to the Delft study, most of the small firms entered production after 1951, when laws regulating parts imports were imposed; medium-sized firms predate them. That study's hypothesis is that the small firms arose to complement the larger firms, which could not meet the burgeoning demand.[69] Therefore, the protected market, combined with strong short-run demand and expectations that it would continue into the future, were more critical than financial subsidies. Investment may have been stretched too thin, but protection and a sellers' market may have made the sector complacent and unconcerned with modernization.

Neither is it likely that Instruction 113 was primarily responsible for the denationalization of the sector. In his 1967 testimony, Sydney Latini claimed that the nationally owned parts sector's inability to import used equipment, a privilege restricted to foreign firms importing under 113, was a very important factor in the denationalization of the industry. Domestic firms were subsequently forced to associate with foreign capital.[70] And, as shown by the examples provided by Ventura Dias, the foreign partner often gained control by investing in this manner. To the extent that Instruction 113 encouraged more joint ventures than otherwise would have occurred, therefore, it may have facilitated the sector's partial denationalization. Nevertheless, this pattern of denationalization might have occurred even in the absence of Instruction 113. The large foreign-owned terminal producers demanded that their Brazilian suppliers be licensed by their suppliers at home. Licensing arrangements often led to shareholding arrangements. Furthermore, licensing is not a viable form of technological transfer in the long run. Baranson concluded from his study on the Latin American auto industry that only through significant ownership and control would technology effectively be transferred and an adequate return guaranteed. Newfarmer also argues that licensing does not ensure an adequate return.[71]

[68] Gordon and Grommers, *U.S. Manufacturing Investment in Brazil: The Impact of Brazilian Government Policies 1956–1960*, p. 57.
[69] Programa Delft, *Pequenas e médias indústrias de autopeças*, p. 38.
[70] Sydney Latini, Testimony before the Parliamentary Commission on Vehicle Cost, October 26, 1967, GEIA Archives.
[71] Richard Newfarmer, *Transnational Conglomerates and the Economics of Dependent De-*

The macroeconomic crisis after 1964 accelerated this tendency. The terminal firms were no longer facing a seller's market and were hampered by price controls, so that they became more concerned about costs. They tried to exert more control over the parts sector. As mentioned, the tighter market and expensive credit made it difficult for the domestic firms to compete against foreign-owned firms. Moreover, the elimination of the "cost-of-exchange" rate discussed in the previous chapter was especially burdensome to domestic parts firms, which had relied on foreign-financed equipment imports. According to Latini's testimony, they were forced to amortize their payments at interest rates of 48.03 cents to the dollar.[72]

With the recovery in 1967–8, and the consolidation in the terminal sector, the industry entered a new cycle. The industry was an established reality. Companies such as Ford and GM made new commitments to passenger-car production, and cars came to dominate overall production. The industry was more competitive. In the industry's initial phase, firms were forced to use whatever parts were available to reach domestic-content levels, but they were also facing minimal competitive pressure. By the late 1960s, investment in parts production therefore became less risky and also more necessary. In some instances, firms vertically integrated to evade domestic cartels.

The image of the terminal TNCs somehow saving the day by vertically integrating and making the industry less inefficient must be qualified, however. Domestically owned small firms may have been somnolent. Yet, TNC diversification policies were clearly detrimental. Also, large independent firms supplied the major parts; the terminal firms generally integrated into less complicated parts, and it is not clear whether these formed a large share of total costs.

Furthermore, not all vertical integration or mergers intended to or succeeded in reducing costs or guaranteeing supply. Some of this activity doubtless resulted from foreign firms' financial advantages and the availability of domestic firms at bargain-basement prices. Facing weak demand, firms were not investing in new plant; those with capital bought up existing capacity.

As in the terminal sector, the position of domestic capital in the parts sector was very unstable and ultimately unsustainable. This was partly a result of the nature of automotive parts. Protection from

velopment: A Case Study of the International Electrical Oligopoly and Brazil's Electrical Industry (Greenwich, Conn.: JAI Press, 1979).

[72] Sydney Latini, Testimony before the Parliamentary Commission on Vehicle Cost, October 26, 1967, GEIA Archives.

imports alone was insufficient to ensure the dominance of local capital. Unlike a consumer good, parts were intermediate goods that were technologically dependent on the terminal sector. The sector could not simply pass along its costs as higher prices to final consumers. Moreover, in these products, Brazilian capital had no intrinsic advantage, such as knowledge of the national market, over foreign capital that might have compensated for its relative weakness in other respects. Therefore, foreign capital received no benefits by maintaining association with domestic capital.

Also, despite GEIA's original intent to maintain the parts sector as the preserve of domestic capital, no policies were introduced either in the early years or subsequently to ensure this outcome. In fact, the automotive plan embodied contradictory objectives. The speed of the program may have pushed the industry to "the point of no return," but requiring 95 percent domestic-content levels within five years most likely worked against the interests of domestic parts producers. In the mid-1960s, when the military regime became more concerned with inflation control and costs, consolidation and mergers were explicitly encouraged, even at the expense of Brazilian firms.

The experience of national capital in the parts sector is indicative of its relatively weak political power and influence on the state. The military government was not concerned about maintaining a strong role for national capital in this sector in the 1960s. According to Gadelha, and Francisco de Oliveira and Maria Angélica Travalo Popoutchi, the process of vertical integration continued into the mid-1970s, when the military government did attempt to preserve a role for domestic capital by imposing tighter domestic procurement policies and domestic-content targets on other sectors; this was when the triple alliance or *tri-pé* among state, foreign, and local capital was being advocated in industries such as petrochemicals.[73] According to the Delft study on auto parts, the parts sector's association, SINDIPEÇAS, was considered to be ineffective in protecting the sector's interests.[74]

In the absence of enforcement capacity, passing decrees against vertical integration would have been unsuccessful. In Mexico, for example, the initial automotive decrees forbade terminal firms from moving into parts except to manufacture engines and those parts they

[73] Gadelha, "Estrutura industrial e padrão de competição no setor de autopeças – um estudo de caso"; and Francisco de Oliveira and Maria Angélica Travalo Popoutchi, *El complejo automotor en Brasil* (Mexico City: ILET and Nueva Imagen, 1979). For a thorough theoretical and empirical discussion on the *tri-pé* in Brazil, see Peter Evans, *Dependent Development* (Princeton: Princeton University Press, 1979).
[74] Programa Delft, *Pequenas e médias indústrias de autopeças*, p. 263.

were already producing in-house. Also, foreign capital was not allowed more than a 40 percent equity position in independent parts firms. In Mexico specifically, there was the problem of *prestanombres*, whereby a local firm "lent its name" as a cover. Moreover, the laws controlling vertical integration were weakened, and Ford and General Motors were allowed to cast their own engine blocks after proclaiming the Mexican foundries inadequate. Mexico also tried to limit models and to prevent market fragmentation in the terminal sector, with little success.[75]

A comparison with the structure of the Japanese and South Korean auto industries is illustrative. In both cases, different organizational structures emerged, in part because of the terminal firms' financial weakness. Automobile companies integrated their suppliers more closely into their operations. Born out of necessity, these new types of relationships addressed some of the problems inherent in the U.S. system of arm's-length supplier relations, which generated coordination problems and did not promote information sharing or the spread of innovation capacity. They are credited with the emergence of "just-in-time" production, now considered part of the Japanese firms' competitive advantage.[76]

South Korea followed the Japanese model, promoting domestic "national champions" in the terminal sector and the development of an extensive supplier network in the 1960s and 1970s. This strategy followed in part from the national terminal firms' limited access to capital and technology. In addition, the government pressured companies to work with small firms so that the benefits of growth could be more widely dispersed. The 1982 Small- and Medium-Industry Systemization Law forbade prime contractors from absorbing subcontractors through stock ownership and provided subcontracting firms financial help. Although there remained an asymmetry between the two due to market power, this system does appear to have reduced the tendency toward vertical integration and promoted technological change.[77]

---

[75] Bennett and Sharpe argue that the fragmentation in the terminal sector led to the fragmentation of parts production. Douglas C. Bennett and Kenneth E. Sharpe, *Transnational Corporations versus the State: The Political Economy of the Mexican Auto Industry* (Princeton: Princeton University Press, 1985).

[76] For a complete discussion, see Womack et al., *The Machine That Changed the World.*

[77] Amsden suggests that Korean-owned terminal firms such as Hyundai subcontract to a greater extent than joint ventures such as Daewoo Motors, in which GM has a 50% share. Before 100% domestic content was required in the 1970s, Daewoo imported more parts than did Hyundai. Then, instead of subcontracting to local Korean

Despite their initial dependence on domestic parts firms in Brazil, the transnational auto firms were neither capital-constrained nor reined in by legislation that enforced a nonvertically integrated industrial structure. Although the space for domestic capital in the parts sector was not as extensive as GEIA had anticipated, the emergence of an auto industry did nevertheless create new opportunities that had not previously existed for national capital and fostered the growth of world-class supplier firms.

firms, Daewoo formed joint ventures with GM's American suppliers who established operations in Korea. See Alice Amsden, *Asia's Next Giant: South Korea and Late Industrialization* (Oxford: Oxford University Press, 1989), pp. 179–80.

6

CONCLUSION

In 1984, a party was given to commemorate the publication of a new book on Brazil's early motor vehicle industry by Sydney Latini, a former secretary of the Executive Group for the Automotive Industry (GEIA). Lúcio Meira, who had directed the GEIA program in the 1950s, took the opportunity to apply historical lessons drawn from that experience to Brazil's current economic problems. Addressing the small gathering at the auto salon in São Paulo, with the annual automotive show in the background providing silent testimony to the legacy he bequeathed, he blasted the government for abdicating its responsibility to the private sector. Describing GEIA as a model of government planning and public–private cooperation, he called for the formation of new GEIAs to confront the problems of the 1980s and to reproduce that heroic effort of the past.

The preceding chapters have shown that GEIA was not solely responsible for the implantation of the auto industry in Brazil, but that a combination of factors led to the success of its program. First, it was shown how GEIA's chances of success were increased by the fact that a strictly economic argument could be made in defense of the industry's establishment. The insights of the strategic trade literature, which defends protectionism to construct new industries characterized globally as oligopolies, were applied with a twist to the Brazilian case. That literature concerns itself with the international distribution of rents between countries, presuming that the new infant industries are domestically owned. In Brazil, the domestic industry was foreign-owned, so that the internal distribution of rents became an important issue. Brazil successfully attracted foreign capital into the industry. The subsidies provided were significant but not as large as previously estimated. Moreover, Brazil redistributed the rents accruing to these firms. In addition, the linkage effects of the investment were significant and helped trigger industrialization.

Second, efficiency in production was not a binding constraint on the effectiveness of this policy. Because of the size of the Brazilian market and the existence of an incipient industrial infrastructure, some firms were able to approach economies of scale, and the costs of domestically produced parts were not as high as in other less-developed countries (LDCs). As a result, it was not necessary to provide *ongoing* subsidies or to charge even higher prices. Also, the nature of the product's market was important. For cars, relatively rich consumers bore the cost of inefficiencies in the early years. The demand was relatively inelastic, which allowed firms to charge high prices, and the state to charge high taxes, without diminishing total revenues. Furthermore, because automobiles were not productive inputs, their high prices did not inflate the cost structure of dependent industries.

Third, GEIA demonstrated some capacity to shield itself from clientelistic pressures and to implement policy in a consistent fashion. It forced firms to submit detailed projects and used them as a basis for overseeing their implementation. The state also had some capacity to play the transnational firms off one another and to create a semblance of oligopolistic competition. Under some circumstances, this even involved price competition. The military government also assumed the power to impose price controls on the industry, mitigating some of the negative consequences of protectionism and forcing the firms to concern themselves with production efficiency.

For a variety of reasons, therefore, the Brazilian automotive industry was not as plagued as that in some other countries by the excesses typically associated with import-substitution strategies. Nevertheless, the sectoral policy could not always shield the industry from more global economic and political phenomena. For example, by the late 1950s, the methods used to finance industrialization and macroeconomic policy in general were not sustainable. The conflicting demands on the state no longer were manageable within the existing institutional and political framework. The problem of state finance became acute as export revenues fell and the coffee sector, rather than financing industrialization through its export revenues, became the recipient of substantial public subsidies. Moreover, foreign exchange receipts declined just when short-run foreign debts were coming due. The automotive industry certainly was responsible for part of this debt but, relatively, its share of the total was small. Because of the predominance of transnational firms in the terminal sector, investment under Instruction 113 played a larger role in foreign financing than in the Target Plan generally. Nevertheless, although the auto industry was a strategic sector, it was not insulated from these macroeconomic changes; the foreign exchange crunch limited the amount of imported spare parts and, hence, production volumes.

Nor could an executive group such as GEIA resolve all the inherent problems of public administration or of the larger constraints imposed on the state in its dealings with transnational firms. GEIA was not completely sheltered from clientelism. As demonstrated by the case of passenger cars, the auto industry was not immune from the contradictory pulls within the administration.

Finally, the policy was less successful with respect to the domestically owned parts sector. With an eye to the U.S. industry, whose structure developed under different circumstances, the planners assumed that the industry would not be as vertically integrated as it turned out to be. Their primary focus was on attracting foreign capital into the terminal sector; the parts sector was secondary. It was assumed that the establishment of the terminal sector would provide the inducement necessary for capital to flow into the parts sector. Given the nature of the industry and the general development model that gave priority to foreign capital, it is not clear what could have been done even if GEIA had devoted more of its attention to the parts sector and had had more instruments at its disposal.

Despite these limitations, GEIA set the timing of foreign investment in the industry and, as a result, changed the face of Brazil's industrial landscape. However, given the confluence of factors behind this sectoral policy's success, simply creating "new GEIAs" to address current industrialization issues, as Lúcio Meira proposed, would not be sufficient to reproduce the same results. As this study has shown, this outcome was dependent on characteristics specific to the auto industry and on the international conjuncture of the time. Still, his suggestion inherently raises the important question concerning the extent to which Brazil's experience can be reproduced and the general lessons it provides. This question can be addressed by highlighting Brazil's attempt to create domestic productive capacity in a different sector – microelectronics – and by discussing the response of the Brazilian auto industry to changing conditions in the 1970s and 1980s, particularly with respect to exports.

The Brazilian Microelectronics Sector

If automobiles were the symbols of advanced industrialization in the 1950s, they had been replaced with computers by the 1970s. With similar motivations, Brazil attempted to create indigenous technological and productive capacity in microelectronics. In contrast to GEIA's motor vehicle program, however, the domestic market in minicomputers was reserved for national firms by prohibiting imports and restricting foreign investment in that market segment. The "market reserve" was then extended to microcomputers, peripherals, and other related items.[1]

The controversy generated by the market reserve policy focused primarily on computers. Computers composed the market segment specified by the initial decrees and were the products most commonly identified with microelectronics in the public mind. Nevertheless, the impact of the microelectronics revolution, and therefore the potential policy impact, extend far beyond this market segment. Unlike automobiles, microelectronics serve as important industrial inputs with ramifications for the entire manufacturing sector. Moreover, this new sector is characterized by rapidly changing technology with revolutionary consequences on process and product development. These differences have profound implications.

As for the automotive sector, an argument could be made that Brazil's market reserve was a legitimate strategy in the face of a concentrated, global industry reaping technological rents. Given the centrality of technological change to the industry, and skepticism about whether foreign firms in other sectors had transferred technology along with production to Brazil, the policy restricted foreign ownership and the licensing of foreign technology. Unlike the case of foreign-owned production, it involved the direct transfer of technology rents from foreign firms that previously exported to Brazil to innovative, domestically controlled firms.

However, it is precisely the rapid pace of technological change and diffusion that complicates import substitution into this sector. As Kenneth Flamm and others have pointed out, the nature of competition in the industry is such that the monopoly held by a firm over technology and over differentiated products is temporary and relatively short term. As a result of imitation and competition, the benefits of decreasing costs have been transferred largely to consumers via lower prices.[2]

These cost declines have been nothing less than spectacular. The dollar cost of information processing has fallen approximately 25 percent per year during the past several decades.[3] As a result, the pace of diffusion has accelerated. Therefore, despite the Schumpe-

---

[1] The market reserve was initially legislated by executive decree. In 1984, Congress passed the National Informatics Law.

[2] Kenneth Flamm, *Targeting the Computer* (Washington, D.C.: Brookings Institution, 1987).

[3] Ibid.

terian rents accruing to the firms, on a macro level these private returns have been swamped by social gains. Users have been the primary beneficiaries of cost-reducing technical change.

As this book has argued, protection or government subsidization may be warranted in cases where the social return of a project outweighs the private return to the investor. In the absence of such compensation, the socially optimal level of investment would not be attained. Nevertheless, the microelectronics industry has special characteristics. Deviations from perfectly competitive market conditions other than externalities are present, such as rapidly changing technology and decreasing costs, as well as widespread potential diffusion. Therefore, the costs of domestic production to users are greater in the short run.

Even in the medium and long run, it is not clear that countries like Brazil can approach the technological frontier. Much of Brazilian production has been at the commodity end of the spectrum – that is, personal computers. Given the enormous research and development requirements of the industry, it is becoming increasingly difficult for new entrants anywhere to appropriate technological rents; the rents from past innovations have financed the following waves of research and development in established, competitive firms. A specialized niche strategy has been successfully undertaken by some new entrants and may be the only viable solution for Brazil.

Due to the particular characteristics of the microelectronics sector, the relevant policy choice may not lie between domestic manufacture versus importation, but between domestic production and domestic use. The greatest benefits derive from diffusion, which is affected by price and quality differentials. Flamm estimates that demand for computer capacity is elastic with respect to price in developed economies. Although similar estimates for LDCs are unknown, the demand profile for the industry would differ from that of the automobile industry in its early stages if it followed this pattern.

This leads to another complicating factor related to the demand for microelectronics. In contrast to consumer durables like automobiles, the sector provides both final and intermediate goods. The ramifications of a technological gap for the industrial sector as a whole are potentially more widespread and significant.

Brazil had previously import-substituted into basic industrial inputs. However, many of those products, like steel, were characterized by relatively stable technology. Relatively high-technology inputs like petrochemicals were financed directly by the state or in association with foreign capital. In contrast, computer technology changes rapidly, and the research and development requirements are huge. The technological base of U.S. computer firms was built with public support. Even today, the U.S. defense department is the largest funder of research on some advanced semiconductors. The amount spent on research and development in Brazil has grown, but from a relatively small base. And given its fiscal crisis, the Brazilian government has been unable to fund large-scale research efforts. More important, microelectronics are not simply production inputs but also change the production process itself and/or the nature of the final good. Historically, higher cost was the major problem associated with the domestic production of previously imported industrial inputs. Generally, this problem could be, and often was, rectified directly through subsidies to the industrial producer. However, financial subsidies alone cannot compensate for inputs that are technologically backward.

The import-substitution process in automobiles was initially a success because its linkage effects were not more dispersed throughout the industrial sector. Final consumers paid for the initial subsidies and inefficiencies, and transferred resources to the state. The state's administrative and fiscal capacities were less strained, as fewer sectors clamored for their own compensatory subsidies.

The microelectronics sector's elevated cost structure and technological lag take on additional significance for those industries that have successfully penetrated foreign markets. During the 1980s, the debt crisis and the depressed internal economy forced some firms to compete abroad. With the help of government programs and subsidies, Brazil's manufactured exports skyrocketed. The playing field changed for these firms. They were no longer competing only behind protective walls with local firms that faced the same inflated cost structure. These exporting firms had to meet international standards.

Because of the sector's rapid technological change and widespread ramifications for industry, Brazil's policy was more problematic with respect to computers than to automobiles in the 1950s and 1960s. The policy generated widespread opposition from industry and consumers, thereby becoming increasingly costly both economically and politically. Under the government of President Fernando Collor de Mello, the policy was all but abandoned.

Brazil's Auto Industry in a Changing World

At the time of the first oil shock in 1973, 80 percent of the oil consumed in Brazil was imported. Concerned with the balance of trade, the government looked to the auto industry as a potential source of foreign exchange. Prior to that time, automobile exports were virtually nonexistent, amounting to only 2.5 percent of production in 1973. Firms had invested exclusively to serve the domestic market. Government policy shifted the incentive structure toward export promotion with the aim of generating a positive trade balance at the industry level.

Although some export incentives were introduced in the late 1960s, export promotion gathered steam in the early 1970s under the Special Fiscal Benefits for Exports (Benefícios Fiscais a Programas Especiais de Exportação [BEFIEX]) program, which was not unique to the automobile industry. To qualify for BEFIEX, firms had to commit to targeted dollar values of total exports and net foreign exchange earnings. The incentives they received in return included exemptions from taxes on imported capital goods, parts, components, and raw materials. Every three dollars in exports was worth one dollar of duty-free imports. Federal and state value-added and sales taxes were waived on exports. Firms also received a credit equal to these waived taxes that could be used toward taxes due on goods produced for the domestic market. Various drawback schemes were also introduced that allowed firms to import goods that would otherwise have been banned for the production of exports. If the export or trade balance target was not fulfilled, firms had to refund these incentives.[4]

The government was motivated primarily by its desire to generate foreign-exchange earnings rather than by broader concerns of industrial policy and attaining economies of scale through exports. Increasing exports were necessary to avoid any import constraint on investment and economic growth. Brazil's response to the first oil shock was to adopt a debt-led growth strategy rather than to impose economic austerity. As a result, the auto industry grew at respectable annual rates, although not as quickly as during the "miracle" years. Total vehicle production topped the magic million mark in 1978, and future domestic demand projections were optimistic.[5]

As Brazil was able to take advantage of the shake-up occurring in

---

[4] In response to complaints from GATT, the original export subsidy of 26% was reduced to 15%. After 1989, export subsidies disappeared altogether, except for old contracts that were grandfathered.

[5] The domestic auto industry had negative repercussions on the balance of payments through its contribution to Brazil's oil import bill. In order to reconcile the potentially contradictory goals of market growth and import reduction, Brazil implemented an ambitious gasohol program. Subsidies were offered to sugar growers in the field and consumers at the pump. The production of gasohol-engined cars began in 1979. In 1982, 95% of new cars sold ran on gasohol.

the global industry after World War II, the country's attempts to increase exports in the 1970s also coincided with another structural shift when U.S. and European firms were forced to respond to the oil shock and the Japanese challenge. By the late 1960s, Japan's revolution in production techniques had produced low-cost, high-quality vehicles suitable for export. Countries responded to Japan's growing share of world production and trade by imposing caps on Japanese imports. Firms responded in various ways. Many restructured their operations in an attempt to cut costs and downsize their product lines. Some firms focused on automating plants at home, whereas others focused on relocating production to low-wage, offshore sites. The search for low-cost production sites, combined with the emergence of new product lines, led to a new wave of foreign direct investment in peripheral producing countries such as Spain and South Korea.

This restructuring and globalization process would create new opportunities, and constraints, for Brazil as well. The conditions that had allowed countries like Brazil to attract foreign investment had begun to change. Foreign investment originally flowed into domestic production at a time when firms remained multimarket, rather than globally integrated, operations. The automotive industry had become increasingly global in the sense that manufacturing and sourcing became cross-national; strategic alliances formed between firms of different national origin, and products and performance standards were more universal. With increased globalization, firms became less willing to make investments only to serve an internal market, and foreign subsidiaries potentially became part of a global strategy, no longer serving only individual, unconnected markets.

However, the legacy of previous investment and government policy does influence firm strategy with respect to new investments and global sourcing patterns. As a result of the stickiness and long-run nature of investment in the auto industry, investments made in one time period affect firms' decisions about exports in the next. Because firms do not automatically view these investments as sunk costs, their subsequent strategies might be different than they would have been in the absence of prior investments. Exports may be based less on a country's competitiveness than on a firm's decision based on existing production locations, which are difficult to change in the short run.

In fact, each major auto company participated in the BEFIEX program but adopted different export strategies.[6] Generally, the U.S.

---

[6] According to Oliveira, the most important incentives from the firms' point of view were the cash credits on exports and the ability to import equipment duty free. Access

firms as represented by Ford and GM responded to the challenges of the 1970s by automating in the United States and by adopting "world car" strategies. They sought to increase economies of scale and to spread research and development costs over more vehicles by increasing product standardization worldwide and by using low-wage production sites as export platforms for engines and components, whose design changes are less frequent and whose scale requirements are less extreme than for finished vehicles. European firms such as Fiat[7] and VW looked to LDCs such as Brazil as low-cost export bases for finished vehicles to other low-income countries with similar demand profiles. Vehicle exports by all firms were directed primarily to regional markets. Ford and General Motors fulfilled their BEFIEX obligations primarily by exporting engines to the United States. European firms exported both engines and finished vehicles. BEFIEX participation meant that firms were not able to alter export targets in response to foreign demand, domestic capacity, and exchange-rate fluctuations, but were bound to fulfill export commitments by a given date.

BEFIEX was also introduced at a time when firms, with the expectation of rapid growth rates, were investing heavily for the domestic market. Given the lumpy nature of auto investment, exports could also serve as a temporary outlet for excess capacity while the domestic market grew. As a result, investment levels were sustained despite the slowdown in domestic market growth compared to the "miracle" years, particularly in the early 1970s.

Despite their growth in numbers, exports remained a small percentage of production, and the industry continued to focus on the domestic market. The industry's "opening" to world markets was asymmetric, in that imported vehicles were still prohibited and imported parts did not grow in tandem with exports. Once the major

---

to imported parts was not as crucial; the law of similars was still on the books for domestically sold vehicles, and the government demonstrated less flexibility with respect to imported parts after the severe foreign-exchange crunch of 1974–5. See Gesner Oliveira Filho, "Comissão para concessão de benefícios fiscais a programa especiais de exportação (BEFIEX) 1973–81" (Master's thesis, University of Campinas, Brazil, 1984).

[7] Attracted by Brazil's market potential, Fiat entered the country in 1973 and began production in 1976. Although the company held minority positions in foreign joint ventures elsewhere, Fiat do Brasil was its first wholly owned foreign subsidiary and accounted for its biggest automotive investment outside of Italy. Fiat overcame the disadvantages of being a latecomer to the Brazilian market by negotiating an attractive incentive package with the state of Minas Gerais, which had been trying to attract an auto plant ever since Simca broke its promise to locate there in the 1950s.

investment push was complete, the sector generated growing trade surpluses.

The optimistic projections of internal demand did not materialize in the 1980s as the full impact of the debt crisis hit. Firms looked to exports as an alternative. The sector as a whole (including parts) was responsible for the largest share of manufactured exports during much of the decade. Exports as a share of passenger car production peaked at 41 percent in 1987 and settled at 18 percent in 1990. Brazil's export success in the 1980s depended partly on fortuitous timing. The export capacity was available from investments planned in the 1970s when projections for internal demand were optimistic and firms made BEFIEX commitments. Rather than building upon a growing domestic market to attain economies of scale, exports came to substitute for, rather than complement, domestic sales for some firms.

Brazil's export momentum had waned by the early 1990s. As a result of the unprofitability of Brazilian exports, caused in part by an overvalued exchange rate, and the enormous uncertainty of Brazil's economy, most firms have effectively canceled all export programs. Brazil's overall capacity to export has fallen. Exports in the 1980s were based on earlier investments; virtually no capacity was added over the decade. Firms made marginal investments to maintain their competitive position in the domestic market.

Individual Firm Strategies[8]

1. Ford and Volkswagen

Ford relied almost exclusively on exporting engines and components to the United States. When originally planned, engine production was considered to be cost-competitive even in the absence of BEFIEX subsidies. Engines were preferred over cars because of their lower transport costs and simpler quality control. The decision to produce engines came at a time when Ford was downsizing and needed new capacity. A more sophisticated, four-cylinder engine of the same family was being built in Lima, Ohio. If the engine had not been produced in Brazil, it would have been produced at the Lima plant.

Ford did experiment briefly in the mid-1980s with exporting Escorts

[8] The following discussion of firm strategy is based on extensive interviews with managers in Brazil and the United States. For a comparison of Brazilian and Mexican export strategies, see Helen Shapiro, "Automobiles: From Import Substitution to Export Promotion in Brazil and Mexico," in David Yoffie, ed., *Beyond Free Trade: Firms, Governments and Global Competition* (Boston, Mass.: Harvard Business School Press, 1993).

to Scandinavia when Ford-Europe was capacity-constrained and when relative exchange rates favored Brasil over England and West Germany, which had previously been supplying these markets. Ford do Brasil had adopted European product lines in the 1970s because they seemed better suited to the domestic market and because Ford–Europe was generating more attractive model lines while Ford–United States was losing markets. The export program was short-lived because Brazilian Escorts became less cost-competitive when the exchange-rate situation reversed itself, European unions protested, and Ford began to turn its attention to East Asia as a potential export source.[9] Brazil was also chosen as the primary source of the Cargo, a truck, for the North American market when Europe was seen as a high-cost production site.

Volkswagen used Brazil as a low-cost production site for finished vehicles for export to other LDCs and continued to produce such models as the Beetle, which had been discontinued in Germany. When Latin American markets collapsed in the early 1980s, VW do Brasil first shifted its exports to the oil-exporting nations in Africa and the Middle East.

Volkswagen and Ford formed the holding company Autolatina in 1987 to rationalize operations in both Argentina and Brazil, which had begun negotiations for freer trade in autos. Brazil had always accounted for a larger share of VW's global production than of Ford's and, before its recent investments in Spain, was VW's primary low-cost production site. Before the union, VW had been receiving funds from its German parent, which were discontinued under the new arrangement. With the introduction of the Fox in 1987, VW do Brasil, now part of Autolatina, began to export almost exclusively to the United States and Canada. VW needed an entry-level product for the U.S. market. Although the car received positive reviews when it was introduced, it quickly lost its competitive edge to Japanese imports. An increasingly overvalued exchange rate and internal cost increases were critical in its price-sensitive market niche. VW could not raise prices sufficiently to cover its losses. Overall uncertainty in Brazil and an aging product were also contributing factors.

As a result of the increasing unprofitability of Brazilian exports and the enormous uncertainty of Brazil's economy, Autolatina had effectively canceled all export programs by 1990, with no plans to replace them. The millions of dollars in high-quality, four-cylinder engine exports were also scheduled to disappear, since Brazil was not chosen

[9] Elizabeth Bortolaia Silva, *Refazendo a fábrica fordista* (São Paulo: Hucitec, 1991), p. 89.

as the production site for the updated model. As the only company that exported finished vehicles to the United States, and for which the United States was practically its only export market, Autolatina was hit especially hard by the overvalued exchange rate. Until 1986, the company's exports had been profitable because of a combination of export incentives, a favorable exchange rate, and a good mix of export products. Starting in 1986, it would have incurred losses on exports if not for BEFIEX incentives, and in 1988, it did suffer losses on exports. According to the firm's calculations, its exports would have been profitable if Brazil's currency had remained at its 1985 parity with the dollar.

2. General Motors

After General Motors began its first "world car" program in the mid-1970s with the introduction of the J car series (Chevrolet Cavalier, Opel, and Monza), GM do Brasil lobbied Detroit to introduce the J car in Brazil. The subsidiary needed a new product line to compete in the Brazilian market, and there was no competition in the market niche that the J car would fill. The domestic market could not justify the large investment needed to build the new engines, however, which had to be manufactured in Brazil to comply with domestic-content requirements. It was decided that GM do Brasil would provide the appropriate engine for the U.S. Pontiac division as well as for the domestic market.

Although producing engines in Brazil was cost effective for GM, even without BEFIEX, the company did not need to build a new plant. It could have supplied engines from its engine plant in New York state. GM do Brasil was also not held in high regard in Detroit. The subsidiary had suffered financial losses in the late 1970s in its non-automotive activities, which were sold off. Capital infusions from the parent were necessary. Roger Smith, the CEO at the time, considered Brazil a "black hole."

Nevertheless, domestic market considerations drove the decision to produce J cars and to export engines, according to GM managers. In 1979–80, the 1990 forecast for domestic demand was two million vehicles. Exports would absorb the excess engine capacity while the Brazilian market grew. Brazil's case for the J car was assisted by the liability suits GM was facing from having shut down its operations in Argentina; exiting the market could have been costly and staying in required new product lines. Although domestic considerations predominated, BEFIEX export incentives helped sweeten the deal. The import-duty exemptions on imported capital equipment were particularly important in reducing the investment costs.

Engine exports were important to GM's financial health in the 1980s, when the domestic market stagnated. Exporting engines from Brazil remained cost effective, although the margins shrank as a result of rising domestic costs and exchange rate appreciation. In 1990, Brazil exported engines to GM-Opel for the first time. Until then, the global sourcing strategy had assigned the U.S. market to Brazil and the European market to Australia. GM was forced to grant Brazil access to the European market because demand was down in both the Brazilian and the U.S. markets as a result of economic recession. Otherwise, GM do Brasil would not have been able to meet its export commitments, upon which its import strategy was dependent.

GM do Brasil never considered exporting vehicles to either the United States or Europe. The U.S. market had a short product cycle, which made competition stiff. Mirroring the overall industry, GM's product line was antiquated. There was no pressure from imports to make frequent model changes, which would have been costly given Brazil's small production volumes. In addition, Brazilian models had followed European product lines since 1968, with a lag. German models were smaller and based on similar gasoline pricing, so were considered more appropriate for the Brazilian market.

As of 1991, GM do Brasil had no new approved export proposal, although it continued to export engines. Like Autolatina, it planned to invest to remain competitive in the domestic market in the face of potential market liberalization but was capital constrained; all funds had to be internally generated.

3. Fiat

Fiat initially considered exporting cars to other Latin American countries from Brazil. Its Brazilian product was always akin to that produced in Europe, so when Latin American markets collapsed in the 1980s, it could shift its exports to Italy. Fiat do Brasil exported the Uno, which, as the smallest and cheapest car of its product line, complemented Italian production. These exports were made feasible with BEFIEX incentives; without them, according to company spokespeople, they would not have been cost competitive.

In most years since 1982, exports accounted for 40 to 50 percent of Fiat's annual production, most of which went to Italy. This export performance made Fiat Brazil's largest private exporter. Fiat do Brasil benefited from rapid growth of the Italian market and from Fiat-Italy's capacity constraints. The company's expectations of Brazil's domestic market growth did not come to fruition, but because its vehicles were introduced practically at the same time as Fiat-Italy's, integration of its operations was easy. Because Italy is a captive market, the company could smooth out cycles in the domestic market through exports. In the face of increasing costs, Fiat's export performance will be hard to maintain. In 1991, which promised to be more problematic for exports, the Italian market was recessed and exports amounted to only 30 percent of production. Exports of Unos were being phased out.

With the BEFIEX program, Brazil was able to leverage privileged access to its domestic market to change firms' investment behavior, as it had in the 1950s. This time, however, the story was more complicated because the firms were already producing there. Therefore, firms acted not only to protect access to the Brazilian markets but also to protect their past investments. Indeed, firms were reluctant to close down a plant until it had been written off or until its product was obsolete. Given the large investments and long time horizon in the industry, trade and investment strategies do not immediately change in response to variation in relative costs.

In general, firm response indicates that, although internationally competitive production costs might be a necessary condition for a firm to begin exporting from a country, it is not a sufficient one.[10] Auto companies do not randomly survey the globe in search of low-cost production sites, despite the images conjured up by the notion of a "world car strategy." This may be an accurate portrayal of firm strategy in labor-intensive industries that can be easily relocated to exploit low wages and government incentives, but it is less so for industries like auto that require large, fixed investments, distribution networks, industrial infrastructures, skilled labor, and a domestic market.

[10] In the mid-1980s, one firm in Brazil found the country competitive in machined castings and forgings because of their high labor content and lower wage rates, which offset productivity differentials. It identified Brazil's greatest cost advantage in engines and transmissions since 70–80% of their content comprises such components. Due to a 50% content of plastic, glass, and other parts in which Brazil is not competitive (and which in this case were also outsourced), it found passenger cars had cost disadvantages. Comparing production costs for small cars in 1988, the company found that ex-factory costs in Brazil compared favorably with those in Spain, unfavorably with those in Japan and Korea, and were about the same as those in the United States. These costs partly reflected the appreciation of the cruzado (which had replaced the cruzeiro), as the growth in industry costs exceeded devaluation by 30 percent from 1986 to 1988, but were also inclusive of export incentives that came to over US$800 per vehicle.

That firms were forced to consider Brazil as a production site when they otherwise might not have speaks to the "success" of the country's import-substitution policy. Once the initial investments were made, firms took these sunk costs seriously. Moreover, these investments increased entry costs for new entrants or for those firms that might consider reentry after leaving the market, increasing the risk of temporarily opting out of a potentially growing market. Although this book did not attempt to calculate the full domestic resource costs of the GEIA program, this pattern of firm behavior does raise questions about how best to assess costs and benefits. It suggests that the initial investment's impact on future investment, foreign capital flows, and exports must be considered in the calculation.

Nevertheless, firms worry about sunk costs only up to point. Occasionally, they carry out their threats to exit markets. It is unlikely that they will subvert operations in their primary markets for less important ones. The evidence indicates that the extent to which a country like Brazil can regulate the behavior of transnational firms is determined largely by the attractiveness of the domestic market. Cost and locational considerations alone are not sufficient to induce investment for export in the absence of domestic market potential.

Additionally, product cycles have quickened, as the need for increased flexibility to match consumer preferences has become more acute. Low wage rates may already have become less important in determining the location of production. Technical change in the industry is no longer as controlled in terms of pace or dissemination. A decade of low investment rates in the Brazilian auto industry has widened the technological gap.

In some ways, high domestic-content policies left a problematic legacy in Brazil for confronting this new global industry. They fostered the development of a domestic parts sector and reduced pressure on the balance of trade, but they also isolated the industry from world norms and kept antiquated models in production because firms changed models infrequently in order to amortize tooling costs. Also, by imposing 90 to 95 percent domestic-content requirements, the Brazilian government sacrificed trade policy – still one of its most potent weapons – as an instrument to shape firm behavior. Because firms had invested to produce at 95 percent domestic-content levels, preferential access to imports was not an issue. When Brazil wanted to promote exports, it could only offer subsidies, especially on investment, and a limited drawback scheme as "carrots" but had virtually no "sticks" to discipline firms for not participating. Access to the domestic market or market share was unaffected because vehicle components were domestically supplied. To force firms to export and/or become more competitive, the government must threaten to open the market to finished vehicles and risk reductions in employment.[11]

At the beginning of the 1980s, the Brazilian auto industry appeared to be on the verge of maturity but was confronted with domestic market contraction and macroeconomic uncertainty. The nature of the industry and Brazil's position within firms' global strategy have made it difficult for the auto firms to find sustainable alternatives to the domestic market and the traditional LDC export markets. Overall, Brazil's strategic value has diminished along with its domestic market, which was always the industry's prime focus. Nevertheless, Brazil still has the largest internal market on the continent, with only one car per fourteen inhabitants (compared to 1:4 in the United States). The question remains as to how attractive a revived internal economy would be to the transnational firms. In the absence of domestic market growth, even if the market is opened, it is unlikely that firms will commit new capital inflows. Furthermore, the impact of regional free trade with Argentina, Paraguay, and Uruguay remains to be seen.

The changes that have occurred in the industry and in the world economy since the 1950s have altered the relationship between the firms and Brazil. Along with the changing domestic situation, these changes will have to be considered explicitly when Brazil defines a new policy toward the automobile industry.

The Limits and Possibilities of State Intervention

Two key lessons emerge from this discussion.

The Nature of the Sector

Gross generalizations about industrial policy can be misleading because of variations across sectors. The success of the Brazilian auto policy was attributable in the early stages to product-specific charac-

---

[11] Mexico provides an interesting contrast. It was in a weaker bargaining position vis-à-vis the transnational auto firms, and more concerned about price stability, when it started its domestic industry in the 1960s and adopted lower domestic-content requirements. In the 1970s and 1980s, the Mexican government proved adept at using firm access to imported parts and components as a way to structure the industry and to force firms to export. Similarly, the South Korean government's control over imports and access to cheap financing gave it considerably more leverage over its auto firms, which were largely domestic. See Shapiro, "Automobiles: From Import Substitution to Export Promotion in Brazil and Mexico."

teristics, such as demand profile and linkages with other sectors. As a sector's characteristics shift over time – that is, if the domestic market matures or if the technology changes – the domain for policy effectiveness will be redefined.

Some sectors are inherently dominated by structural constraints over which policy can have little effect. As Brazil's experience with microelectronics demonstrates, if a domestically produced good becomes too costly or too technologically backward relative to international standards, and if it affects a variety of users, the efficiency constraint may become binding. The policy will become too costly to maintain, both economically and politically. In such cases, the strategy is likely to produce a noncompetitive industry that requires an ongoing transfer of resources, paid either directly by the consumer or through state subsidies, or both.

Administrative Capacity of the State

A potentially large market and relatively advanced industrial infrastructure are not sufficient to duplicate Brazil's experience with respect to rent redistribution; the state's capacity to wield "carrots" and "sticks" must be considered. This involves an analysis of technical competence not only at the top but of the bureaucracy as well. A public sector decimated in terms of personnel and infrastructure by fiscal austerity imposes serious constraints on industrial policy.

It is also hard to generalize even within one country about the capacity of the state as a whole. Even if there are many claims on the system, state intervention need not degenerate into rent-seeking activity if parts of the state apparatus can be insulated and provided with sufficient authority to implement a plan.

The degree to which this is possible also varies by sector. It may be harder to regulate an industry with a large number of firms; this aspect explains some of the difficulties in shaping the structure and performance of the Brazilian parts sector. A state may have *less* rather than *more* difficulty controlling rent-seeking activity when dealing with a concentrated industrial structure, if one assumes it has the appropriate instruments at its disposal and the capacity to wield them.

The state's bargaining power vis-à-vis the private sector also changes over time. This may have to do with changing fiscal or political capacity or the maturation of the industry in question. With respect to transnational firms, it can be affected by their global strategy and the country's position within it.

These are the main lessons from Brazil's early experience with the automotive industry and the ones that must be taken into account when asking how the GEIA experience can be reproduced. GEIA was a necessary but not sufficient condition for the observed results; the program succeeded only because of underlying economic conditions and the nature of the public–private interface.

Recent development literature argues that state intervention invariably leads to rent-seeking activity and its negative effects. Demonstrating how this is not always the case does not deny the existence and potentially deleterious effects of rent-seeking activity. Indeed, government intervention by definition redistributes income and provides rents. Only in an unimaginable apolitical world would this not be the case. The fundamental issue, however, is not the potential existence of rent-seeking activity but the conditions under which the state can intervene effectively. In the rush to identify villains responsible for the failures of development policies, historical lessons provided by cases such as the Brazilian automotive industry should not be forgotten.

APPENDIX A: DATA EXHIBITS ON THE BRAZILIAN AUTO INDUSTRY

Table A.1. *Motor Vehicle Projects Approved by the Executive Group for the Automotive Industry (Grupo Executivo da Indústria Automobilística [GEIA],) 1956-1957*

1.	Fábrica Nacional de Motores (FNM) FNM (heavy truck) and Alfa Romeo J.K. (passenger car) The automobile project was originally to be implemented by Fabral S.A., an association of Brazilian capital and Alfa Romeo.
2.	Ford Motor Co. Exports, Inc. Trucks F-600 and F-350 (medium) and F-100 (light)
3.	General Motors do Brasil S.A. Trucks HD-6.503 (medium) and Chevrolet 3.104 (light)
4.	International Harvester Máquinas S.A. S-184 (heavy truck)
5.	Mercedes-Benz do Brasil S.A. Trucks L-312 and LP-312 (medium), LP-315 (heavy); Bus 0-321-4; Passenger Cars 180 D and B (cars were never produced)
6.	S.A. Industrial de Motores, Caminhões e Automóveis, Simca do Brasil Vedette (passenger car)
7.	Scania Vabis do Brasil S.A. Scania Vabis (heavy truck) originally produced by Vemag. The firm became an independent company in July 1960.
8.	Toyota do Brasil S.A. Indústria e Comércio Toyota Jeep
9.	Vemag S.A., Veículos e Máquinas Agrícolas DKW Vemaguet (utility vehicle), Candango (jeep), and DKW Belcar (passenger car)
10.	Volkswagen do Brasil, Indústria e Comércio de Automóveis, S.A. Kombi (utility vehicle) and Luxury Sedan 113 (passenger car)
11.	Willys-Overland do Brasil S.A. Willys Jeep, Willys Rural and Military Small Truck (utility vehicle), Dauphine and Aerowillys (passenger cars) The automobile was originally a project of Chrysler-Willys do Brasil S.A..

Table A.1. *(continued)*

Approved but aborted projects

12.   Borgward do Brasil S.A.
       Isabella (passenger car)

13.   Chrysler-Willys do Brasil S.A.
       Plymouth Savoy-1956 (passenger car) Later became the Willys project,
       Aerowillys.

14.   Fabral S.A., Fábrica Brasileira de Automóveis Alfa
       AR/103/B (passenger car) This project was later implemented by the FNM.

15.   Indústria Nacional de Locomotivas (INL)
       Krupp Truck

16.   Máquinas Agrícolas Romi S.A.
       Romi BMW (passenger car) The firm later produced the passenger car Romi-
       Iseta independent of GEIA auspices.

17.   N.S.U. Brasileira S.A., Indústria e Comércio de Veículos Motorizados
       Prinz (passenger car)

18.   Rover do Brasil S.A. Indústria e Comércio
       L. Rover Jeep

Table A.2. *Firm Ownership 1956-1960 and 1968*

***

Original Eleven Firms

Predominantly Brazilian capital
        FNM
        Vemag
        Willys
50% Brazilian
        Mercedes-Benz
        Simca
Foreign controlled
        Ford
        General Motors
        International Harvester
        Scania Vabis
        Toyota
        Volkswagen

1966 - Chrysler buys 92% of Simca in France and International Harvester.
1966 - VW takes over Vemag.
1967 - Ford gains control of Willys through buying controlling shares of Kaiser and Renault.
1967 - Alfa Romeo gains control of FNM.

Eight foreign-controlled firms in 1968
        Chrysler
        FNM
        Ford
        General Motors
        Mercedes-Benz
        Scania Vabis
        Toyota
        Volkswagen

Table A.3. *Production Projections Based on Original Twenty-nine Projects*

| | Trucks | | | Utility | | | |
	Heavy	Medium	Light	vehicles	Jeeps	Cars	Total
1958	7,260	27,870	5,520	11,010	17,670	21,800	91,130
1959	10,490	47,690	9,512	17,664	23,480	61,050	169,886
1960	16,820	66,560	12,576	21,144	27,350	87,800	232,250
Total	34,570	142,120	27,608	49,818	68,500	170,650	493,266

Source: Presidência da República, Conselho do Desenvolvimento, "Programa de Metas, Tomo III: Alimentação, Indústrias de Base, Educação; A Meta da Indústria Automobilística" (Rio de Janeiro, 1958).

Table A.4. *Production Projections Based on Twenty-four Projects and the 1960 Target of 170,000*

	Trucks	Utility vehicles	Jeeps	Cars	Total
1957	18,800	2,600	9,300	--	30,700
1958	32,000	13,000	14,000	8,000	67,000
1959	55,000	17,000	18,000	20,000	110,000
1960	80,000	25,000	25,000	40,000	170,000
Total	185,800	57,600	66,300	68,000	377,700

Source: ANFAVEA, *Indústria automobilística brasileira* (São Paulo: ANFAVEA, 1961).

Table A.5. *Actual Production by Vehicle Type 1957-1971*

	1957	1958	1959	1960	1961	1962	1963
Passenger cars	--	2,189	11,963	37,818	54,978	74,887	86,024
Utility vehicles	9,164	14,273	18,083	19,514	17,621	22,247	13,432
Small trucks							
Mixed use	1,656	9,165	18,508	24,446	30,153	35,455	36,638
Cargo	1,217	4,684	7,900	9,576	12,339	18,935	14,067
Trucks							
Medium	14,886	25,518	35,013	35,529	25,935	36,107	20,366
Heavy	3,121	4,496	3,340	4,262	2,943	2,636	2,485
Buses	498	658	1,307	1,896	1,615	927	1,179
Total	30,542	60,983	96,114	133,041	145,584	191,194	174,191

Table A.5. (continued)

	1964	1965	1966	1967	1968	1969	1970	1971
Passenger cars	97,768	103,415	120,154	132,152	161,500	237,733	249,913	342,214
Utility vehicles	11,853	9,496	14,426	8,140	7,328	5,193	4,674	5,642
Small trucks								
Mixed use	34,917	35,252	37,909	38,361	41,341	42,588	93,757	95,530
Cargo	14,675	12,065	17,067	15,028	21,860	21,938	25,250	29,420
Trucks								
Medium	19,873	19,982	29,047	26,783	39,520	37,587	35,158	33,952
Heavy	2,376	2,671	3,252	1,778	2,470	2,982	3,230	4,916
Buses	2,245	2,306	2,754	3,245	5,696	5,679	4,058	4,393
Total	183,707	185,187	224,609	225,487	279,715	373,700	416,040	516,657

Source: ANFAVEA, Indústria automobilística brasileira (São Paulo: ANFAVEA, various years).

Table A.6. *Brazilian Motor Vehicle Production and Exports, 1957-1990*

Year	Total vehicle production (units)	Vehicle exports (units)	Vehicle exports as percent of production (%)	Passenger car production (units)	Passenger car exports (units)	Passenger car exports as percent of production (%)
1957	30,542	--	--	1,166	--	--
1958	60,983	--	--	3,831	--	--
1959	96,114	--	--	14,495	--	--
1960	113,041	--	--	42,619	--	--
1961	145,584	380	0.3	60,205	--	--
1962	191,194	170	0.1	83,876	--	--
1963	174,191		0.0	94,764	--	--
1964	183,707	57	0.0	104,710	--	--
1965	185,187	129	0.1	113,772	--	--
1966	224,609	210	0.1	128,821	--	--
1967	225,487	35	0.0	139,260	--	--
1968	279,715	9	0.0	165,045	--	--
1969	353,700	25	0.0	244,379	--	--
1970	416,089	409	0.1	306,915	52	0.0
1971	516,964	1,652	0.3	399,863	656	0.2
1972	622,171	13,528	2.2	471,055	6,611	1.4
1973	750,376	24,506	3.3	564,002	13,891	2.5
1974	905,920	64,678	7.1	691,310	47,591	6.9
1975	930,235	73,101	7.9	712,526	52,629	7.4
1976	986,611	80,407	8.1	765,291	62,079	8.1
1977	921,193	70,026	7.6	732,360	56,636	7.7
1978	1,064,014	96,172	9.0	871,170	77,388	8.9
1979	1,127,966	105,648	9.4	912,018	76,486	8.4
1980	1,165,174	157,085	13.5	933,152	115,482	12.4
1981	780,883	212,686	27.2	585,834	157,228	26.8
1982	859,304	173,351	20.2	672,589	120,305	17.9
1983	896,462	168,674	18.8	748,371	132,804	17.7
1984	864,653	196,515	22.7	679,386	151,962	22.4
1985	966,708	207,640	21.5	759,141	160,626	21.2
1986	1,056,332	183,279	17.4	815,152	138,241	17.0
1987	920,071	345,555	37.6	683,380	279,530	40.9
1988	1,056,332	320,476	30.3	782,441	226,360	28.9
1989	1,013,252	253,720	25.0	731,992	164,885	22.5
1990	914,671	187,314	20.5	663,084	120,377	18.2

Source: See Table A.5.

Table A.7. *Domestic Market Share for Motor Vehicles, 1960-1969 (%)*

Year	Ford	GM	Volkswagen	Willys	Total
1960	14.4	13.7	21.3	29.3	78.7
1961	9.6	9.4	32.5	29.4	80.8
1962	11.4	9.9	28.1	32.1	81.5
1963	10.3	7.0	33.7	29.6	80.5
1964	8.8	7.5	36.2	28.3	80.9
1965	9.2	5.9	40.5	26.2	81.9
1966	10.3	7.1	42.4	24.5	84.2
1967	7.4	7.6	51.4	20.1	86.5
1968	24.8	8.9	55.4	--	89.1
1969	25.1	14.9	50.4	--	90.4

Table A.8. *Domestic Market Share for Passenger Cars, 1974-1989 (%)*

Year	Chrysler	Fiat	FNM	Ford	GM	VW
1974	4.0	--	0.5	19.1	20.6	55.6
1975	2.2	--	0.7	17.6	20.1	59.2
1976	2.5	--	0.7	17.9	20.3	57.9
1977	2.2	9.4	0.5	14.4	17.0	55.9
1978	1.8	11.5	--	15.7	19.3	51.1
1979	1.5	12.5	--	15.8	18.6	51.2
1980	0.8	13.6	--	15.2	21.5	48.7
1981	--	10.5	--	19.2	24.0	45.9
1982	--	10.5	--	17.5	26.7	44.9
1983	--	10.6	--	19.8	28.0	41.6
1984	--	10.4	--	20.5	27.4	41.7
1985	--	13.0	--	20.6	27.2	39.2
1986	--	12.9	--	19.6	26.0	41.4
1987	--	15.3	--	20.7	28.7	35.1
1988	--	11.4	--	20.4	28.9	39.3
1989	--	11.8	--	19.8	30.6	37.4

Source: The Economist Intelligence Unit, International Motor Business, "Short Term Prospects to the Brazilian Motor Industry," October 1990.

Table A.9. *Individual Firm Projections of Output and Actual Output*

		1957	1958	1959	1960	1961	1962
1. General Motors							
Projected							
Trucks	HD-6503	5,370	9,840	20,190	29,460	--	--
	3104	--	2,520	4,512	6,576	--	--
Total		5,370	12,360	24,702	36,036	--	--
Actual							
Trucks	HD-6503	4,868	7,896	14,011	13,938		
	3104	--	1,453	3,153	4,238		
Total		4,868	9,349	17,164	18,176		
% of plan		91	76	69	50		
2. Ford							
Projected							
Trucks	F-60	6,000	8,000	13,000	21,800		
	F-350	--	1,600	2,000	2,200		
	F-100	2,250	3,000	4,000	6,000		
Total		8,250	12,600	19,000	30,000		
Actual							
Trucks	F-60	4,756	7,495	10,860	9,838		
	F-350	--	0	1,623	3,866		
	F-100	1,217	3,231	4,755	5,388		
Total		5,973	10,726	17,238	19,092		
% of plan		72	85	91	64		
3. Mercedes-Benz							
Projected							
Trucks	L-312	--	1,200	--	--		
	LP-315	--	1,000	1,950	3,300		
	LP-321	--	5,800	9,200	9,200		

Table A.9. (continued)

	1957	1958	1959	1960	1961	1962
Bus	—	1,350	3,300	3,900	—	—
Automobiles	—	5,000	9,000	12,000	—	—
Total	—	14,350	23,450	28,400	—	—
Actual						
Trucks L-312	—	2,238	—	—	—	—
LK-312	—	565	—	—	—	—
LP-312	—	412	—	—	—	—
LP-321	—	6,740	7,587	7,312	5,494	7,763
LKP-321	—	316	538	—	—	—
LAP-321	—	—	1	250	96	73
LS-312	—	11	—	—	—	—
Heavy trucks	—	411	841	1,027	302	461
Bus and bus chassis	—	366	851	1,100	1,101	640
Total	—	11,059	9,818	9,689	6,993	8,937
4. Toyota						
Projected						
Jeeps	—	1,820	3,180	4,500	—	—
Actual						
Jeeps	—	—	489	295	—	—
% of plan	—	—	15	7	—	—
5. Volkswagen						
Projected						
Kombi	4,000	5,500	7,000	9,000	—	—
Automobile	—	5,000	9,000	15,000	—	—
Total	4,000	10,500	16,000	24,000	—	—
Actual						
Kombi	371	4,819	8,383	11,299	—	—
Automobile	—	—	8,445	17,059	—	—
Toal	371	4,819	16,828	28,358	—	—
% of plan	9	46	105	118	—	—

6. Vemag			
Projected			
DKW Vemaguet	500	1,200	1,200
DKW Candango	--	2,300	3,050
DKW Belcar	750	4,250	5,500
Scania Vabis	--	540	720
Total	1,250	8,290	10,470
Actual			
DKW Vemaguet	1,166	2,524	4,446
DKW Candango	8	1,968	2,481
DKW Belcar	0	1,773	3,097
Scania Vabis	162	428	586
Total	1,336	6,693	10,610
% of plan	106	81	101
7. FNM[a]			
Projected			
Truck FNM	3,600	4,200	6,600
Actual			
Truck FNM	3,202	2,079	2,543
Car			414
Total	3,202	2,079	2,957
8. International Harvester			
Projected			
Truck S-184	2,000	3,000	5,000
Actual			
Truck S-184	--	841	1,227
% of plan	--	28	25

Table A.9. (continued)

	1957	1958	1959	1960	1961	1962
9. Willys Overland						
Projected[b]						
Willys Jeep	--	8,900	12,950	15,000	15,000	--
Willys Camioneta	--	--	4,410	10,464	10,944	--
Total	--	8,900	17,360	25,464	25,944	--
Actual						
Universal Jeep	--	13,099	15,626	16,738	16,032	21,005
Rural Jeep 4x4	--	2,704	6,938	5,721	5,089	6,654
Rural Jeep 4x2	--	--	655	2,625	3,522	5,249
Pick Up Jeep	--	--	--	305	4,915	6,921
Interlagos	--	--	--	--	--	218
Aerowillys	--	--	--	6,124	7,747	9,508
Dauphine	--	--	528	7,491	5,294	7.197
Renault Gordini	--	--	--	--	2	4,585
Total	--	15,803	23,747	39,004	42,601	61,337
10. Simca						
Projected						
Automobile	--	3,000	6,000	12,000	--	--
Actual						
Automobile	--	--	1,217	3,633	--	--
% of plan	--	--	20	30	--	--
11. Borgward						
Projected						
Automobile	--	1,500	3,500	5,000	--	--
12. Chrysler-Willys						
Projected						
Automobile	--	3,000	19,000	22,000	--	--
13. Rover						
Projected						
Jeeps	--	1,500	3,000	4,800	--	--

14. Fabral			
Projected	--	--	--
Automobile	--	3,900	6,000
15. Romi			
Projected	--	--	--
Automobile	1,400	2,800	4,300
16. N.S.U.			
Projected	--	--	--
Automobile	400	3,600	6,000
17. I.N.L.			
Projected	--	--	--
Krupp Truck	300	800	1,200

[a] The original Fabral plan was to produce 3,900 cars in 1959 and 6,000 in 1960.
[b] The original Chrysler-Willys plan called for 3,000 cars in 1958; 19,000 in 1959 and 22,000 in 1960.

Source: Individual firm projects submitted to GEIA, GEIA Archives, Conselho do Desenvolvimento, Ministério da Indústria e Comércio, Rio de Janeiro; Presidência da República, Conselho do Desenvolvimento, *Indústrias de Base Tomo III* (Rio de Janeiro, 1958); and ANFAVEA, *Indústria automobilística brasileira* (ANFAVEA: São Paulo, various years).

Table A.10. *Actual Production by Individual Firm*

	1957	1958	1959	1960	1961	1962
FNM						
Car FNM 2000	--	--	--	414	454	378
Truck FNM	2,912	3,990	2,077	2,463	2,040	892
Bus chassis	290	10	2	80	184	34
Total	3,202	4,000	2,079	2,957	2,678	1,304
Ford						
Truck F-600	4,756	7,495	10,860	9,838	7,984	11,753
F-350	--	--	1,623	3,866	2,167	3,454
F-100	1,217	3,231	4,755	5,388	3,877	6,506
Total	5,973	10,726	17,268	19,092	14,028	21,713
General Motors						
Truck C6503	4,660	7,752	13,683	12,962	8,941	11,769
C3104	--	1,453	3,026	3,285	3,175	3,970
Camioneta C3116	--	--	8	355	532	968
Bus chassis	208	144	328	552	178	151
Camioneta C3103	--	--	63	59	52	28
C3112	--	--	56	538	98	106
Misc.	--	--	--	425	713	1,988
Total	4,868	9,349	17,164	18,176	13,689	18,980
International Harvester						
Medium trucks	--	--	721	877	762	711
Heavy trucks	--	--	120	350	262	561
Bus chassis	--	--	--	--	--	9
Total	--	--	841	1,227	1,024	1,281
Mercedes-Benz						
L 312	4,033	2,238	--	--	--	--
LK 312	337	565	--	--	--	--
LP 312	1,100	412	--	--	--	--
LP 321	--	6,740	7,587	7,312	5,494	7,763
LPK 321	--	316	538	--	--	--
LAP 321	--	--	1	250	96	73
LS 312	47	11	--	--	--	--
Heavy trucks	--	411	841	1,027	302	461
Bus and chassis	--	366	851	1,100	1,101	640
Total	5,517	11,059	9,818	9,689	6,993	8,937
Saab-Scania (originally under Vemag)						
Truck Scania Vabis	--	84	302	422	339	722
Bus chassis	--	138	126	164	152	93
Total	--	222	428	586	491	851
Simca						
Cars Chambord	--	--	1,217	3,570	5,641	6,120
Presidence	--	--	--	63	173	120
Ralley	--	--	--	--	--	449
Utility Jangada	--	--	--	--	--	215
Total	--	--	1,217	3,633	5,814	6,904

Table A. 10. *(continued)*

	1957	1958	1959	1960	1961	1962
Toyota						
Landcruiser jeep	--	--	489	295	--	--
TB 430 L (Utility)	--	--	--	--	7	627
Vemag						
Camioneta DKW	1,166	1,642	2,524	4,446	4,695	7,805
Car DKW	--	2,189	1,773	3,097	4,642	7,123
Jeep - Candango 4	8	1,174	1,968	1,977	858	386
- Candango 2	--	--	--	504	714	229
Total	1,174	5,005	6,265	10,024	10,919	15,544
Volkswagen						
Kombi	371	4,819	8,383	11,299	16,315	14,563
Sedan 1200/1300	--	--	8,445	17,059	31,025	38,430
Karmann-Ghia	--	--	--	--	--	759
Total	371	4,819	16,828	28,358	47,340	53,752
Willys Overland						
Universal jeep	9,156	13,099	15,626	16,738	16,032	21,005
Rural jeep 4x4	119	2,704	6,938	5,721	5,089	6,654
Rural jeep 4x2	--	--	655	2,625	3,522	5,249
Pick up jeep	--	--	--	305	4,915	6,921
Interlagos	--	--	--	--	--	218
Aerowillys	--	--	--	6,124	7,747	9,508
Dauphine	--	--	52	7,491	5,294	7,197
Renault Gordini	--	--	--	--	2	4,585
Total	9,275	15,803	23,747	39,004	42,601	61,337

Source: See Table A.5.

Table A.11. Domestic Content

A. Original GEIA guidelines (%)

	12/31/56	7/1/56	7/1/58	7/1/59	7/1/60
Trucks	35	40	65	75	90
Jeeps	50	60	75	85	95
Utility	40	50	65	75	90
Cars	--	50	65	85	95

B. Domestic content by firm (%)

1. FNM

Planned:

	1/57-6/58	7/58-6/59	7/59-12/59
Truck (weight)	74.8	81.9	90.5
Truck (value)	59.3	63.8	87.9

Actual (weight):

	12/31/58	6/30/59	6/30/60	6/30/61	6/30/62
Truck	72.9	79.3	(79.5)	89.1	85.9
Car	--	--	(65.0)	65.0	49.9

2. Ford

Planned (weight):

	6/30/57	7/1/57-6/30/58	7/1/58-6/30/59	7/1/59-6/30/60	7/1/60
F-100	40.2	51.6[a]	69.9	75.3	95.9
F-350	40.2	46.0	67.2	76.0	92.9
F-60	36.3	40.4	68.6	78.3	91.1

Actual (weight):

	6/30/59	6/30/60	6/30/61	6/30/62
F-100	72.2	80.0	90.5	88.0
F-350	70.0	79.0	91.6	87.6
F-600	--	84.0	90.4	90.8

3. General Motors
Actual (weight):

	6/30/59			6/30/60		6/30/61	6/30/62
	Motor	Parts	(Total)	Total	(Total)	Total	Total
Chevy 3104	61.3	70.4	(73.0)	76.0	(70.3)	90.4	93.9
6503	61.3	73.9	(67.3)	79.0	(79.2)	87.3	95.4

4. International Harvester
Actual (weight):

	6/30/59	6/30/60		6/30/61	6/30/62
	(Total)	Total	(Total)	Total	Total
Truck	(67)	83.2	(67.3)	91.1	86.4

5. Mercedes-Benz
Planned (value):

	12/31/56	7/1/57		7/1/58	7/1/59	7/1/60
	Motor	Parts	(Total)	Total	Total	Total
L	36.0	40.1	(32.9)	65.1	75.0	90.0
LP 312	44.3	48.1	(41.3)	71.0	75.0	90.0

Actual (weight):

	6/30/59			6/30/60		6/30/61	6/30/62
	Motor	Parts	(Total)	Total	(Total)	Total	Total
LP 321	69.4	80.3	(79.7)	80.0	(88.3)	94.2	98.1
LAP 321	—			80.0	(77.1)	82.5	98.1
O 321-H	69.4	82.3	(60.2)	94.0	(75.8)	90.1	89.8
LP 331	66.6	75.4	(67.2)	89.0	(76.3)	90.1	88.1

6. Simca
Planned:

	6/30/58	6/30/59	6/30/60	After
Car (weight)	50.0	60.0	80.0	99.0
Car (value)	50.0	58.0	87.0	97.0

Actual:

	6/30/59	6/30/60		6/30/61
	(Total)	Total	(Total)	Total
Car (weight)	(46.5)	67.7	(67.7)	96.2

7. Toyota
Planned:

	6/30/57	6/30/58	6/30/59	6/30/60	6/30/62
Jeep (weight)	60.1	75.0	86.2	96.4	83.3
Jeep (value)	58.3	71.3	80.0	92.9	

Table A.11. (*continued*)

Actual:

	6/30/59	6/30/60	6/30/61	6/30/62
Jeep (weight)	60.0 (60.1)	60.0 (60.1)	60.1	84.9

8. Vemag

Planned:

	1/7/57-6/30/58	7/1/58-6/30/59	6/1/59-6/30/60	1/7/60
Jeep DKW (weight)	60.0	75.0	85.0	95.0
Jeep DKW (value)	50.0	63.0	77.0	89.0

Actual (weight):

	6/30/59			6/30/60		6/30/61 Total	6/30/62 Total
	Motor	Parts	(Total)		(Total)		
Car DKW	18.0	65.5	(65.4)	85.0	(85.3)	95.2	96.4
Vemaguet	20.0	65.2	(65.1)	79.0	(73.4)	95.8	88.4
Jeep DKW	25.0	75.2	(75.2)	82.0	(82.0)	95.2	93.6
S-V	63.0	62.7	(65.6)	75.0	(65.6)	90.3	81.6

9. Volkswagen

Planned:

	12/1/56	7/1/57	7/1/58	7/1/59	7/1/60	7/1/61
Sedan (weight)	--	--	25.5	41.2	66.2	90.7
Sedan (value)	--	--	21.2	39.1	65.4	85.9
Kombi (weight)	40.2	67.6	76.9	86.1	90.1	--
Kombi (value)	42.4	58.1	66.7	77.7	82.8	--

Actual (weight):

	6/30/59			6/30/60		6/30/61 Total	6/30/62 Total
	Motor	Parts	(Total)		(Total)		
Sedan	61.8	38.7	(38.2)	73.3	(68.4)	92.0	94.0
Kombi	61.8	70.9	(70.9)	91.0	(91.0)	94.6	92.6

10. Willys

Planned:

	October 1959-July 1960	After
Aerowillys (weight)	86.6	95.0
Aerowillys (value)	82.2	94.0

Actual (weight):

	6/30/59			6/30/60		6/30/61	6/30/62
	Motor	Parts	(Total)	Total		Total	Total
Jeep	83.0	82.4	(82.4)	95.2	(95.2)	98.5	98.7
Rural Willys 2x4	83.0	67.0	(67.0)	97.9	(97.9)	98.9	98.9
Rural Willys 4x4	83.0	67.0	(67.0)	93.8	(97.8)	98.8	99.0
Aerowillys	--	--	--	85.3	(85.3)	92.8	98.8
Dauphine	--	--	--	70.2	(70.2)	94.8	96.9

III. 1960 Average domestic content level per vehicle type (nonweighted)

Passenger cars	73.7	(78% of GEIA target of 95%)
Trucks	76.9	(86% of GEIA target of 90%)
Utility vehicles	87.4	(97% of GEIA target of 90%)
Jeeps	79.1	(83% of GEIA target of 95%)

a Changed from 52.9 and 43.4 after GEIA complained of improper calculations.

Sources: FNM: 1959 data from ANFAVEA, Indústria automobilística brasileira (São Paulo: ANFAVEA, 1959); 1960 data from ANFAVEA, 1960; data in parentheses and for 1961 and 1962 from Instituto Brasileiro de Geografia e Estatística (IBGE), Anuario Estatístico do Brasil, various years. (Eros Orosco in A indústria automobilística brasileira [Rio de Janeiro: CONSULTEC, 1961] claims 1960 figures are suspect.) Ford: Ford Project. General Motors, International Harvester, Mercedes-Benz, Simca, Vemag, Toyota, Volkswagen, and Willys: same as FNM. (Eros Orosco claims that the 1960 figures for the Kombi are suspect.)

Table A.12. *Brazilian Vehicle Exports, 1970-1990 (US$ thousands)*

Year	Vehicles	Engines	Components	Total
1970	2,790	534	5,598	8,922
1972	24,935	144	29,067	54,146
1974	118,712	17,386	67,671	203,769
1976	233,579	67,442	84,721	385,742
1978	373,641	132,078	104,689	610,408
1980	729,948	210,620	160,600	1,101,168
1981	1,066,045	188,459	311,911	1,566,415
1982	715,853	188,853	250,128	1,154,834
1983	594,036	293,862	299,160	1,187,058
1984	669,247	350,272	413,931	1,433,450
1985	746,410	407,176	450,153	1,603,739
1986	667,461	280,514	539,585	1,487,560
1987	1,522,382	259,027	671,707	2,453,116
1988	1,645,636	261,714	710,336	2,617,686
1989	1,489,257	304,252	776,500	2,570,009
1990	975,127	220,710	701,647	1,897,484

Source: See Table A.5.

Table A.13. *Brazilian Trade Balance in Automotive Industry (US$ thousands)*

Year	Imports	Exports	Trade balance
1940-1950	420,547	--	(420,547)
1951	256,846	--	(256,846)
1955	232,403	--	(232,403)
1960	83,505	39	(83,466)
1965	8,256	3,192	(5,064)
1970	69,128	8,922	(60,206)
1972	97,642	54,146	(43,496)
1974	347,947	203,769	(144,178)
1976	235,088	385,742	150,654
1978	292,889	610,408	317,519
1980	524,185	1,101,168	576,983
1981	468,702	1,566,415	1,087,713
1982	318,386	1,154,834	836,448
1983	367,729	1,187,058	819,329
1984	394,618	1,433,450	1,038,832
1985	435,522	1,603,739	1,168,217
1986	656,240	1,487,560	831,320
1987	826,327	2,453,116	1,626,789
1988	695,606	2,617,686	1,822,080
1989	678,110	2,570,009	1,891,899
1990	733,095	1,897,484	1,164,389

Source: See Table A.5.

254

Table A.14. *Motor Vehicle Production – Selected Countries (thousands of units)*

Country	1960	1965	1970	1975	1980	1985	1990
Japan	482	1,876	5,289	6,942	11,043	12,271	13,487
United States	7,905	11,138	8,284	8,987	8,010	11,653	9,778
West Germany	2,055	2,976	3,842	3,186	3,879	4,446	4,977
France	1,369	1,642	2,750	2,861	3,378	3,016	3,769
Italy	645	1,476	1,854	1,459	1,612	1,573	2,121
Spain	58	229	536	814	1,182	1,418	2,053
USSR	524	634	916	1,964	2,199	2,232	NA
Canada	398	847	1,160	1,424	1,374	1,933	1,923
United Kingdom	1,811	2,177	2,098	1,648	1,313	1,314	1,566
Belgium	--	167	272	222	260	266	386
South Korea	--	--	29	36	123	378	1,322
Brazil	133	185	416	930	1,165	967	915
Mexico	50	97	193	361	490	398	821
Sweden	129	206	311	367	315	461	410
Poland	36	60	118	257	431	349	NA
China	23	41	87	140	222	443	NA

Source: MVMA World Motor Vehicle Data and ANFAVEA.

APPENDIX B: JOSÉ ALMEIDA'S CALCULATION OF SUBSIDIES PROVIDED TO THE BRAZILIAN AUTOMOTIVE INDUSTRY

In his book, *A implantação da indústria automobilística no Brasil* (Rio de Janeiro: Fundação Getúlio Vargas, 1972), José Almeida states that between 1956 and 1961, US$339.7 million and Cr$21 million were invested in the terminal and auto parts sectors in Brazil. Exchange and fiscal subsidies provided to the industry amounted to US$301.3 million, or 89 cents per dollar of foreign investment.

In his unpublished manuscript, "A indústria automobilística brasileira," prepared for the Instituto Brasileiro de Economia, Centro de Estudos Industriais, at the Fundação Getúlio Vargas, and upon which the book was based, Almeida provides the raw data and methodology by which he arrived at this estimate. These data cover both the terminal and auto parts sectors. Also, his methods of calculation differ from those used in Chapter 4.

I.   *Direct Investment under Instruction 113*
          (US$ millions)

1956	13.8
1957	56.3
1958	76.7
1959	47.0
1960	56.3
1961	3.5
1956–61	253.6

Subsidy: No subsidy is calculated for investment under Instruction 113. Perhaps he assumed, as did Eugênio Gudin, that this subsidy only compensated foreign investors for an overvalued exchange rate.

II.   *Financing at the Cost of Exchange*
          (US$ millions)

1956	16.2
1957	2.3

1958	23.4
1959	17.6
1960	12.9
1961	2.7
1956–61	75.1

Subsidy: To evaluate this subsidy, Almeida amortizes each year's financing over a five-year period, beginning three years after the loans were incurred. For example, the US$16.2 million in financing for 1956 was amortized in five individual payments of US$3.240 million from 1959 to 1963. He measures the cruzeiro subsidy per dollar of financing as the difference between the free exchange rate at the time of payment minus the cost-of-exchange rate *at the time* the loan was incurred. He then multiplies this subsidy rate times the value of the loan payment and converts the cruzeiro amount into dollars at the free exchange rate at the time of payment.

As discussed in Chapter 4, the subsidy was in fact calculated at the time of payment and the cost-of-exchange rate was abolished in 1961, before most of these loans came due. Almeida's method overestimates the subsidy by taking the nominal exchange rate at the time of payment, which was rising rapidly with inflation.

The value of the subsidy according to these calculations comes to US$67.9 million, or 90.5 percent of the total financing.

III. Almeida calculates a subsidy for equipment imported from countries with inconvertible currencies, which was paid for on delivery at the cost of exchange. These imports were not included in the Chapter 4 calculations, as parts producers were the primary importers of this type of good. From 1958 to 1961, US$11 million worth of equipment was imported; the subsidy came to US$5.8 million or 53 percent.

IV. *Parts Imports*

As mentioned in Chapter 4, there is some discrepancy between my data on parts imports and Almeida's. Almeida's valuation of the subsidy is also different. He evaluates the subsidy as the difference between the average general category rate and the free exchange rate.

Imported Parts
(US$ millions)

		Subsidy
1957	30.7	4.0
1958	41.3	20.2

January–June 1959	71.4	37.5
July–December 1959	24.7	0.7
1960	30.3	1.4
January–March 1961	0.9	0.3
Total	199.3	64.1

V. *Fiscal Subsidies*

The method used in Chapter 4 to measure the cruzeiro subsidy rate per dollar of investment was borrowed from Almeida. He calculates the total subsidy on his estimations of foreign investment as stated previously.

Subsidy
(US$ millions)

1957	30.7
1958	52.5
1959	38.6
1960	41.8
1957–60	163.6

VI. *Total Subsidy*

Foreign Investment
(US$ millions)

	Instruction 113	Financing	Imports paid on delivery	Total
1. Investment	253.6	75.1	11.0	339.7

Subsidy
(US$ millions)

	Instruction 113	Financing	Imports paid on delivery	Total
1. Exchange subsidy	0.0	67.9	5.8	73.7
2. Fiscal subsidy				163.5
3. Subsidy on parts				64.1
4. Total subsidy				301.3

Almeida compares the subsidy of US$301.3 million to the total investment of US$339.7 million to arrive at the 89 cents per dollar figure.

INDEX